P9-DFC-534

Childhood Bullying and Teasing:

What School Personnel, Other Professionals, and Parents Can Do

Dorothea M. Ross, Ph.D.
Division of Behavioral and
Developmental Pediatrics
University of California, San Francisco

5999 Stevenson Avenue
Alexandria, VA 22304-3300

CHILDHOOD BULLYING AND TEASING: WHAT SCHOOL PERSONNEL, OTHER
PROFESSIONALS, AND PARENTS CAN DO

10 9 8 7 6 5 4 3

American Counseling Association
5999 Stevenson Avenue
Alexandria, VA 22304

Aquisitions and Development Editor
Carolyn Baker

Managing Editor
Michael Comlish

Cover design by Brian Gallagher

Library of Congress Cataloging-in-Publication Data

Ross, Dorothea M.
    Childhood bullying and teasing: what school personnel, other professionals, and
parents can do / Dorothea M. Ross.
        p.   cm.
    Includes bibliographical references and index.
    ISBN 1-55620-157-5 (alk. paper)
    1. Bullying — United States.   2. School discipline — United States.   I. Title.
LB3011.5.R67   1996
371.5′8—dc20   96-14476
                                                                         CIP

"I don't like fighting but I keep having fights. you see there are some nasty people and they surround me and the only way out is fighting. Here is what Daniel said. When me and Daniel were out in the playground Daniel started being nasty to me and when we were lining up he was being really nasty to me and when we were in line he said mummy was a fucking bitch. So I kicked him. Gareth and Jo are bullies to. They keep going round haveing fights. Some thing is realy going to have to be done about the bullieing because nice people keep getting bullied and hert."

—*Account written by a 7-year-old boy (Hagedorn, 1993)*

Contents

Preface

RONALD STEPHENS of the National School Safety Center has described bullying as a form of terrorism that encompasses a group of antisocial behaviors, including assault, intimidation, extortion, some forms of vandalism, cruel teasing, and unwanted physical contact, especially of a sexual nature. Bullying in the schools is a serious problem. Estimates of incidence vary, but it is believed that close to 20% of American school children are directly involved as either bullies or victims. The fallout from bullying involves a much larger number, the bystanders who witness the brutality of it and all too often see it go unpunished. Bullying can create a climate of fear that permeates a school and becomes a deterrent to learning.

Despite the serious short- and long-term effects of bullying, most schools in this country have made little or no attempt to deal with the problem. The reasons for this failure are diverse and, for the most part, uninformed. For many school administrators the problem of bullying has been eclipsed by that of weapon-related violence. (The possibility that bullying could be an antecedent of such violence has not been explored.) Some school personnel are unaware of the extent of bullying, and many of those who are aware are reluctant to acknowledge that the problem exists or are blatantly unsympathetic (the "boys will be boys" viewpoint). Some believe it to be a transient problem with character building attributes and, as such, best left to work itself out. Others do nothing because they do not know what to do. The end result of all these points of view is school environments in which bullies flourish and victims deteriorate.

I first became interested in the problem of childhood bullying when many school-age children, who came to our Department of Pediatrics complaining of recurring stomach aches for which no physiological basis could be found, also reported being cruelly teased at school. In 1973 I wrote a program based on the principles of social learning theory (see Chapter 8) that was designed to empower these children to combat the teasing themselves. It was an immediate success. As a pediatric psychologist, I was not surprised that when the children learned how to put an end to the teasing, their recurring stomach aches also disappeared.

In the early 1980s, as part of a major study of childhood pain, we asked children with leukemia what their worst pain experience had been. We expected the answers to be some of the often excruciating treatment-related pains that these children must endure. To our astonishment many children said that their worst pain was to be teased about their appearance (for example, baldness, extreme pallor) when they returned to school. Once again the teasing program successfully put an end to the teasing.

At this time there was virtually no interest in either the media or the school and clinical domains in the problem of teasing or in the other components of bullying, such as acts of physical aggression, intimidation, and extortion. Many teachers and parents dismissed bullying as "something we all go through," "character building," or as a transient problem of little importance. However, beginning in the late 1980s, interest in childhood bullying increased sharply as a result of the pioneer work of Dan Olweus in Scandinavia. Olweus reported chilling figures on the prevalence of bullying, demonstrated the efficacy of a whole school campaign against bullying, and, perhaps most important of all, made it clear that the potential long-term effects on both the bully and the victim far outweighed the immediate misery of being bullied. By the early 1990s the procedures for whole school campaigns were supplemented by specific interventions that could further enhance their effects. All of these procedures are described in detail in this book. They are neither difficult nor expensive to implement, but they do require adults who believe that childhood bullying is a serious problem and who are committed to sustained action against it. This book has been written for these concerned adults and for the children whose lives are being blighted by the stress of being bullied.

The basic premise of this book is that bullying is intentional, a purposeful act, and therefore one that can be controlled provided that there is strong commitment and concerted action on the part of all those involved: school personnel, other professionals, parents, and children.

The goal is to bring together in a readily accessible form the research and other findings on childhood bullying and victimization along with the kinds of intervention that have proven effective or have the potential for combating these problems. The fact is that enough is known *now* to launch a major campaign.

Since the early 1980s childhood bullying has aroused increased investigative interest and has emerged as a subject in its own right.

Beginning with the first studies of prevalence in Scandinavia, the issue of childhood bullying has moved slowly up in the public agenda. Major studies, first in Scandinavia and then in the United Kingdom, have demonstrated the efficacy of mounting whole school campaigns against bullying. One offshoot has been considerable progress in designing intervention options that target specific facets of the problem. Another has been new awareness that parents and teachers often are part of the problem but seldom are equipped to become part of the solution. A third is the realization that the silent majority of children who are not directly involved in bullying could become a viable force in combating it in the school setting. In addition, many of the old myths and beliefs that held progress in a strait jacket have been discarded. There is, for example, new awareness of the complexity of the bullying problem: Longtime views of bullies and their victims as homogeneous groups have given way to the recognition of subgroups of bullies and victims. The notion that bullying is a transient problem primarily of childhood and adolescence and one that will work itself out if left alone or ignored has been discarded in the face of unequivocal evidence of the potentially serious immediate and long-term effects for both bullies and their victims in the absence of intervention.

In this text, the problem of childhood bullying is discussed within the theoretical framework of Lazarus's (1966) cognitively oriented theory of stress and coping. This theory provides a perspective of the plight of the different subgroups of bullies and victims as well as a theoretical basis for the interventions that best fit their needs. Some of these interventions are described in detail at appropriate points.

Major sources of data that have made impressive contributions to the current state of our knowledge of bullying and victimization are discussed throughout the text. Included are the seminal contributions by Dan Olweus, among them the Norwegian nationwide study of bullying that was begun in 1983 and the whole school campaign against bullying, as well as a body of earlier research on this topic. In England, investigators on the ongoing Sheffield Bullying Project conducted a large group of studies under the able and creative leadership of Peter K. Smith. This group tested the efficacy of the whole school approach and also has branched out to related studies of specific interventions and other bullying-related topics that have cast new light on childhood bullying. In the United States, a major body of research on victimization has been built up since the mid-1970s by David Perry and his colleagues on the Perry Victimization Project. This work constitutes the most important contribution to date to our understanding of the problem of victimization.

At the present time we have a substantial body of information on the characteristics of the subgroups of bullies and victims, the antecedents of bullying and victimization along with their immediate and long-term effects, and the types of bullying. All of these findings are described, along with critical comments on the problem of defining bullying and the controversy about two hypotheses about victimization. Also included are two particularly insidious types of victimization: racial bullying and sexual harassment.

Although teasing is considered in most contemporary research to be a component of bullying, it is accorded only secondary status. Investigators generally view it as much less severe than the other components of bullying. We disagree with this evaluation. and believe that teasing merits separate consideration when it occurs in the absence of any of the other components of bullying. The reasons for this stance are twofold. Unlike most of the other components of bullying, teasing is not invariably of an antisocial nature: It can be as cruel and destructive as bullying or it can be fun, playful, and a helpful factor in the socialization process. This difference must be understood if adults are to respond appropriately when teasing occurs. For this reason, both kinds of teasing are discussed in some detail. It is difficult for victims to cope effectively themselves with most of the components of bullying. In contrast, most teasing victims can learn to cope with teasing and manage teasing incidents without adult help when no other components of bullying are involved. Four interventions that children can learn for stopping ongoing cruel teasing are described in detail.

The book concludes with a topic of great importance, the prevention of the early onset of bullying, that is, primary prevention. No such programs exist specifically for bullying. However, primary prevention programs for the preschool and early school years have been developed for antisocial aggression of a general nature, and these have a clear application to bullying. The folly of relying solely on secondary prevention programs is discussed. A serious omission in all of the foregoing primary and secondary programs is the failure to use individuals in the community as a preventive resource. It is our opinion that the community should become an integral part of the overall preventive strategy, and the rationale for this innovative inclusion is discussed.

It is recognized that, even with the sequence of primary and secondary preventive programs proposed here, bullying and teasing will not be completely eliminated. Certain child rearing and temperament combinations, coupled with the existence of a particular kind of vulnerable child, virtually ensure a small, but hard-core, group of bullies likely to be resistant to school-based and/or home intervention. This group would need intensive psychiatric treatment. But with early serious and concentrated effort on the part of school personnel and reasonable cooperation from the home, bullying and cruel teasing could become relative rarities as the majority of children learn to look on these behaviors as despicable.

Childhood Bullying and Teasing represents an important addition to the counseling literature. It will enable school counselors and those in private practice to make a difference to the many children who yearn to be free of the bullying that makes their lives a period of unremitting misery.

To work effectively with these victims, as well as with their bullies, counselors should be aware of the multiple causes and nature of bullying and victimization, the typologies of bullies and victims, the immediate and long-term effects on both the bullies and their victims, and the appropriate intervention procedures that are available. These topics are discussed in detail along with vignettes and case studies illustrating the problems in bullying and victimization and potential solutions. The verbatim comments of both groups provide insight into the differing views that bullies and victims have about behavior such as cruel teasing, racial bullying, and sexual harassment.

Although research on the problem of bullying has lagged behind research on other antisocial behaviors, the information in this book is more than sufficient for counselors and other professionals to assign high priority to the problem *now*.

Acknowledgments

THE MOST IMPORTANT contribution to this book came from Sheila Ross, who gave generously of her expertise, creativity, and time throughout the writing of it. Her commitment and enthusiasm never wavered. The quality of the book has been greatly enhanced by her cogent comments and expertise in writing and editing.

I wish to express my deep thanks to Mark Roberts, Headmaster of the Rectory Paddock School in Orpington, Kent, England, for his continuing interest in this book and for his sustained contributions of information about childhood bullying that I could not otherwise have obtained.

I would also like to thank the investigators and other professionals who took the time to respond to my questions and, in some cases, went back to their original data to do so: Elizabeth Boyle, John Cobb, John Coie, Helen Gofman, Suzanne Horowitz, Jean La Fontaine, David Lane, John Lidstone, Robert Maher, Dan Olweus, David Perry, Erling Roland, Mark Rosenberg, Alberta Siegel, and Ronald Slaby.

A number of my colleagues sent me their prepublication materials, and I wish to express my appreciation for their generosity: Michael Boulton, David Finkelhor, Becky Kochenderfer, Gary Ladd, David Lane, David Perry, Kenneth Rigby, Ronald Slaby, Philip Slee, Peter K. Smith, and Richard Tremblay.

The material in this book was greatly enhanced by the inclusion of case studies and the verbatim comments about bullying and teasing of a number of children who talked freely and cooperatively. Warmest thanks are extended to these children, their parents, and the psychologists and pediatricians who permitted me to reproduce these otherwise unobtainable materials.

Special thanks are due to the reference departments of the Bainbridge Island and Seattle Public Libraries, the Seattle Law Library, the University of California, San Francisco Libraries, and the University of Washington Libraries for their help in locating relevant books and articles.

Several reviewers' constructive criticisms of the final version helped immeasurably, especially those from Carolyn Baker, Arthur Horne, and David Perry.

The support of Thomas Boyce and Mary Rita Crittenden of the Division of Behavioral and Developmental Pediatrics, University of California, San Francisco, is greatly appreciated.

Carol Lindahl put the manuscript on disc, efficiently, intelligently, and cheerfully, despite deadlines. We are particularly indebted to Sunny Martineau, who stepped in and helped with skill and enthusiasm when a computer breakdown threatened to hold up production.

It has been a pleasure to work with Carolyn Baker, Acquisitions and Development Editor of the American Counseling Association, whose enthusiasm and belief in the book remained constant.

About the Author

DOROTHEA M. ROSS is a Research Psychologist in the Division of Behavioral and Developmental Pediatrics at the University of California, San Francisco. She earned her Ph.D. in developmental psychology at Stanford University and her M.A. and B.A. degrees in psychology at the University of British Columbia. Her honors and awards include the Distinguished Contribution Award of the Society of Pediatric Psychology. Dr. Ross is nationally known for her research on children with special learning needs and is coauthor of two books on hyperactivity and one on pain in children. Part of the work on the latter book involved conducting a large research project on pain in children. She was appalled to discover that children with leukemia rated as their greatest pain not the excruciatingly painful medical procedures that they had undergone, but the teasing about their baldness and illness-related appearance changes on their return to school. What should have been a joyful return to normal life instead became a nightmare. Dr. Ross developed the Ross Teasing Program to help these and other children whose lives are made miserable by being teased. The success of this program provided the impetus for the present book.

1 Childhood Stress: Appraisal and Coping Strategies

CHILDREN IN OUR SOCIETY typically encounter a diversity of potentially stressful and challenging events that require varying degrees of action and adaptation on their part. Mild stress is unlikely to be hazardous to a child's well-being, but more severe stress can be harmful. One group of children who experience stress that often exceeds moderate amounts and that is at times unbearable are those who are subjected to bullying and teasing. However, such stressful experiences do not always have a negative impact on the child. Instead, they can provide a basis for the development of healthy coping skills resulting in positive growth in the form of feelings of competence and mastery behavior. Because it often is not possible or even desirable to eliminate stressors from a child's life, it is important to help the child cope effectively with the stressors that inevitably occur. To do so the adult must understand how children appraise stressors, the cognitive and behavioral efforts that they may make to modify the stressors or mediate their impact, the sources of help in the form of social support that may be available to them, and the fact that being in control of a stress situation does not guarantee stress reduction. Lazarus's theory of stress and coping (1966) embodies such a conceptual framework. An important component of his model of stress is that it sets the child's responses to a stressor in a transactional context that allows bidirectional influences between the child's cognitive and behavioral responses to stress and other aspects of his or her environment. This chapter begins with a general discussion of childhood stress and then moves on to Lazarus's theory and its potential for understanding the stress engendered by bullying and teasing.

The cardinal rule in helping a child cope with an event that is perceived as threatening is to accept the child's appraisal as fact no matter how unreasonable it seems to the adult. Nothing is harmless if the child believes it to be a threat and feels his or her resources to be inadequate. Adults generally find it difficult to accept a child's appraisal of an event as stressful when they do not perceive it as such. They erroneously believe that they are competent to make that decision for the child and, having done so, deny the existence of any problem or minimize it as this mother did:

> The operation on eight-year-old Betty's scalp involved shaving a patch of hair. "I look funny," she said, begging to stay home from school. "The other kids are going to tease me." But her parents insisted. "If they tease, don't pay any attention," her mother said, certain that this time-honored solution would soothe such a minor problem. But by 10 A.M. Betty was at home, sobbing. She had slipped away and walked two miles rather than face the gibes of her schoolmates. (Collier, 1988, p. 7)

Empirical evidence that even professionals may be unaware of how stressful some events are for children is contained in a series of studies on children's versus professionals' perception of stressors by Yamamoto and his colleagues at the University of Colorado. In the first of these Yamamoto (1979) asked fourth- through sixth-grade children (n = 367) to rate the following 20 commonly occurring events. The children's judgments of the stressfulness of each of the 20 events were analyzed and ranked from 1 (least upsetting) to 7 (most upsetting). As a group, the 367 children rated a *new baby sibling* to be the least upsetting of the 20 events and *losing a parent* as the most upsetting:

- *School-related events:* Giving class report (2); losing in game (4); picked last on team (5); not making 100 (6); ridiculed in class (9); a poor report card (13); wetting in class (17); academic retainment (18).
- *Fear-arousing events:* Going to dentist (3); scary dream (7); getting lost (10); having an operation (11); parental fights (16); going blind (19); losing parent (20).
- *Misbehavior:* Sent to principal (12); suspected of lying (14); caught in theft (15).
- *Change events:* New baby sibling (1); moving to new school (8).

There were no differences associated with grade, gender, or personal experience with the 20 events either in this study or in a repetition of it (Yamamoto & Byrnes, 1984) that reported similar ratings. Note that two major sources of potential stress, bullying and teasing, were not included. In the United States during the 1970s there was virtually no clinical or research interest in these topics. Yamamoto and Felsenthal (1982) next asked 197 men and women (39 clinicians, 97 teachers, and 61 teacher training students) to make professional judgments of how upsetting the events were for children and also to infer the judgments that children would make. The three sets of adults' ratings were in close agreement with each other (correlations across the 20 events were all above .90) regardless of their specialty, experience, or gender, and these professional ratings considerably overlapped the inferred ratings. The ranks of the three groups were almost identical on the stressors that were judged to be the most severe (wetting in class, going blind, losing parent). However, there were some notable discrepancies on other events between the children's ratings (Yamamoto, 1979) and those of the adults for both the professional ($r = .70$) and inferred ($r = .68$) judgments. Consider, for example, the differences in the ratings of school-related events and having an operation (Table 1.1). All but one of the school-related events (inferred judgment of academic retainment) were seen by the adults as *less* stressful than having an operation, and by the children as *more* stressful. Particularly disconcerting was the fact that increased training was not associated with greater skill in seeing events from the child's point of view: the professionals were only slightly better on inferring judgments of the 20 events than the teacher training students. The disparities between these adult and child ratings, as well as the similarities between the professional and student teacher ratings, suggest that from the beginning of professional training there should be a strong emphasis on the child's viewpoint, a focus that is clearly lacking in most traditional medical and education programs.

Taken together this series of studies provides strong support for Anthony's contention that ". . . stress as experienced by the child and stress as estimated by the adult observing the impact of the stress on the child are frequently of very different orders of magnitude" (1974, p. 106). It follows that stress event scales and check lists should not be developed on the basis of adults' views in the absence of validation by children.

DETERMINANTS OF THE CHILD'S PERCEPTION OF STRESS

A major contributor to the difficulty that adults have in evaluating the degree of stress experienced by the child in a specific situation stems from the fact that the child's reaction cannot be predicted accurately solely from the apparent degree of threat in that situation. This is true even for events such as unexpected divorce or parental death, that would appear to be highly stress producing. Instead, the child's reaction is in part a function of the complex interplay of a cluster of dispositional factors such as developmental level, temperament, and personality; social experiences and rela-

Table 1.1   Ranks and Scale Values by 197 Professionals and
367 Children

Life Event	Professional Judgment		Inferred Judgment		Children	
	Rank	Scale Value	Rank	Scale Value	Rank	Scale Value
Academic retainment	11	5.51	14	5.73	18	6.82
Sent to principal	7	4.51	6	4.64	12	5.75
Poor report card	5	4.36	4	4.32	13	6.23
Having an operation	15	5.79	13	5.63	11	5.51

Reproduced with permission of the authors and publisher from Yamamoto, K., & Felsenthal, H. M. Stressful experiences of children: professional judgments. *Psychological Reports, 1982, 50*, 1087–1093. © Psychological Reports 1982.

tionships; previous stressful experiences and history of success or failure in dealing with them; and the interpersonal context in which the event occurs (Sorensen, 1993).

It is clear that, given the multiplicity of factors that may contribute to the child's reaction, two children who are similar in many respects might perceive the same event quite differently in terms of stress potential. An event that may be appraised by one child as stressful may not be perceived as such by the other. What causes apprehension in one may prove challenging to the other. Of particular importance are the meaning of the event for the child in terms of the degree of threat evoked and the demands that the situation makes, that is, what actions must be taken to manage the stressor effectively (Lazarus & Folkman, 1984).

Consider the hypothetical case of two same-age boys who must move to new schools in the middle of the school year. Both boys have experienced some teasing and bullying related to being overweight. A combination of maternal overprotection, a highly reactive temperament, and child-rearing practices that encourage the transformation of apparently minor daily irritants into overwhelming adversities predisposes one boy to perceive the move as highly threatening and so he experiences undue anxiety and fears of what may happen in the new school. These negative emotions divert his attention and impede effective coping; he does not manage the new situation well, comes across as tentative and timid, and soon experiences some active rejection, verbal harassment, and mild bullying, thus reinforcing his appraisal of the move as highly threatening.

The second boy has a more even temperament, is less prone to overreact, and generally is more adaptable, having been encouraged to view changing circumstances as opportunities for positive growth. Although he recognizes the potential threat in the new school situation, he views the move as a challenge that he must face up to and consequently generates fewer negative emotions. He is therefore in a position to focus on managing effectively in the new school. His manner is friendly without being pushy, he laughs off comments about his weight, and soon wins the acceptance of the peer group.

The different reactions of the two boys are important because it is unlikely that they are isolated events. Instead, they probably represent the boys' typical patterns of response. The failure of the first boy to cope effectively may result in anxiety and frustration predisposing him to later difficulties in adaptation to stressors. In contrast, the successful coping on the part of the second boy should enhance his general flexibility and resilience, which in turn increases the probability of successful adaptation to subsequent potential stressors.

Many children tend to fall apart in the face of stress, and the resultant loss of confidence makes it more difficult for them to cope with future stressors. If a general pattern of failure to cope persists, their confidence may be severely diminished. Sometimes even single stressful incidents that they are unable to handle effectively may be so traumatic that they cannot cope at all with subsequent similar incidents. A 7-year-old boy who had only one line to say in his first play was unable to say anything and ran from the stage. Despite kindly reassurances about the commonality of stage fright, the incident had a lasting effect:

> . . . then when I had to do a book report and they were all looking at me, I was like that again. So now I got book report fright and lots of other frights and I know if I have to get up at the front and say things, I'll mess up again. (D. M. Ross, Case studies, University of California, San Francisco, 1977–1979)

Children who are subjected to bullying and teasing often experience moderate to severe stress over fairly long periods. These children constitute the largest and also the most neglected group of special needs children in both the United States (Greenbaum, 1989) and the United Kingdom (P. K. Smith, 1991). Their plight can best be understood within the framework developed by Lazarus (1966) for his theory of stress and coping. This theory provides both a perspective of the problems that confront these children and a theoretical basis for the kinds of intervention that should be beneficial to them.

LAZARUS'S THEORY OF STRESS AND COPING

Lazarus (1966) has assigned the elements of the stress process to three categories that are constantly in transition, with potentially overlapping boundaries and variations in complexity. *Daily hassles* are the minor irritating and distressing demands of daily living that characterize everyday transactions with the social environment. These include such events as having to give a book report, having an immunization shot, and stern reprimands from teachers. The more taxing day-in and day-out long-term irritants, such as being a latch-key child after school or being on a juvenile diabetic regime, are *chronic life strains*. The most dramatic events, which often have a severe impact on the child, are *major life events* such as the death or serious illness of a family member, a highly destructive fire, or family disruption by violence or divorce.

Although some stressful events can be relatively uncomplicated short-term transactions that fall into only one category, other stressors may present a complex set of changing conditions with a consequent shifting in status over time from one category to another. Bullying, for example, often starts at the level of daily hassles, with tentative and sporadic probes by the bully to determine whether the potential victim is a suitably vulnerable target. When the choice proves to be satisfactory, that is, when the victim becomes visibly upset and is clearly too intimidated by fear of reprisal to counterattack or report the bully, being bullied often becomes a chronic life strain as it increases sharply in frequency and intensity. Escalation to the status of a major life event, as feelings of helplessness and hopelessness build up over time with a concomitant increase in anticipatory terror, is well documented in the literature (Besag, 1989; Hammond, 1989; La Fontaine, 1991).

Appraisal is a universal phenomenon in which people of all ages constantly assess the significance of ongoing events for their own well-being. Within Lazarus's (1966) theoretical formulation, two major sequential forms of appraisal converge to shape the meaning of events for children (Folkman, 1984). The first is *primary appraisal*, through which means they assess the significance of the events in respect to their well-being. If the events are perceived as threatening, as is often the case even for first-time bullying, the children engage in *secondary appraisal*. They evaluate the options available for managing the demands of the situation and their competence in dealing with it. The question that children ask themselves here is whether something could be done to change or improve this situation and, if so, are they capable of doing it? The actions that could be taken are called *coping resources*.

Coping Resources

Coping resources are the cognitive and behavioral efforts that children may invoke to manage or change a stressful or threatening event or mediate its impact. In this definition, coping refers to efforts to manage the demands of the situation regardless of how adaptive or successful these efforts are in handling the stress. In other words, coping is defined independently of both the quality of the coping efforts and their outcome. The coping resources that the child can invoke in attempting to manage the stress situation fall into two clusters: Efforts that the child undertakes without help from others are called *personal resources*; those in which help is sought from others are *social support resources*. These clusters may be used independently of each other, sequentially, or concurrently.

Personal Resources

These resources are coping efforts that have the dual function of problem solving and regulating emotional distress. *Problem-focused coping* refers to attempts to alter the threatening situation itself by such direct actions as deliberately avoiding the stressor or working out a solution to the problem. For example, a child who is being bullied at school may forestall the bullying by arranging to be with a protective social network of peers and older siblings when in the school setting. *Emotion-focused coping* refers to the use of reappraisal of the stressor so that it seems less threatening and consequently elicits less intense negative emotions such as anxiety or acute embarrassment. A 9-year-old girl who was teased constantly about her rapidly developing breasts was upset at first, but later came to think of her tormentors as "backward" in terms of understanding incipient adolescence. Both forms of coping are used in most stressful situations: The predominance of one over the other varies as a function of the child's appraisal of the threatening situation as controllable or uncontrollable. The child deals directly (problem-focused coping) with stressors that he or she believes to be controllable and uses reappraisal (emotion-focused coping) to adapt to those that are perceived as uncontrollable.

Evidence that even young school-age children use these forms of coping comes from a study by Band and Weisz (1988). They asked children aged 6, 9, and 12 years to recall stressful events involving six different situations (loss/separation, medical procedures, conflicts with authority figures, peer difficulties, school failure, and physical accidents). Next, the children were asked to describe how they responded to each stressor. Their responses were coded as *primary control* (taking direct action), *secondary control* (doing their best to adapt to the stressor), or *relinquished control* (failing to cope). Note that these labels describe behaviors that are identical to Lazarus's (1966) personal resources categories. Styles of coping varied apparently as a function of the perceived controllability of the stressor. School failure, for example, elicited high levels of primary coping, presumably because the children thought that they could do something about their grades, whereas medical stressors evoked secondary coping (such as self-distraction), possibly because the children knew from experience that resistance was pointless. With increasing age, self-reports of primary coping tended to decline and secondary coping increased: As children mature they become much better judges of when to openly and actively resist and when to try adapting to stress situations. Of particular interest were the frequency and quality of the children's coping. Only 3.5% of all the children's descriptions involved relinquished control, and only 7.7% of all coping efforts reported were judged by adult raters to be ineffective.

Direct actions may not be adaptive or even realistic in terms of outcome, particularly when used by young children. A 6-year-old boy who had to undergo daily painful burn dressings said, "When they come for me I tell them it's the kid in the other bed" (Savedra, 1977). With older children the direct action often consists of trying one coping tactic after another. Sometimes a boy who is being repeatedly bullied will seize on one kind of direct action such as avoidance and engage in a series of avoidance strategies, for example, convincing his mother that he is too ill to go to school, becoming "ill" in school and being allowed to go home, playing truant, taking a circuitous route to school to avoid the bully, hiding somewhere in the school until the bell rings, performing badly in class in an effort to be detained after school, and so on. When these direct actions consistently fail, the child must recognize that it is time to accept that the stressful situation calls for a different approach. Flexibility is needed here, with the child being able to recognize the necessity for change, rather than persisting doggedly along the failure route. As Folkman (1984, p. 843) has noted, a time-honored principle of effective coping is to accept that a stress situation is uncontrollable and abandon direct attempts at altering the situation, and then to turn to emotion-focused coping in order to adapt to the situation or tolerate it. Emotion-focused coping can be used to change the meaning of a stress situation and, in the process, increase the child's feeling of control, with a consequent lessening of distress (Silver & Wortman, 1980). Consider, for example, the girl who has been subjected to a prolonged period of vicious racial teasing and has tried unsuccessfully a variety of direct actions. She finally accepts that there is nothing that she can do to prevent it and turns to a reappraisal of the situation: She places the blame for the teasing squarely on herself by deciding that it is her own fault for being the color that she is. Although this conclusion is irrational, she is likely to experience some relief because now she feels that she has some control over the situation because she is to blame for it; a substantial part of her distress had been due to her feeling that she had no control whatsoever over the teasing. An adult's reaction to this strategy may be that the relief it provides is only temporary. To the child, however, it offers a solution to the problem and consequently, it is stress reducing.

In this example, failure led to intentional reappraisal, but successful direct action also may trigger it off spontaneously. When children use direct action in a stressful situation with some success, there may be a concomitant, almost automatic, shift in their original appraisal of a stressor. The stressor may not seem nearly so formidable when they are able to gain some control over it.

Social Support

In addition to the personal resources available to children, in the form of actions that they can take to manage stressors, there exists another source of relief from the psychological distress caused by threatening events. This source is *social support* in the form of help or comfort from others in their environment. Children who are confronted with stressors that they cannot handle, such as bullying, can in theory seek and obtain social support from their network of family, friends, and school personnel. In practice, however, the availability of a social network does not automatically guarantee support in times of stress. The quality of the child's relationship with his or her social network and the extent to which the network believes in the child's need for help and its members are able and willing to do so will determine the outcome of calling on them for help.

In the following example, an 11-year-old girl sought but did not obtain social support from her mother, then used a variety of direct actions before changing her appraisal of the situation and acting on it. The girl was given a dress by her grandmother that was "so totally weird it was awesome." She complained bitterly to her mother when she was teased mercilessly about it at school. When her mother insisted that she continue to wear the dress to school, the girl next tried avoidance by wearing another dress but leaving for school before her mother was up. This gambit only served to increase her mother's determination that she wear the dress. The girl then tried unsuccessfully to negotiate an agreement with her mother that she would always wear to her grandmother's house but not to school. Although knowing that punishment was inevitable, she finally decided that her only option was to destroy the dress: ". . . there was no way I could get out of wearing it to school so I got my Mom's big scissors and I chopped it up" (D. M. Ross, Case studies, University of California, San Francisco, 1977–1979).

The most common reason for children not getting help with the problems of teasing and bullying is that the members of their social networks, particularly their parents, siblings, and teachers, refuse outright to give it. They may brush the children's complaints aside with such platitudes as "it happens to everyone," "it's part of growing up"; or they may tell them to fight their own battles, coupled with derogatory comments such as "Don't be a wimp." Typical of this attitude is a quote about Hillary Clinton:

> Not so tough at age 4, the first lady . . . came running home, scared of a bully. Rodham (her mother) blocked her path and said, "There is no room for cowards in this house. You have to go back outside and deal with problems like this." (Fournier, 1994, p. A20)

Sometimes parents mask their unwillingness to help their children by blaming them. They suggest or imply that it is the children's fault, thus further eroding their confidence and increasing their vulnerability to further problems in social relationships.

For children in Canada and England who do not see seeking support from individuals in their own social network as a feasible alternative, there is another option: the telephone hotline. This is a widely publicized, toll-free national telephone counseling service called Kids Help Line (Canada) and Childline (England) that offers advice, comfort, and protection to any child up to the age of 18, for 24 hours a day, 7 days a week. Children can talk to trained professional counselors as often as they choose without saying who or where they are. They are guaranteed complete confidentiality. Often the effect of this anonymity results in their revealing information that face-to-face discussion might never elicit. So many calls about bullying were made to Childline in 1990 that a short-term satellite line called the Bullying Line was set up. This latter option is discussed in Chapter 6.

When a child who is being bullied is unable to obtain support from the social network, it can be particularly damaging because often the child has explored other options first and only seeks social support as a last resort. When this final option fails, the child is likely to be overwhelmed with a feeling of hopelessness that in turn can put the child at risk for depression and suicide (Kashani, Reid, & Rosenberg, 1989):

> This 15-year-old boy lived with his mother, his father having left the family. . . . During the school year which ended in his death he had been continually bullied by other boys and had confided this to his principal, his mother and the truant officer following inquiries into his frequent absences. His note said: "Day after day it's the same with no way out. I can't stop them; I ought to be able to stand up for myself but I can't.

Nobody will stand up for me because nobody really cares about me and I can see why." (Leach, 1986, p. 654)

Age may be a factor, too, in the failure to get social support for the problem of bullying. Many children are averse to seeking help from parents and school personnel because of their own misguided ideas about the inappropriateness of seeking help at their age. Often they are embarrassed and humiliated by their own failure to cope with the bullying, even when the odds are overwhelmingly against them. As an example, consider the reasoning of a 13-year-old boy who was being relentlessly persecuted by a pair of 12-year-olds who were both significantly taller and heavier than he was:

> I'm 13, for Christ's sake. How can I tell my folks that I'm buying off (protection money) some 12-year-old kids to keep them from messing me up again? My dad already says I'm a sissy. I'd *never* hear the end of it. The three times they did beat me up I told him it was a rough football game. He liked that. (C. W. Andersen, personal communication, December 6, 1994)

It is essential, then, for children to know not only when direct action should or should not be attempted before seeking social support, but also when they are justified in seeking this support and when it is mandatory to make use of its availability.

Sociometric Status

In a study on the relationship between peer-nominated sociometric status and sources of social support, Munsch and Kinchen (1995) asked 247 adolescents in seventh and eighth grade to describe their attempts to obtain social support for help with a recent stressful event. To assess sociometric status, adolescents were asked to write down the names of classmates who fitted specific behavior descriptors such as popular, social isolate, and rejected. Sociometric status did not prevent the subjects from seeking social support, but it did affect the amount of support that those in their social networks were willing to provide. Parents provided support regardless of their children's social status: It made no difference, for example, whether or not the children were popular or social isolates, controversial (disruptive, aggressive, deviant) or average. Nonparental adults were also relatively unaffected by such differences. Peers, however, were greatly influenced by sociometric status in deciding whether to provide social support. Contrary to predictions, rejected adolescents did not receive the lowest levels of support; surprisingly, it was the popular adolescents whose ratings were lowest. Munsch and Kinchen speculate that this finding may be due to popular children being perceived as competent and self-reliant and, consequently, less in need of social support in dealing with stressors.

In discussing the benefits of social support, Cohen and Wills (1985) have suggested two explanations for its positive effect. According to their *buffering model,* children seek social support, particularly from family or friends, because they see them as potential allies who can protect them from the impact of the stress by eliminating it. Sometimes a child is so confident of the availability of social support that no attempt is made to use personal resources. An 8-year-old leukemic girl who was completely bald from chemotherapy stated that she never made any attempt herself to stop children who teased her about her baldness:

> I don't even tell them to stop it or get lost or anything, I just tell my brothers (both older) and they march up to the kid who's teasing me and they say, "We know *something about you* and if you *ever* tease Anne Marie again or do anything to her we'll tell *everybody!*" And then they march off and that kid never teases me again or even comes near me. (J. Porter, personal communication, September 11, 1992)

The *direct social support model* (Cohen & Wills, 1985) posits an increase in well-being on the part of the child regardless of the actual amount of concrete support given. Sometimes just the presence of family or friends bolsters the ability of the child to cope with the stressor. In a study of childhood pain (Ross & Ross, 1988) we asked children, "What would have helped most when you were (child's report of worst pain ever)?" Almost the entire group (99.2%) felt that the "thing that helped most" regardless of the kind of pain was to have one or both parents present. In response to a question about what specific actions of the parents had helped, the children freely acknowledged that more often than not there was nothing that the parent could actually do but emphasized again how much having them there had helped. That just having an empathic listener can serve to attenuate stress is evident in this 8-year-old boy's comment:

> I thought if I got any more scared about it (scheduled tonsillectomy) I'm gonna go screaming crazy so I talked to my Mom about it. Like I told her *everything* starting with praying the doctor would die or something so I couldn't have it. And there wasn't anything she could do to stop it, you know, but after I told her *everything,* even the very bad stuff, I still didn't feel good about it but I wasn't scared silly any more. (D. M. Ross, Case studies, University of California, San Francisco, 1977–1979)

An integral part of the secondary appraisal process concerns the child's judgment about whether or not controlling the stressful event is possible. Knowing that specific personal and/or social coping resources are available that can lessen the impact of a stressor

(Bandura's [1977a] "outcome expectancy") is only the first step toward control. The child also must have confidence in his or her ability to implement the coping resources needed to mediate the impact of the stressor (Bandura's "efficacy expectancy"). The relationship between being in control and stress is an interesting one. Being in control does not always lead to stress reduction (Folkman, 1984). In teaching children how to combat teasing, Ross (1973) encouraged them to use the strategies in the real-life teasing situation only when they had provided unequivocal evidence in test situations that they could use them successfully and also felt ready and eager to confront the teaser. When they met these prerequisites we believed that they felt in control. Even so, some of the most able and confident children clearly found the first trial stressful. A 10-year-old girl reported that

> I did all the things right but Mary Helen (the teaser) came up real close and gave me that terrible look and it got very scary. But I just moved back a bit so as I wouldn't be touching and I kept staring at her and asking questions over and over even when she started shouting. My insides were shaking so hard I wondered if she could see the shakes. Then all of a sudden she went off and she yelled at me that she'd be back. (D. M. Ross, Case studies, University of California, San Francisco, 1977–1979)

Nor does believing an event to be uncontrollable always result in increased stress (Folkman, 1984). Sometimes this belief results in a kind of passive resignation, a relaxing about the problem.

Appraisals of control are transitory rather than static phenomena. In Lazarus's theory (1966) the child and the environment are in a bidirectional relationship in which new information from the environment and/or from coping efforts can result in changes in the child's appraisal. Consider, for example, the case of an 11-year-old boy who initially was pessimistic about his ability to combat cruel teasing and who was then taught how to react to the teaser. When he first put what he had learned into action, he immediately saw that the teaser was disconcerted by the new tactics. The boy then realized that, for the first time, he had a coping resource that could appreciably influence and perhaps even eliminate the misery of being teased. That his appraisal of control then shifted sharply in his favor was evident from his report:

> I just get there (to school) and I see Greg—waiting. And he goes, my terrible fumble in the playoff, my funny accent, my weirdo brother—you name it. And I'm *really* zeroing in on him so as to report back, but I yawn *real wide* and I look *real interested*—like, you know, at the guys shooting baskets? And all of a sudden Greg grabs my arm and he goes, "Parker!

Hey, Parker! You hear me?" And he sounds kinda different, like more sort of worried than nasty, you know? So I turn my head real slow and I give him my zombie look and I say, "What?" And he doesn't say nothing. And right then *I* know it's [teasing program] starting to work on him! And I jerk my arm away and I go, "See ya, Greg," and I leave him still talking. I *never* done that before. (D. M. Ross, Case studies, University of California, San Francisco, 1977–1979)

The reciprocal influence between the environment and the child does not always operate in the child's favor. Bullying that is repeated over time, for example, commonly results in depressed affect (Kashani et al., 1989) and the child becomes increasingly sad, dejected, and irritable. This behavior pattern may then adversely influence the responses of others, particularly the child's peers, who could provide valuable social support. Instead, what often happens is that the downward spiral leads to more and more negative interactions with those who were once friendly and a concomitant increase in the social isolation of the child.

Within this transactional framework, stress can be viewed as an imbalance or poor fit between the child's personal and/or social coping resources on the one hand and the demands of a threatening event on the other (Lazarus & Folkman, 1984). The poorer the fit between the coping resources and the threatening event, the greater the stress. It follows that stress is not a property of the child, as is a response such as poor self-esteem. Nor is it a property of the environment, as school examinations or noxious medical procedures are. Instead, stress is ". . . a particular relationship between the person and the environment that is appraised by the person as taxing or exceeding his or her resources and endangering his or her well-being" (Lazarus & Folkman, p. 19).

Comment

To help a child cope effectively with a stressor such as bullying, the adult *must* accept the child's appraisal of the stressor as fact and work from that position. Often a stressor that the adult sees as a daily hassle seems like a major life event to the child. Initial efforts should focus on helping the child to cope by means of direct actions (problem-focused coping) because success by this route engenders a feeling of mastery and of being in control. However, if the stressor is clearly uncontrollable, adaptation in the form of emotion-focused coping could be the best solution. Most stressful situations lend themselves to a combination of the two forms of coping. It should be noted that being in control of the stressor does not invariably lead to stress reduction; nor does perceiving a stressor as uncontrollable always result in increased stress. If the stressor is one that makes help in the form of social support from parents or school personnel imperative (as many bullying problems do), it is important that the child see this source of help as mandatory rather than optional. When help is given, the degree of fit between the coping resource and the stressor is of prime importance. The adult should eliminate the stressor for the child only if a good coping resource–stressor fit is not a viable alternative.

2 Bullying: An Overview

CHILDHOOD BULLYING has a long history. This overview focuses on the first empirical study of bullying, which was conducted in Scandinavia under the leadership of Dan Olweus, and discusses a cluster of findings from this important study beginning with the prevalence data. Two topics of particular importance here are the dissent among investigators about the definition of bullying and the marked difference between the child's concept of bullying and that of adults.

Contrary to many contemporary media reports, childhood bullying is *not* a 20th-century phenomenon. According to classical fiction of the 19th century (for example, *Tom Brown's Schooldays* [Hughes, 1857] or *Oliver Twist* [Dickens, 1838]) and historical accounts of childhood (Ariès, 1962; Rose, 1991; Walvin, 1982), children have long been subjected to bullying by their families, peers, teachers, and other adults. Rose (1991) has described English public schoolboy society of the mid-Victorian period as barbaric and goes on to relate how the oldest boys in a boarding school

. . . got sadistic pleasure out of making younger boys box each other for their amusement, and if they failed to keep up at football they were made to cut large thorn sticks out of the hedges and were flogged with them till bloody. (p. 177)

A respected 19th-century surgeon, Chevalier Jackson, stated that the perpetual torment and bullying that he was subjected to throughout most of his school years was so severe that he always thought of the day he left school at 17 to enter the University of Pittsburgh Medical School as the happiest day of his life (Killinger, 1980). During his high school years a group of older boys had waited for him regularly after school, ambushed him, and swung him around by his feet until the pressure in his head was unbearable. Sometimes they choked him almost to a point of unconsciousness.

Often they filled his lunch box with rotten eggs and, on several occasions, plunged him into the watering trough.

Twentieth-century accounts of children whose schooldays were marred by cruel bullying abound in the autobiographies of men such as Graham Greene (1971), a distinguished author, and Sir Ranulph Fiennes (1988), a world-famous explorer. At age 6, Fiennes attended the Forres School in South Africa, where a sadistic bully known as the Forres Monster warned his hapless victims that if they ever reported him their lives would become one long nightmare. Fiennes was as mesmerized by fear as the next boy and the bullying soon assumed the status of a major life event (Lazarus, 1966). Fortunately, direct action in the form of buying the bully off solved the problem, although at some cost to Fiennes: "I began to give Gertz my prize marbles, catapult, biltong sticks, anything to placate him" (Fiennes, 1988, p. 4).

Later he was sent to Eton. When he had been there a month he was accused of being a tart. In Eton slang a tart is a boy who sells himself for sexual activities in return for favors and is regarded as the lowest form of life. Many attractive boys, including Fiennes, were unjustly accused of being tarts. When denial had no effect, Fiennes sought social support from his peers, to no avail. Once again, the bullying took on the status of a major life event (Lazarus, 1966) and the fact that it was clearly uncontrollable induced a feeling of such profound hopelessness in the hapless victim that he contemplated suicide. In describing the misery he endured at Eton, Fiennes (1988) wrote:

> No leper or spy can have suffered as much as I did as I struggled to live . . . for two years with the shouted taunts and the subtle cruelties of my fellow Etonians. . . . There was no one for me to run to . . . I contemplated the option of suicide with growing seriousness. . . . (p. 17)

Current literature for children and adolescents also contains many fictional (for example, Golding's [1955] *Lord of the Flies*) and nonfictional (Grunsell's [1990] *Bullying*) accounts of bullying. A list of books on this topic is contained in the Annotated Bibliography.

Bullying is not restricted to childhood. Recent books (Bing, 1992), articles in periodicals (Adams, 1992; Berle, 1989; Bly, 1988; Finley, 1992; Fitzgerald, 1992), and an increasing number of newspaper reports (Rhoden, 1993) of the bullying of adults attest to the fact that bullying thrives in adulthood. Bullying is prevalent in adult social groups characterized by well-established power relationships and low supervision and is particularly likely in groups from which it is difficult for an adult to leave because of financial considerations, family obligations, or tenure. A recent questionnaire survey

(Dean, 1995) in English schools yielded 4,000 reports of the bullying of teachers by school principals and parents. Many teachers have escaped the bullying by resigning or taking early retirement; but in some bullying situations, such as a wartime military establishment with a tradition of painful initiations (Tattum, 1989) or a custodial institution in which the brutalization of new inmates is the rule (Prestage, 1994; Williams, 1995), it is virtually impossible to escape. In the United States the classic studies of Polsky (1962) and Feld (1977) have described the sadistic attacks on prisoners by those further up in the power hierarchy.

Although bullying has long been a problem in contemporary society, prior to 1970 investigative interest in the bullying of children was at best sporadic (see Farrington, 1993, for an excellent review of this literature). The first significant contribution to the problem came from Peter Paul Heinemann (1973), a Swedish physician who became so appalled by the bullying that he observed in school playgrounds that he wrote several articles and then a book about bullying. Heinemann used the term *mobbing*, a term taken from the work of Lorenz (1966), to describe childhood bullying. His interpretation of mobbing was as group violence against a *deviant* individual who had disturbed the group's ordinary activity. This view was a forerunner of the provocative victim category of Olweus (1978).

Heinemann's expressions of concern were well received by Scandinavians who, as Munthe (1989) has pointed out, are known for a long tradition of tolerance and caring for each other. Heinemann's publications gave substance to a pervasive unease that Swedish teachers and parents had had about bullying. They also focused attention on the important research of Dan Olweus, who, in the early 1970s, had begun a longitudinal study of bullying that is still ongoing. Olweus is unquestionably the leading authority in the world on the problem of childhood bullying. Over the past quarter century, no other body of research on bullying is comparable in either size or complexity (Besag, 1989). The longitudinal study (Olweus, 1978), which began with 900 sixth- through ninth-grade Swedish boys, is representative of his contribution to the field. The remarkable feature of this study was the breadth and depth of information about bullying and victimization that Olweus collected years before any other investigator attempted a major study on the topic. We briefly discuss some of the findings, many of which have since been confirmed by other investigators.

Of particular relevance to the topic of intervention was Olweus's finding, subsequently confirmed by others, that the well-entrenched dichotomy of bullies and victims was a gross oversimplification.

Instead, Olweus (1978) identified distinct subgroups within both populations, which meant that one form of intervention would not fit all bullies or all victims. These categories have since been confirmed (Stephenson & Smith, 1989) and extended by others (Besag, 1989; Mitchel & O'Moore, 1988). A second important refinement of our understanding of bullying was Olweus's distinction between direct and indirect bullying. *Direct bullying* refers to face-to-face confrontations, open attacks including physical aggression, and threatening and intimidating gestures, whereas *indirect bullying* is a more subtle behavior pattern requiring a third party and including social exclusion and isolation, rumor spreading, and scapegoating. Björkqvist, Lagerspetz, and Kaukiainen (1992) have added a third category, *direct verbal aggression*, such as name calling.

Several of the child-rearing antecedents of bullying, such as parental use of power-assertive methods, were identified by Olweus (1980), and all have been documented by others (Mitchel & O'Moore, 1988; Patterson, DeBaryshe, & Ramsey, 1989). These antecedents of bullying will be discussed in greater detail in Chapter 3.

A common assumption that bullies are characterized by an underlying anxiety and insecurity was discounted by Olweus's findings, obtained from direct measures in the form of personality tests and indirect ones through hormonal assays. At a later point in the study, Olweus obtained information on the negative, long-term outcomes of bullying, such as the increased probability of a criminal record by early adulthood. This finding has been documented in many other investigations (Beale, 1993; Eron & Huesmann, 1987; Farrington, 1993; James, 1994). For those who had been victimized in childhood, Olweus (1993b) found evidence of encouraging, but not uniformly positive, long-term outcomes in young adulthood.

In the early 1980s an abrupt and dramatic change occurred, particularly in Norway, in the status of the problem of bullying. The catalyst for this change was a 1982 newspaper report that three 10- to 14-year-old boys from different schools in Norway had committed suicide apparently as a result of severe, long-term bullying by their peers (Olweus, 1991). The effect of these tragedies was to set off a chain reaction in Norway: Shock and uneasiness in the citizenry fueled mass media outrage, which in turn led to widespread concern in the school administration culminating in alarm and a call for action in government circles.

Although the suicides were the trigger for these reactions, sensational events such as these often are a nine-days' wonder that quickly fades from public awareness. A potentially useful conglomeration prevented this from happening. Prior research by Olweus (1978) showed conclusively that the suicides could not be attributed to isolated instances of bullying. There already was a database of information on bullying that had begun to accumulate not only in Norway, but also elsewhere (see, for example, the Finnish research of Björkqvist, Ekman, & Lagerspetz [1982] and of Lagerspetz, Björkqvist, Berts, & King [1982]). Perhaps most telling was the availability of a group of experienced investigators, headed by Dan Olweus and Erling Roland, who were ready to launch an attack on the problem.

The result of this timely combination of events and personnel availability was a government-supported intervention program, the Nationwide Campaign Against Bullying (referred to here as the Campaign), launched by the Ministry of Education in 1983 under the leadership of Olweus with Roland and a team of experienced investigators. The goals of the Campaign were to reduce bullying sharply in the primary and secondary Norwegian schools while fostering the active involvement of teachers and parents in this change process.

Three sets of program materials were developed: a 32-page booklet about bully–victim problems and their management for the schools; a 4-page booklet on bullying for parents; and an inexpensive 25-minute video cassette, for purchase or rental, on two children who were bullied.

To provide an instrument to assess the problem of bullying, Olweus (1983) developed the Bully/Victim Questionnaire. (An English version of this Questionnaire [Olweus & Smith, 1995], is available. For information contact Dr. P. K. Smith, Department of Psychology, P.O. Box 603, University of Sheffield, Sheffield, S10 2UR, UK.) Olweus defines bullying or victimization in general terms as follows: "A student is being bullied or victimized when he or she is exposed, repeatedly and over time, to negative actions on the part of one or more other students" (Olweus, 1993a, p. 9).

Olweus's Questionnaire definition of bullying (1983) has been slightly modified by investigators in other countries to accommodate language differences. A representative example is that provided by Smith and Sharp (1994):

> We say a child or young person is being bullied, or picked on when another child or young person, or a group of children or young people, say nasty and unpleasant things to him or her. It is also bullying when a child or a young person is hit, kicked, threatened, locked inside a room, sent nasty notes, when no one ever talks to them and things like that. These things can happen frequently and it is difficult for the child or the young person being bullied to defend himself or herself. It is also bullying when a child or young person is teased repeatedly in a nasty way. (p. 13)

Olweus's Questionnaire covers aspects of the bullying problem such as the frequency and types of bullying, its location, who does the bullying, how often children report bullying to teachers or family, and what action, if any, teachers take in cases of ongoing or reported bullying. In empirical investigations by members of the Sheffield Bullying Project (Ahmad & Smith, 1990), the Questionnaire has proven to be reliable and valid and to show "reasonable" agreement with peer nominations. One week before the Campaign started in September 1983, the Bully/Victim Questionnaire was made available to comprehensive primary and secondary Norwegian schools (n = 3,500). Eighty-five percent of these schools subsequently participated in the Campaign.

Of particular interest to investigators in other countries are the core components of the Campaign's school-based intervention program. To achieve the goal of reducing the existing bully–victim problems in the school environment and community (secondary prevention) and to prevent the onset of new problems (primary prevention), it was important to create a school environment characterized by warmth, positive interest, and commitment on the part of school personnel. Firm rules about acceptable school behavior were established; when violations occurred nonhostile, nonphysical sanctions were unequivocally applied.

Olweus (1993a) specified two prerequisites: one was *awareness* on the part of school personnel and parents of the prevalence of bully–victim problems in their school; the other was *involvement*, that is, a genuine interest in working on the problem of bullying. To accomplish these two tasks, a number of procedures and activities were implemented that targeted the whole school population as well as the children's parents. Included in this group of school-level activities were a questionnaire survey to establish prevalence and a school conference day to draw up a general plan of action for the school and have the staff meet the parents. One of the goals of the plan of action was to improve the physical attributes of the playground and have better supervision of play time. A contact telephone was recommended for children and adults who wished to report bullying or discuss bully-related problems anonymously. Teams of teachers were formed to work on the social milieu of the school, and study groups were set up for concerned parents.

At the classroom level students were asked to agree on a set of rules about bullying, with the goal of reducing bully–victim problems. Class meetings were held to talk about bullying and other problems. Role play and relevant fictional and nonfictional accounts were incorporated into the curriculum along with cooperative learning activities in which small groups of students worked on a common task with the evaluation of it focusing on the performance of the group. Mutual positive dependence was created by the nature of the task, such as the requirement that the group produce one paper on the task. Whole class activities that were fun, for example, a class picnic, and ones that were instructive, for example, attending a PTA meeting, were included.

At the *individual level* the teachers had serious talks with children who had bullied others and with their parents, emphasizing the school's policy of zero tolerance of bullying. Discussion groups were made available to the parents of bullies and victims. Much was accomplished by pairing children who needed help with those who were more able. In certain cases, bullies and/or victims were assigned to a new class.

The school programs used in the Campaign are noteworthy for their simplicity: no major expenditure of funds, no flashy equipment or materials; instead, the will to effect a change backed up by a supportive administration and school personnel committed to sustained interest and effort. With these components, Olweus (1993a) achieved excellent results: a decrease in bully–victim problems of 50% or more and fewer new victims, with improvements being even greater after 2 years than after 1 year. Marked improvement occurred in the social climate of the school with a concomitant increase in satisfaction with school life. Reductions also occurred in instances of bullying outside the jurisdiction of the school and in general antisocial behaviors. Given these results, it is commendable that Olweus regards the plan for the school programs as in transition and subject to change pending further research and increased use of it in the schools. Such caution is exemplary and rare.

As part of the Campaign, two other projects were commissioned. One was a large-scale project, the Bergen Study, designed to assess the efficacy of the intervention program. It involved 2,500 children, ages 10 to 15, in grades 4 through 7, attending 28 primary and 14 junior high schools in Bergen. Also participating were 1,000 parents and between 300 and 400 teachers and other school personnel. Over a 2½-year period data collection was scheduled five or six times from children and school personnel and three times from parents. To ensure a fair evaluation of the intervention project, Olweus (1993a) provided continuing and fairly intensive support to the schools over the intervention period.

The second project, the Swedish Study, was designed to compare bullying in Norway and Sweden. The Bully/Victim Questionnaire was administered to 17,000 students in three Swedish cities and to 32,000 students in three same-size cities in Norway. Olweus's (1993a) conclusion was that there were great similarities in the bullying problems of the two countries, although overall the problems were somewhat greater and more serious in the Swedish schools.

The findings of the Campaign and those of all studies on bullying are influenced to a considerable extent by the way in which bullying is defined. If a definition specifies that there must be several attacks before the behavior can be regarded as bullying, then the respondents' answers concerning frequency will be considerably lower than would be the case if single instances of attacks were also regarded as bullying. Because definitions play such a vital role in interpreting research findings, we first discuss the problems involved in defining bullying, including what is known about the child's concept of bullying, before moving on to the results of the Campaign.

THE PROBLEM OF DEFINITION FOR RESEARCH

Defining even an apparently uncomplicated behavior such as bullying can create dissension. Yet, if exchanges of prevalence data and other findings are to have any validity, it is essential that they be based on one definition acceptable to the research and clinical communities. This problem is one that has long complicated and slowed advances in the behavioral sciences. Because the formal study of bullying is a relatively recent phenomenon, it is a great pity that the field already has lost cumulative benefits that could have accrued from the many excellent investigations had their researchers shared a common viewpoint. It can be seen from Table 2.1 that in terms of definitional accord the field was in a state of disarray by the early 1990s.

Points of Dispute

Long-standing Bullying

How many bullying interactions must occur, or over what period of time must bullying continue, if it is to meet this temporal criterion? It is baffling why this has become a criterion and it is another example of an adult interpretation being superimposed on the child. It is the child's view of a stressor that defines it as such, whether or not it is the first occurrence or one of a series, is irrelevant. So if the child perceives an experience as bullying, then it is bullying. Olweus (1993a, p. 9), however, defends *long-standing* or *repeatedly over time* as a way of excluding "nonserious" events. He and Roland require that the negative actions must have occurred at least once a week for a month or more for the behavior to be considered a serious problem, whereas Lowenstein (1978) advocates a 6-month period.

Table 2.1 Definitions of Bullying

- *Askew* (1989). Bullying is a continuum of behavior that involves the attempt to gain power and dominance over another.
- *Lane* (1989). Bullying includes any action or implied action, such as threats, intended to cause fear and distress. The behavior has to be repeated on more than one occasion. The definition must include evidence that those involved intended or felt fear.
- *Olweus* (1993a). A student is being bullied or victimized when he or she is exposed, repeatedly and over time, to negative actions on the part of one or more other students.
- *Smith and Thompson* (1991a). Bullying intentionally causes hurt to the recipient. This hurt can be both physical or psychological. In addition, three further criteria particularly distinguish bullying: it is unprovoked, it occurs repeatedly, and the bully is stronger than the victim or is perceived to be stronger.
- *Stephenson and Smith* (1989). Bullying is a form of social interaction not necessarily long-standing, in which a more dominant individual (the bully) exhibits aggressive behavior that is intended to and does, in fact, cause distress to a less dominant individual (the victim). The aggressive behavior may take the form of a direct physical and/or verbal attack or may be indirect. More than one bully and more than one victim may participate in the interaction.
- *Tattum* (1989). Bullying is a willful, conscious desire to hurt another person. It can be occasional and short-lived, or it can be regular and long-standing.

Other investigators (Smith & Thompson, 1991a, p. 1) state explicitly that "something that just happens once or twice would not be called bullying," which implies that short-lived incidents should be excluded. Imposing a temporal lid as the criterion rather than a qualitative evaluation of the incident means that if the following incident only occurred once it would not be regarded as bullying: "I was 11 . . . a gang of six girls pushed me downstairs, smashed my face against a wall, cut off my hair and threatened to stab me" (Buchanan, 1992, p. 8).

At the other end of the continuum are investigators (Stephenson & Smith, 1989; Tattum, 1989) who contend that attacks do not have to be long-standing to be classified as bullying. Some investigators (see, for example, Askew, 1989; White, 1987) do not set any temporal criterion. Adherence to a temporal criterion is not in the best interests of effective management of bullying. Interventions would not be introduced at the earliest point, when it is probably easiest to stop the bullying and the least damage has been done to the victim.

The only compelling argument for long-standing attacks comes from the acknowledged importance of an anticipatory fear component in victims (Besag, 1989; Greenbaum, 1989; Mellor, 1991). Their accounts suggest that bullying generally results in two kinds of quite severe distress: One is the immediate upset that results from the physical or psychological sequelae of bullying, such as physical pain, humiliation, or reaction to loss or damage to one's possessions; the other is the anticipatory terror that occurs from the spoken or implied threat of future attacks, which often becomes more severe over time. It is this latter kind of distress that is assumed to be absent in bullying that happens only once or twice. This is a major assumption to make in view of the reactions of victims to first-time bullying:

> Nine year old Mark was walking home from school when a gang of bullies set upon him. His arm was broken, his money was stolen and his books were destroyed. His self-confidence was also destroyed. He became withdrawn, hated to go to school and eventually had counseling to help him through the trauma. He knew the boys who had attacked him, but refused to tell who they were. He was frightened of what they would do if he told. (Elliott, 1991, p. 8)

Number of Bullies Involved

Most investigators, including the leading Scandinavian researchers Olweus (1993a) and Roland (1989a), agree that there may be one or more bullies and one or more victims. However, a contingent of other Scandinavians, headed by Pikas (1989) contends that there must be at least two bullies, a view that has evoked considerable criticism. In a sense the criticism is unjustified because what Pikas has done is to identify a criterion for a *variant* of bullying, which Heinemann (1973) called *mobbing*, rather than a criterion for bullying in general. Accepting only Pikas's criterion would have the same effect as accepting the temporal criterion: A spuriously low frequency rate for bullying would result, with a negative effect on prevention and intervention efforts.

WHEN IS A BEHAVIOR BULLYING?

Besag (1989) has pointed out that a definition encompassing all possible facets of child-instigated physical hurt and psychological distress would be too cumbersome to be productive. One criterion might be to look at a specific behavior in terms of its underlying motive rather than its face value. Consider theft, for example. Instead of deciding that all theft is or is not bullying, ask what is the motive underlying the theft. If it is to demonstrate power over the victim or to strike fear or feelings of helplessness and no attempt is made at secrecy because the perpetrator is confident that the victim fears reprisals following disclosure, then the theft should be regarded as bullying. Note that secrecy may also be an element of bullying when bullies engage in a series of antisocial acts, such as theft or vandalism, and make every effort to hide their identity because the goal is to strike terror in the victim with anonymous relentless persecution. Applying the motive criterion eliminates behaviors that have some of the elements of bullying but clearly cannot be construed as bullying. For example, *initiation rites* that children or adolescents participate in of their own volition in order to be accepted in a club or other organization are not bullying, although often there is an element of physical or psychological cruelty in them. *Good-natured scuffling, wrestling, pushing,* or *shoving* (with the goal of standing up for one's rights or protecting one's territory) without animosity or ill will, is not bullying. Nor are *clearly thoughtless or accidental actions* that unintentionally cause physical hurt or psychological distress but lack the conscious desire to inflict pain on others. Of relevance here is an unpublished survey of attitudes to bullying (O'Connor, 1995) conducted as part of the Sheffield Bullying Project. The respondents ranged in age from 5 to 20. A surprising finding was that this group viewed unintentional negative actions by others as bullying. Truly accidental behaviors, however negative, are *not* bullying. It is important for young children to learn to discriminate between bullying and genuine accidents. The response of the perpetrator provides one basis for making this distinction. Bullies seldom, if ever, apologize, show concern, or try to help a victim. Discuss the incident with the child in these terms. Note that the accomplished bully often falls back on the unintentional category with the excuse, "It was just an accident," offered so earnestly and convincingly that to the discredit of the gullible adult no censure follows.

The Child's Concept of Bullying

In a questionnaire on bullying, the provision of a definition by the adult implies that the adult's concept of bullying concurs with that of the child. If, in fact, they differ, the child's responses will have little value. If valid responses are to be obtained, it is essential to explore the child's concept of the topic and phrase questions accordingly. Although this step in questionnaire development frequently is overlooked, there is some evidence supporting the necessity for it.

Consider, for example, the finding reported by Lane (1989). In interviews with a random group of 100 students from an English mixed secondary school, a number of incidents were described that adults would have considered to be bullying but that the students did not view as such:

A 15-year-old boy was fearful of another group of boys. They would play threatening games on him to see how scared he would get.

A fifth-year girl, who intensely disliked a Muslim girl in her class, organized her friends to ignore her. For added fun she then pretended to be friends, persuaded the girl to organize a party at her house, and then ensured that no one came. (p. 97)

Lane (personal communication, December 29, 1994) stated that in this group "frightening games generally were seen as outside of bullying , and nasty behavior was defined as bitchy, even horrid, but not as bullying."

One of the best sources of information on the child's concept of bullying is the short-term satellite line of Childline, the Bullying Line: except that the descriptor *bullying* was used to indicate the problem this line was intended for, there was no definition of bullying and no guidelines for how to talk about the problem. Children phoning Childline described a wide range of behavior as bullying that could, as La Fontaine (1991) has pointed out, present problems of definition to investigators because it implies that children include far more behaviors under the heading of bullying than adults do. Evidence in support of this possibility comes from studies carried out by investigators on the Sheffield Bullying Project (Madsen & Smith, 1993; O'Connor, 1995; Smith & Levan, in press).

Imbalance of Power

Most investigators concur that bullying involves an imbalance of physical or psychological power, with the bully, or bullies, being either stronger or perceived to be stronger than the victim. Casting doubt on this assumption is the statement by Thompson and Smith (1991) that in "talking to children their perceptions (of bullying) easily shade over into including any situations involving unprovoked aggression, whether or not the odds are . . . uneven" (p. 141).

Bullying as Long-standing

Many investigators (see, for example, Olweus, 1993a; Roland, 1989a; Smith & Thompson, 1991a) also believe that victimization must be long-standing to qualify as bullying. La Fontaine (1991), however, has pointed out that

bullying as long-standing violence . . . implies that short-lived incidents victimizing children are excluded. Yet many of the children who telephoned the Bullying Line were referring to quite recent incidents . . . the children clearly thought that (these incidents) already qualified to be counted as bullying. (p. 12)

In the unpublished survey of attitudes (O'Connor, 1995) referred to earlier the respondents did not think that negative actions had to be repeated in order to constitute bullying.

Distortions

The characteristics of the respondents may distort responses. Bullies may minimize the frequency or severity of their bullying because they perceive these episodes differently from how their victims and uninvolved observers do (Besag, 1989). Quite cruel bullying may be viewed as "just messing around a bit." Victims, however, may consciously exaggerate aspects of the bullying to put themselves in a better light, or they may underreport if they lack confidence in the promised anonymity of the questionnaire and fear reprisal.

Definition in This Text

Bullying refers to intentional and generally unprovoked attempts by one or more individuals to inflict physical hurt and/or psychological distress on one or more victims. There must be an imbalance of physical or psychological power, with the bully actually being stronger or perceived to be stronger than the victim. The bullying may be direct, with face-to-face physical or verbal confrontations, or indirect with less visible actions such as spreading rumors or social exclusion. Although a single attack on a victim can be accurately described as bullying, the term more often refers to a series of negative actions that occur frequently over time. This definition is almost identical to that of Stephenson and Smith (1989), which we think is the best in the current bullying literature. The only difference is that our definition includes the qualifier "generally unprovoked," because it allows for the behavior of the provocative victim.

The Norwegian Nationwide Survey

From the schools participating in the Campaign, Olweus selected a representative sample of 715 schools, with 130,000 children ranging in age from 8 to 16, for the Norwegian Nationwide Survey. The pretest data from this sample provided a wide range of information about the bullying problem: prevalence figures, and age and gender differences are discussed here.

Prevalence

Olweus (1993a) estimated that 15% of the students in the Norwegian comprehensive schools were actively involved in the bullying sequence. To be considered a bully, a child had to have bullied others one or more times per week. Five percent of the school population were involved in more serious bully behaviors. Although Norwegians were reportedly shocked by the prevalence of bullying (Olweus), they had no grounds for hoping that the findings were exaggerations of the problem. With most investigators using slight modifications of Olweus's Bully/Victim Questionnaire (1983), subsequent studies of prevalence in England (Smith & Sharp, 1994), Ireland (O'Moore & Hillery, 1989), the Netherlands (Haeselager & van Lieshout, 1992), Australia (Rigby & Slee, 1991), Japan (Hirano, 1992), and Canada (Ziegler & Rosenstein-Manner, 1991) have reported an even higher prevalence of bullying than that found in Norway.

The conclusions of the two principal investigators, Olweus and Roland, about the prevalence data were notable for their restraint. Olweus (1984) stated that bullying was a considerable problem in Norwegian and Swedish comprehensive schools and one that must be taken seriously. Roland (1989a, p. 27) merely pointed out that the 1983 findings were generally consistent with previous prevalence reports from other Scandinavian countries and said, "It became obvious that there was work to be done!" Other investigators have been similarly cautious: Michele Elliott (1993a, p. 8), founder of Kidscape, said, "Although we do not know the true extent of bullying, it is probably safe to say that it is one of children's major concerns"; and Caroline St. John Brooks (1985) contended that it is almost impossible to tell exactly how much bullying goes on in the United Kingdom because of the mixture of secrecy and exaggeration that surrounds bullying. Their restraint is commendable because there are potential pitfalls in collecting prevalence data on bullying that limit the confidence one can have in exact prevalence figures while not detracting from the established fact that bullying is a serious problem. We briefly consider some of the pitfalls.

Age as a Restrictor

Olweus reported that first-grade children were unable to handle the questionnaire format, even when the person administering it read the items to the class, and Roland (1989a) found that even children in third grade had the same problem. This finding raises questions about the validity of Olweus's (1985) second- and third-grade prevalence data. Mechanical problems of this kind should be identified in the preliminary stages of questionnaire development.

Teacher Nominations of Bullies and Victims

On the basis of teacher–peer agreement, Olweus (1985) has expressed confidence in the accuracy of teacher nominations. However, investigators from non-Nordic countries do not share this confidence. Smith and Sharp (1994, p. 11) contend that "most teachers are only aware of a fraction of the bullying which may be going on," and O'Moore (Nash, 1989) found that teachers seriously underestimated the amount of bullying in that they were able to identify only 4 in 10 of the persistent bullies. The disparity in viewpoint may be attributed to certain characteristics unique to the Scandinavian public school system; for example, in order to foster psychological closeness, the classes are very small, and for the first 6 years, children have the same teacher (Munthe, 1989).

Olweus's (1985) report on the prevalence of bullying in Norway proved to have a catalytic effect: From a minor problem requiring minimal attention, bullying became a serious one demanding immediate action. The effects spread beyond the Nordic countries to other continental European countries, the United Kingdom, the United States, Canada, and Japan. Organizations such as Kidscape were established to combat bullying, multidisciplinary meetings were convened in the United States (Greenbaum, 1989) and Europe (O'Moore, 1988), and the media produced articles, television dramas, and talk shows that focused on bullying. Parents became more demanding and protective of their children's rights, filing lawsuits when school districts failed to acknowledge and remediate bullying by other students (Greenbaum). Bully-related suicides began to be attributed to bullying rather than to "accidental death" (Prestage, 1993). Although some of the media reactions, fueled by the flurry of outrage, were unjustified (Britain is the "bullying capital of Europe " *The Guardian* of September 28, 1989, trumpeted), in the main the public outcry underlined the need for an attack on the problem and served as a stimulus for it.

Grade Level Differences in Bullying

In the prevalence data (Olweus, 1985, 1993a) the percentage of victims decreased with increasing age and grade level, with the incidence of victims being twice as high in the primary grades than in the secondary grades (see Figure 2.1). In contrast to the steady decline in victims, the number of bullies remained fairly stable. In the lower grades most of the bullying was carried out by older children, particularly boys. In fact, relative age rather than chronological age is a factor here: The boys who bullied were most often the oldest in the group, with the number of boy bullies peaking in the final years of both primary and secondary school (see Figure 2.2). Boys who bullied in the final year of primary school were much less active in terms of bullying when they first entered secondary school. These trends in the Norwegian data were consistent with similar analyses of the Swedish (Olweus, 1993a) and Sheffield Bullying Project data (Whitney & Smith, 1993) but not with those of Perry,

Figure 2.1. Percentage of Students, by Grade, Who Reported Being Bullied by Other Students. From *Bullying at school: What we know and what we can do*, (p. 15), by D. Olweus, 1993a, Cambridge, MA: Blackwell. Adapted by permission.

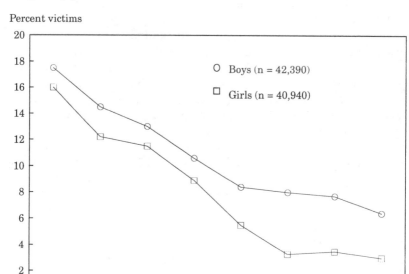

Kusel, and Perry (1988), who did not find that grade was a signifi-cant determinant of victimization. The difference in results could be a function of age changes in bullying being different in the United States, or it may be due to the method of data collection: Perry et al. (1988) used peer nominations rather than self-report.

Olweus (1993a) has stated that "the most remarkable result from these analyses is that bully and victim problems in primary schools were considerably more marked than previously assumed" (p. 16). Certainly the finding that one third of the boys and girls in the second grade reported being bullied is surprisingly high, and this figure is even more disconcerting in view of Smith and Levan's (in press) speculation that ". . . if the age trends in the Whitney and Smith (1993) data were extrapolated backwards, one could predict an even greater incidence of being bullied in 5- to 7-year-olds." The latter hypothetical prevalence figures suggest that the child enter-ing kindergarten could be at high risk for being bullied and so should be given training in coping with bullies prior to entering school.

Figure 2.2. Percentage of Students, by Grade, Who Reported Bullying Other Students. From *Bullying at school: What we know and what we can do*, (p. 16), by D. Olweus, 1993a, Cambridge, MA: Blackwell. Adapted by permission.

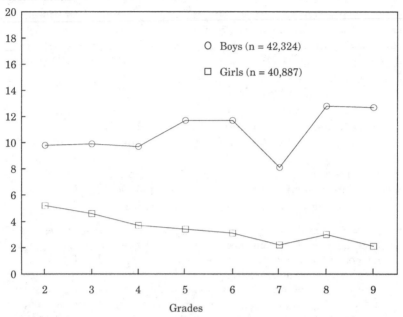

Percent victims

A number of explanations for the high prevalence of victims in the lowest grades have been explored. Several investigators (Besag, 1989; Olweus, 1993a; Thompson & Arora, 1991) have attributed the high rate to the fact that there are more older children in a position to bully the youngest ones. Smith and Levan (in press) point out that this explanation would predict a marked increase in victims when students first enter secondary school because once again they are the youngest in the school, but the prevalence data (Olweus; Whitney & Smith, 1993) for the primary-secondary transition period clearly negate this prediction. Interview data on bullies (Thompson & Arora) have led to the suggestion that younger children are less socialized and therefore are more prone to bully others. However, bullying only decreases slightly across age level, if at all (Olweus; Whitney & Smith).

Level of Cognitive Development

Cognitive development may influence prevalence figures. Smith and Levan (in press) have demonstrated that 6- and 7-year-old children interpret bullying more broadly than older children do, that is, they interpret more events as bullying. For example, the children in their study included occasional aggressive behavior (as opposed to the repeated, long-standing bullying in most definitions), fighting in which there was no imbalance of power, and often omitted any mention of intent to hurt (a critical feature of many definitions). In the Sheffield study of attitudes toward bullying (O'Connor, 1995), there was evidence that young children tend to exaggerate the incidence of bullying. The younger children in Childline (La Fontaine, 1991) and the 5-year-olds in Madsen and Smith's (1993) study exhibited the same patterns in their responses.

Another possible explanation that we offer stems from a report by an experienced head teacher (Frost, 1991) of interviews with 5- and 6-year-old children in a junior school that were conducted 2 weeks after they had started in the new school. Over 50% reported being bullied in the 2-week period, and only 5% said that they had never been bullied. Frost pursued the question further possibly because she doubted the accuracy of their reports:

> . . . on further examination, it seemed that the time scale was confused. Once children had identified someone as a bully the impression and memory remained very strong, even if not reinforced by future experience. Having experienced bullying, the perpetrator then remained a person to be feared by the victim and further interaction involving that person was always viewed at best negatively, or sometimes fearfully, hence *the bullying persisted in the victim's mind*. (p. 31, italics added)

It follows that some of the reported bullying could have occurred before school started, but persisted in the children's minds so strongly that they believed it had occurred more recently than was the case. Assuming that the bullying episodes caused the victims to feel helpless and not in control and their parents to be upset about the incidents, a heightened sense of trauma should result (Dalenberg, Bierman, & Furman, 1984). Trauma may distort memory by producing fear structures (Foa & Kozak, 1986; Pitman, 1988), that are cognitive networks that link all the associations and connotations related to the traumatic event and the meanings attached to them. Fear structures are easily triggered and hard to extinguish, particularly if they encompass cues from the child's ordinarily safe environment (Foa & Kozak; Foa, Steketee, & Rothbaum, 1989) as they did for the children that Frost (1991) interviewed.

Gender Differences

One of the most consistent findings throughout the bullying literature of several continents concerns the higher incidence of bullying in boys than in girls (Ahmad & Smith, 1994). This finding, reported in 1980 by Roland and in 1985 by Olweus is consistent with studies of gender differences in aggression (Maccoby & Jacklin, 1974; Parke & Slaby, 1983). Tieger (1980) had expressed doubts of the veracity of such differences in 1980. Roland subsequently expressed similar doubts. On the basis of his "exhaustive" interview study conducted with 10- to 12-year-old children (n = 300), he reported that girls were involved almost as often as boys, both as bullies and as victims. Unfortunately, the study is unpublished and unavailable in English (E. Roland, personal communication, April 15, 1994).

The differences reported by Roland could be a function of the data collection method, for example, interviews versus questionnaires. In terms of the quality of information obtained, well-conducted interviews can provide a rich body of material (see, for example, Ross & Ross, 1988) when carefully constructed open-ended questions are used. It also is possible that girls may not see their behavior as bullying when they exclude someone or spread rumors. Adults would see a lot of the physical aggression that boys indulge in as more representative of bullying than the girls' less direct attacks. Perhaps in the socialization process this difference is conveyed to girls. If a child is beaten up by another child, the victim's mother is likely to say, "The big bully," but if a child is excluded from a formerly friendly group, the mother is more likely to condemn the behavior as "mean."

There are also gender differences in bullying behavior associated with age. Boys who bully tend to be 1 to 2 years older than their victims, who may be boys but quite often are girls. The percentage of boy bullies is quite stable at different age levels. Bullying in girls declines slightly with age (Olweus, 1993a). Girl bullies are more likely to be the same age as their victims, who are generally other girls, and sometimes girls will join in with boy bullies in indirect bullying of other boys:

> Harold . . . was my ninth-grade classmate. . . . He was tall, pimply-faced and "walked funny." New that year, incredibly shy, he was first made a goat by the boys who, for a prank, elected Harold class president and then jeered at his blushing, stumbling attempts to lead a meeting. The girls quickly climbed on the bandwagon. At slumber parties we phoned him with giggling, sultry invitations to "come on over, Harold." At school we teased him just for the fun of watching this shy, gangly boy squirm. (Zablow, 1991, p. 39)

Both Olweus (1985, 1993a) and Roland (1980) concur that boys used direct bullying four times as often as girls and were victims twice as often, trends that are consistent with more recent research (Björkqvist et al., 1992; Lagerspetz, Björkqvist, & Peltonen, 1988; Whitney & Smith, 1993). However, when direct bullying is broken down into its physical and verbal components, there are no gender differences for direct verbal bullying (Björkqvist et al., 1992; Lagerspetz et al., 1988; Rivers & Smith, 1994). Girls report more indirect bullying, a consistent finding in all studies from Olweus (1985) to the present. Indirect bullying was more likely to involve boys and girls against a victim, whereas direct physical or verbal bullying was less likely to do so.

RELATIONSHIP BETWEEN SCHOOL CHARACTERISTICS AND PREVALENCE OF BULLYING

The Norwegian prevalence data (Olweus, 1993a) show unequivo-cally that bullying is not evenly distributed over any population, that is, any school district, specific school, or class. Other investigators have confirmed this finding with junior secondary (Smith & Sharp, 1994) and secondary schools (Arora & Thompson, 1987; Siann, Callaghan, Glissov, Lockhart, & Rawson, 1994). In addition Stephenson and Smith (1989) have reported that within one cluster of schools the probability of being bullied was four to five times greater in some schools than in others. The question then is what characteristics of a school are associated with higher or lower prevalence of bullying.

School and Class Size

Commonsense reasoning would suggest that the sheer numbers of students in big-city schools with large classes would be associated with higher rates of bullying, but this is not the case. Neither school nor class size was a significant factor in the prevalence of bullying in the Norwegian National Survey (Olweus, 1993a), the earlier Swedish data (Olweus, 1978), or the Finnish studies (Ekman, 1977; Lagerspetz et al., 1982). Although these findings may be partly related to the smaller school and class size characteristic of most schools in Nordic countries, international research also discounts size within the range of size variations that are generally found (Rutter, 1983).

In the case of small schools with cross-age grouping, such as that in the one-room rural school, results are mixed. Olweus (1993a) found that bullying was more of a problem in these schools than in the larger primary schools in Norway; but in England, two of the three schools that according to teacher reports had no bullying used cross-age grouping (Stephenson & Smith, 1989). One possibility for the contradictory results may relate to age range, with the Norwegian schools having a wider range in age than the English ones.

Competitiveness for High Grades

Another reasonable hypothesis attributes bullying to competition for top grades. This is essentially a frustration-aggression model in which the aggressive behavior of the bully can be attributed to the frustration of failure in school. However, a detailed causal analysis of the longitudinal data from the Swedish Study (Olweus, 1993a) gave no support for this idea. Although there was a moderate association between poor grades and bullying behavior, there was no evidence of a *causal* relationship. A similar finding targeted to delinquent behavior has been reported by a Canadian team (Tremblay, Masse, Perron, Leblanc, Schwartzman, & Ledigham, 1992).

Coeducational Versus Same-Sex Schools

In 1971 Dale published in book form the results of a survey that showed that in England coeducational schools are one variable that can have a powerful effect in reducing bullying, whereas single-sex schools lack this advantage and that, in fact, bullying thrives in them. The subjects were 175 men and 620 women in English colleges of education who had each attended at least one coeducational and single-sex school. Dale made within-sex comparisons of respondents who had been in coeducational schools prior to entering a same-sex school, and those who had attended same-sex schools first and then coeducational schools. Both men and women strongly believed that disapproval of bullying engaged in by the opposite sex was a contributor to the reduction of bullying. Typical of the responses were the following: "The girls would scorn any boy whom they heard was a bully. This seemed to be a very effective deterrent"; "If this [girls bullying girls] happened the boys usually made life so unpleasant for the offensive group that they stopped" (Dale, 1991, pp. 147, 149).

This study is rarely mentioned in texts or cited in journal articles on bullying, yet methodologically it was excellent and the findings were important. To the best of our knowledge, it is the only study of the effects of the opposite sex on childhood bullying. It was years ahead of the surge in interest in bullying and, as a three-volume text, it was one of the earliest reports on bullying in the schools. Dale's (1971) work has been unfairly ignored, to the detriment of progress in the field.

Variables in High Bullying Schools

Although there is some evidence that social disadvantage in the form of poor housing, low socioeconomic status, and unusually large families, plays a part in making a school into a high bullying school, it is not one of the important variables. Instead, one of the most important contributors is a school climate of opportunity for bullying (Olweus, 1993a). Poor supervision by teachers or others during periods of free play, recess, the noon hour, and on the school bus sends a clear message to bullies. The failure of school personnel to address the problem of teasing in a decisive way was noted by Olweus (1984): 40% of primary students and 60% of junior high school students surveyed reported that teachers tried to stop bullying only "once in a while" or "almost never." This reluctance to act also is a recurring theme in the United States. In a survey of middle-school and high school students in a rural Midwestern community (Hazler, Hoover, & Oliver, 1993, p. 16), the respondents were clearly troubled by the fact that school personnel did nothing about the bullying: "They knew about it and did nothing. Our school is lazy that way" (boy, age 15). "They know; they just don't care. They sit in the teachers' lounge and gossip" (boy, age 18).

In informal interviews with high school students in an urban northwestern high school (D. M. Ross, 1995), a 15-year-old girl's response reflected a prevailing view that weapons were a more important issue to school personnel than bullying: "They only care if the guys got guns. Who cares if kids get beat up but not killed?" As Hoover and Hazler (1991) have pointed out, when school personnel tolerate or ignore bullying, they send a negative message about the worth of the individual who is bullied.

For secondary-school children there is more indirect bullying in corridors and classes (Whitney & Smith, 1993). Indirect bullying combined with teacher indifference or contempt for the victims virtually ensures that the victims will get no help. If the teacher is a bully, and there is one in most schools (Pyke, 1994; Smith & Sharp, 1994), the combination becomes even more potent. When inadequate supervision is combined with crowded conditions in halls or playground areas, coupled with insufficient supplies of play materials, an unusually high amount of physical contact results, with much pushing, shoving, and grabbing (Opie, 1993; Opie & Opie, 1959), again, an open invitation to the bully contingent.

In the many studies reported throughout this text the predominant view is that the problem of bullying is handled inadequately by the schools. The findings from these studies should not be viewed as a blanket indictment of all schools. Many make little or no systematic effort to confront the problem of bullying, but there is an encouraging number of other schools working diligently on this problem. In addition, a number of teachers are making largely unheralded efforts in their own classrooms to counteract the indifference of their school administrators. Later chapters describe some of these positive attacks (see, for example, the discussions in Chapter 6 on bully courts, student watch groups, and conflict resolution programs).

Where Does Most Bullying Happen?

Although many parents think that most bullying occurs on the way to and from school, this is not the case. Almost all the studies on bullying support the finding that most bullying occurs in the school environment (La Fontaine, 1991; Olweus, 1993a; Smith & Sharp, 1994). Olweus (1991) reported that there were twice as many students bullied at school, with this ratio rising to three times as many at the junior high school level, than was the case for going to and from school. However, anxious parents have grounds for concern because victims get significantly less help from others at this time than they get when bullied at school (Olweus, 1993a).

Comment

There is no question that Olweus's early investigations (1978, 1981) have significantly advanced our understanding of bullying. Although some of his findings have been consistent with the commonly accepted view of bullying, for example, boys bully more than girls and typically bully younger children, others, such as the prevalence data, were an unpleasant surprise. Some well-entrenched beliefs were disproved: Opportunity was a far more important variable in bullying than school or class size, and more bullying was reported in school (where parents mistakenly believe that their children are safe) than on the way to and from school.

3 Bullies

BULLYING IS A COMPLEX PROCESS that has not yet been effectively managed. One reason for this failure may be that the predominant view of it is far too simplistic. The stereotype of bullies as louts from broken homes in high-crime, lower-class neighborhoods, combined with the belief that bullying is a normal part of growing up and so is a transient problem, has served to justify brushing bullying incidents aside as minor problems. This stance receives further support through the use of the euphemism "bullying" to describe actions, such as assault and extortion, that would be of criminological concern if the perpetrators were adults (Finkelhor, 1995; La Fontaine, 1991).

If efforts at intervention and prevention are to have any success, it is essential that the complexity of the bullying phenomenon be acknowledged. For example, there are distinct subgroups of bullies and victims; a sphere of perpetrators, victims, peers, parents, and school personnel all directly or indirectly involved in the immediate problem; and serious long-term effects on the bully severe enough to justify the descriptor "lifelong losers." Bullies are not born, they are created. A cluster of contributory causes helps to set the child on the path to bullying. These include attributes of the parents that are reflected in their patterns of child rearing and characteristics of the child that elicit negative reactions from caregivers and peers. Although adults in the home and school are clearly part of the bullying problem, they can also be part of the solution *if* they know how to react when bullying occurs. To this end we discuss the failure of many parents and school personnel to take appropriate action about the problem of bullying. We begin with the subgroups that Olweus (1978) has identified within the population of boys.

OLWEUS'S TYPOLOGY OF BULLIES

In 1978, Olweus distinguished between the aggressive bully, whom he regarded as the typical bully, and the passive bully and he added a third small group, bully-victims, who bullied others and were themselves bullied. At that time Olweus was working mainly with boys, but he has since acknowledged (Olweus, 1993a) that much less is known about the characteristics of girls who bully. In this section the discussion focuses on boys who bully, using the framework of Olweus's categories with the exception of the bully-victims. This group is something of an enigma: Although they have bully characteristics, their victim qualities seem to predominate. For this reason we discuss this group in Chapter 4.

Aggressive Bullies

Olweus (1978) has described aggressive bullies as belligerent, fearless, coercive, confident, tough, impulsive, and having a low tolerance for frustration coupled with a stronger inclination toward using violence than that of children in general. Their salient characteristics are an inflammatory combination of physical strength, a stable, but aggressive, personality pattern, a concern with power fueled by a strong need to dominate others, and a tendency to overreact aggressively in ambiguous confrontations. Slights or hostility are seen where neither exists: As Dodge (in Greenbaum, 1989) has noted, aggressive bullies see the world with a paranoid's eye.

The term *bullying* clearly implies that a victim is part of the process. An interesting confirmation of this pairing has come from Floyd's (1985) intensive studies of videotapes of bully–victim interactions:

> Bullies seem to need a victim and may work hard to create one. . . . It is striking to see a sort of choreographed victimization, a dance goes on. It is as though they court each other and often it seems as if neither can leave the other alone. (p. 11)

There is a tendency among school personnel to view bullying and aggression as interchangeable. Although bullying is a subset of aggression (Smith, 1991), boys who bully differ in some respects from chronically aggressive boys. Consider, for example, popularity with peers. In a comparison between bullies and a randomly selected group of same-age boys, Olweus (1991) found that the two groups did not differ in popularity, whereas Foster, DeLawyer, and Guevremont (1986) found chronically aggressive boys to be less popular than their peers. One possible reason for this difference may be that bullies are not indiscriminately aggressive toward other children; instead, they reserve their aggression for a few selected victims. However, aggressive children tend to strike out at many children, so there would be a larger group of victims with good reason to dislike them. Olweus has reported that aggressive bullies often are popular in the early school years, a finding that has some support from the Sheffield Bullying Project (Smith & Sharp, 1994). But their popularity generally diminishes in the upper grades, along with their academic performance (Olweus, 1993a). It is likely that younger children admire or are drawn to the macho image, but then draw away as their own critical faculties concerning friends and leaders become more discerning. Victims are generally depicted as less popular than bullies or children who are not involved in the bullying problem (Boulton & Smith, 1994; Perry et al., 1988). The foregoing studies have in common the assessment of popularity by indirect techniques such as sociometry. Taking a different tack, Boulton (1995) used direct observations of 71 boys of 8 to 10 years of age who had been identified by peer nominations as bullies, victims, or boys not involved with bullying problems. The observations were made of free play on the school playground, an excellent choice of location because the playground is the most commonly reported site of bullying for boys of this age (Whitney & Smith, 1993). The study focused on the nature of the playground activity for each of the three groups.

Social networks are defined by how many different children a target child interacts with in a nonaggressive way during an observation period. The three groups did not differ statistically on this measure, although there was a tendency for bullies to be in larger groups than victims. Bullies spent the most time with other children than the other two groups, whereas victims spent more time alone. An important source of social support that could provide the victims with protection against bullies, that is, a large network of friends, was lacking. Victims spent more time in positive social contact with others, such as talking, than the other two groups, but they spent less time in rule games, such as football. As Boulton (1995) has pointed out, this could be a reflection of their lack of game skills rather than their victim status. The overall impression of the bullies' behavior was that for the most part they were involved in friendly interactions with a large group of others, but they also engaged in more aggressive behaviors than either of the other two groups and tended to be with other bullies rather than with victims.

Although the Boulton (1995) study was an impeccable example of careful training of observers and sound observational methodology that included a period designed to habituate the children to observers, the fact remains that the observers were visible to the children.

In an ingenious observational study of playground behavior in two middle-class Toronto schools, Pepler, Craig, Zeigler, and Charach (1993) bypassed the visible observer problem by using strategically placed cameras and hooking remote microphones up to several children during play periods. Bullying was frequent: During the 52 hours of recording there were 400 episodes of bullying, or an average of one every 7½ minutes. In only 4% of the cases did teachers intervene. However, many of the bullying interactions were of a subtle and fleeting nature, the average length being 38 seconds. Although the brevity of the interactions appears to exonerate the teachers for failing to intervene, a more likely explanation suggests an underlying indifference because one boy was tormented by a group of bullies for 37 minutes without teacher intervention. It is unlikely that the use of microphones had any significant effect on the behavior of the other children. Those hooked up were neither bullies nor victims and reasonable explanations unrelated to bullying were given to them.

The credo for the aggressive bully group is that of the macho aggressor who believes that there are two kinds of people, those who dominate and those who submit (Miedzian, 1992). Many preadolescent bullies do not feel remorse when inflicting pain. Instead, they may escalate the attack to elicit the evidence of pain and submission that confirms that domination and control have been achieved (Perry, Williard, & Perry, 1990). Although physical force is seen as a legitimate means of domination to be used against anyone, including those in a position of authority, Olweus (1993a) found that "harassment with nonphysical means (words, gestures, looks) is the most common form of bullying among boys" (p. 19). It is evident from the following comment by a 9-year-old boy that "the look" can strike terror in the victim:

> I try hard not to catch his eye in class but it's like he's pulling me, it's an awful feeling. I'm helpless and when I do look at him he gives me this look and I know what it'll be like at recess and what's going to happen to my lunch money. (J. Carmichael, personal communication, December 4, 1991)

The bullies' perception of bullying incidents is significantly less severe than that of their victims, for example, "just messing around." When they are caught out, they are noted for their skillful avoidance of any blame: Exasperated school personnel often describe them as "slippery." They view their own behavior from an egocentric stance and have little empathy and no remorse for their victims: Often they feel that the victim deserved the bullying, claiming "he asked for it."

In place of empathy is a cold, calculated attitude that leads to premeditated and heartless attacks:

> If you're a bully like me, you use your head. Toughness isn't enough. You beat them up, they report you. Then where are you? . . . I'm an aggressor of marginal violence. . . . I am ingenious. I am patient. . . .
>
> The Industrial Museum is a good place to find children. I cut somebody's five- or six-year-old kid brother out of the herd of eleven- and twelve-year-olds he's come with. "Quick," " I say. I pull him along the corridors, up the stairs, through the halls, down to a mezzanine landing. . . . I rush him into an auditorium and abandon him. He'll be lost for hours. . . .
>
> I'm best at torment. . . .
>
> I sidle up to a kid at the movies. "You smacked my brother," I tell him. "After the show, I'll be outside." (Elkin, 1987, pp. 173, 175).

Implications of Lazarus's Theory for Intervention

Consider the aggressive bully's behavior within the framework of Lazarus's theory (1966). Stressors in the form of danger are everywhere, in fact, the bully views his world with a paranoid eye (Greenbaum, 1989). Ambiguous actions by others, which most children would consider inconsequential, often are rapidly appraised by the bully as stressors that are threatening and controllable, a combination that within the bully's frame of reference merits direct aggressive action. Typically, there are no deterrents to his aggression: It is buttressed by his previous successes with the use of power, the unqualified social support of his own group, and his impaired capacity for empathy for the victim.

Intervention must focus on changing both the speed and content of his appraisal of ambiguous events. The immediate and aggressive response can be actively discouraged with a combination of consequences, such as deprivation of privileges and peer disapproval of aggression, with reward for nonaggressive responses. The bully must learn to look at events as controllable (if indeed control is called for) by strategies other than force. The goal here is a shift from aggression-based appraisals to assertive ones in everyday interactions. Developing a sense of empathy would facilitate these changes by providing a kind of logic for making them (in addition to the incentive of avoiding punishment).

Bullies frequently are depicted as unhappy children, a view supported by Rigby and Slee (1992) in their study of secondary school pupils. They reported that the tendency to bully others was negatively correlated with feelings of happiness and positive attitudes toward school. Note that in this study the data were not analyzed in terms of Olweus's (1978) typology of bullies.

Passive Bullies and Anxious Bullies

Olweus (1978, 1993a) viewed the passive bullies as "fairly mixed" with some insecure members. A similar group was identified by Stephenson and Smith (1989) and labeled as anxious bullies. Of all the bullies in their study, 18% (almost all of whom were boys) were in this category. Anxious bullies rarely provoke others or take the initiative in a bullying incident, but once the bullying is under way, usually at the instigation of an aggressive bully, they actively participate. The actions of the aggressive bully have a disinhibitory effect by appearing to legitimize the bullying, and this effect is strengthened in the anxious bullies on seeing the aggressive bully rewarded (Bandura, 1969). The fact that the anxious bullies are so eager to align themselves with the more powerful and, relatively speaking, more popular action-oriented aggressive bully has earned them the descriptors "camp followers" and "hangers-on." They appear to buy the approval of the aggressive bullies with intense loyalty. If, for example, adults intervene in bullying that is initiated by the aggressive bully and impose sanctions, the passive bullies often are blamed and accept the punishment without any attempt to implicate the aggressive bully.

Altogether, the anxious bullies are a sad group. They are much less popular than the aggressive bullies, have few likeable qualities, low self-esteem, and home problems. They often have disruptive temper outbursts contributing to peer problems, and at school they have great difficulty concentrating.

Implications for Intervention

For many passive bullies the problem is that their admiration for the aggressive bullies and their need to be affiliated with them color their appraisal of situations so that they, too, see danger that is often nonexistent. By striving to imitate the aggressive bully, the passive bully does himself a disservice: The changes he is striving for are superficial. What he most needs are changes that will facilitate peer acceptance of him, such as increased confidence and self-esteem, social and friendship skills, improved academic and athletic performance, and assertiveness. Before such modifications can be attempted, however, a radical change must occur in the passive bully's appraisal of the aggressive bully, resulting in a diminished desire to be affiliated with him. Live and symbolic modeling procedures (Bandura, 1969) could be used to demonstrate that the aggressive bully is in many respects despicable and not one to emulate. The probability of successful intervention with this rather pathetic group would be markedly greater if active parental cooperation could be obtained.

Comment

The tendency to assign new descriptors to groups of bullies already identified and labeled does not serve to advance our understanding of the bully problem. For example, bullies with many of the same characteristics as the passive bullies (Olweus, 1978) have since been described in more detail by Stephenson and Smith (1989), who refer to them as anxious bullies, and by Mitchel and O'Moore (1988), who label them neurotic bullies. Smith and Thompson (1991) add to the confusion by suggesting "that some people object to the terms 'bully' and 'victim' as having dangerous possibilities in labeling children in undesirable ways . . . it may be better to talk only of 'bullying behavior' rather than of 'bullies' per se" (p. 6). Because the term *bullying* is in itself a euphemism for ugly behavior with criminal aspects, further efforts at watering down its meaning can serve no useful purpose. Almost everyone has exhibited behavior along the bullying continuum, but such occasional lapses should not be equated with the quality of bullying that is the topic of this text. Adding new subgroups of bullies without adequate documentation also should be discouraged. Elliott (1991), for example, has reported two new typologies in the Kidscape study. One was the spoilt brats who had been overindulged and overprotected from censure by their doting parents and who hit out at anyone who got in their way. This behavior pattern sounds more compatible with a classical frustration-aggression sequence than with bullying behavior. The second new group of bullies were the victims of abuse or neglect, who had been made to feel inadequate, stupid, and humiliated. Such children would deny and hate their vulnerability and when confronted with another child with some visible weakness would, according to Elliott, attack the other child in an effort to destroy this reminder of their own weakness. Elliott adds that "the sad fact is that the bully is really attacking himself—it is self-hatred that makes a bully" (p. 10). Much more information is needed before such children qualify as a subgroup in their own right. It is possible, for example, that they may find a better fit in the bully-victim group.

What the field needs is a standard terminology based on specific behavioral criteria. New typologies should be added only if supporting documentation demonstrates that the children being included really are bullies, and if there is no significant overlap with any of the established groups of bullies.

BULLYING IN GIRLS

Bullying in girls shares some common ground with bullying in boys; for example, girls do exhibit direct physical and verbal bullying although to a lesser degree (Olweus, 1993a; Smith & Sharp, 1994), but some of their bullying behaviors are far more subtle (Maslen, 1994). Crick and Grotpeter (1995) have offered an interesting explanation for the gender differences. They propose that when children inflict harm on peers they choose ways that frustrate or damage the priorities or goals that are valued by their respective gender peer groups. For boys, physical dominance, instrumentality, hierarchy, and prestige are important within the peer group context (Block, 1983), and thus much of their bullying takes the form of direct physical attacks, threats, and intimidation. These concerns are of less importance to girls, who are more likely to focus on relational issues in peer interactions such as establishing close friendships with other girls. A similar line of thought proposed earlier by Wachtel (1973) held that boys generally bully for power, which is in line with the fact that they tend to bully younger boys and girls. Girls, however, strive for close affiliation with others and affirmation that they are "in" and their victims are "out" (Wachtel, 1973) and, consequently, are more likely to engage in behaviors such as social exclusion (Roland, 1989a), the often unexplained withdrawal of acceptance, and the spreading of malicious gossip. Their targets are almost exclusively other girls within their own age range (Roland, 1989a). A 14-year-old girl said:

> These girls were my friends last year. I thought. Now they ignore me like I'm a total stranger and they spread horrible rumors like Dad's in jail (father was on military duty) and I got expelled from my last school because I've got a sex disease. . . . (Adlam, 1991, p. 20)
>
> A 15-year-old girl complained, "I was made fun of . . . because of the way I looked. Now I'm being talked about. It really hurts." (Hazler et al., 1993, p. 17)
>
> Marie, who was in the sixth grade, began developing physically more quickly than her classmates. Older students who rode the school bus with her began to tease her about her development and told her she was getting bustier than her classmates because she wanted sex. They teased her about being sexual, calling her "horny" and "whorey." Other female students began to avoid her in order to not be involved with the teasing, and they told Marie to leave them alone because they didn't

want to be around someone who wanted sex. Marie was not able to defend herself and felt alone and isolated. (Horne, Glaser, & Sayger, 1994, p. 2)

In addition to the above form of isolation, other bullying tactics sometimes favored by girls include manipulation of friendships and one of the more visible (but still relatively subtle) bully behaviors called scapegoating. Pipher (1994) describes it as a universal American phenomenon. A particularly vicious kind of scapegoating, "germs," is directed as often at attractive, bright, outgoing girls as at the more obvious targets for bullying. It consists of first picking girls for no apparent reason to be made miserable for weeks or months by suggesting that they are contaminated with highly infectious germs; any girl who touched a germ would be infected unless she immediately passed the germs along by touching another girl. Pipher, in observing this phenomenon, found that a considerable amount of between-class time was spent getting rid of germs from contact with undesirables.

Crick and Grotpeter (1995) refer to this set of bullying behaviors that some girls exhibit as *relational aggression*. In their study of third- and sixth-grade children (n = 491), they demonstrated the validity and distinctiveness of this category of behavior. They found that girls were significantly more relationally aggressive than boys. In comparison with their nonrelationally aggressive peers, relationally aggressive girls were more likely to be at risk for social-psychological adjustment difficulties, were more often rejected, and reported significantly higher levels of internalization problems such as loneliness, depression, and isolation. In order to develop an effective program for eliminating or reducing the incidence of relational aggression in girls, it would be necessary first to determine whether a causal relationship exists between rejection and relational aggression and then to establish its direction.

RACIAL BULLYING AND SEXUAL HARASSMENT

Two kinds of bullying that warrant special consideration relate specifically to a victim's race or gender. The reactions of victims to such bullying differ from reactions to other kinds of bullying because when race or gender is the stimulus for the bullying, the victims feel not only that they are being attacked, but also that their whole race or gender are the targets.

Racial Bullying

Although the complexity and seriousness of racism justify its treatment as a problem in its own right, it is included here because in the school setting it frequently manifests itself as bullying. Racism in any form is an issue that no school should ignore (Cohn, 1988; Kelly, 1990), but as bullying, it is particularly insidious. There is a paucity of research on racial bullying, but small-scale studies have shown clearly that ethnic minority children are at risk. In a study of English secondary-school children Riley (1988) reported that seven out of ten children, who were nominated by peers as bullies, were found to have racist attitudes. At recess, the groups of ethnic minorities and the other students were polarized. Although racial bullying is often regarded as a recent variant of bullying in general, this is not the case (Stainton Rogers, 1991). Black and Asian children in London have long been singled out as this account recorded prior to World War I shows: "The lower type of kid would treat me rough: they used . . . to knock me hat off me head. . . . They called me names; they called me 'Blackie' . . . 'Darkie' (Humphries, Mack, & Perks, 1988, p. 129). Almost a century later, this attitude is still evident in London: "at playtime there are many bullies. . . . They kick me and call me 'black,' 'chocolate,' because of my color and they don't like us because we are Indian" (Akhtar & Stronach, 1986, p. 23).

Name calling continues to be one of the most painful and pervasive forms of racial bullying. The critical difference between racist name calling and other forms of name calling is that the latter are individualized taunts that relate specifically to the victim (for example, "fatty" or "carrot top") whereas racist names refer not only to the victim but also to his or her family and whole race (e.g., "Jew boy") (Swann, 1985). A 17-year-old girl, the target of vicious racist name calling, said: "I think it's worse than being hurt physically, because physical hurt heals quicker than being called names" (Cohn, 1988).

When Does Racism Begin?

Racism begins in the preschool years (Klein, 1994; Kureishi, 1986) and is often transmitted intentionally from parents to children. The following dispiriting exchange occurred between a 4-year-old girl and a teaching assistant at the Stanford University Nursery School:

CHILD: My Mom says to never, never play with Nathan because he's a Jew boy.

TEACHING ASSISTANT: Why does it matter that Nathan's a Jew?

CHILD: Because Jews are bad people.

Community attitudes exert a pervasive influence that may further cement the parental teachings. Pipher's (1994) description of the small Midwest community where she grew up was permeated with racism:

> Our town took great pride in having no black or Native American citizens. Restaurant signs that read, "We have the right to refuse service to anyone," were used to exclude non-whites. Adults told racist jokes and held racist beliefs about ethnic groups they had never met. My father warned me never to dance or talk to Negroes when I went to college or people would think I was low-class. Terms like "jewing people down" and "Indian giver" were part of the language. (p. 241)

In discussing the intergenerational transmission of racial prejudice, Davey (1983) said that the crux of the problem of racism is an implicit consensus in our society about the status of different ethnic groups. Children learn from this consensual perspective how to evaluate different groups.

Racism in the Schools

Although racial bullying is a serious problem in some schools (Kelly & Cohn, 1988), in most schools very little is done to counter it possibly because school personnel often are as reluctant to admit that there is a problem as they are to acknowledge bullying in general: "There is no problem at all about racism in this school" (principal of an elementary school in which racial bullying on the school bus was a major problem); "The parents and children are overreacting" (response of principal about complaints of well-documented racial bullying) (Akhtar & Stronach, 1986, p. 23).

It is bad enough that school personnel are reluctant to admit that a racism problem exists, but what makes matters infinitely worse are the many teachers who have racist tendencies (Gillborn, 1992) that they convey implicitly or explicitly:

> A young Sikh published his own account of the regular verbal and physical harassment that he had experienced in the seven years he had spent at schools in the South. Much of that harassment was directed at his hair and turban, both regarded as sacred symbols. Sometimes teachers would join in or even initiate the jokes. The main effect, he said, was to erode his self-confidence and capacity to concentrate on learning. (Tattum, 1989, p. 15)

Teachers who brush aside complaints of racial bullying or harassment or who blame the victim are tacitly condoning racist behavior. A victim support coordinator said: "one Indian girl . . . suffered years of verbal abuse in school, to the point where her health was suffering. . . . When she would complain to teachers . . . they would say, 'Don't be silly, everyone's called names'" (Klein, 1994, p. 9). Schools should handle instances of racial bullying and parents' complaints of it in the same way that bullying in general is managed, as described in Chapter 5.

What Can Parents Do?

When children are the targets of racial bullying, their parents should follow the general procedures described in Chapter 5. However, when they are subjected to racial name calling, ignore the problems of those engaging in this antisocial behavior, and make no attempt to change their attitudes or to reason with them. This is a waste of time. Apart from encouraging target children to say in a very firm voice, "Stop that, I don't like it when you call me names" and then to continue with their activity or walk away, focus on helping the children in other ways. For both groups attack the problem *directly* by listening sympathetically and offering reassurance about their right to feel angry (at the same time being clear about not retaliating with physical attacks because this immediately puts them in the wrong); briefly discuss the ignorance underlying racial name calling; then mention incidents from your own past, how you felt, and how you handled them. Occasionally, when the children are present, one parent should talk about a current incident in which he or she was the target, and then discuss with the other parent what happened, how it felt, and so on. Make a distinction between this specific experience in which *one* person made racist remarks and the danger of stereotyping, that is, of believing that because a white person called you names, then *all* white people are suspect. Acknowledge that it often looks as if a very large number of people fall into the negative category, but stress that this does not justify regarding all people in a negative way.

Much can be done *indirectly* to protect and strengthen children who are targets of racial prejudice. Ask the children's librarian at the public library for books on racial and other kinds of prejudice; read them to the children and sometimes discuss them with the whole family. Work on the children's social skills so that they can handle commonly occurring interactions with adults with ease. Particularly practice how to respond to unjustified criticism: for example, what to say if you were unavoidably late, or could not complete an assigned task. Too often in this kind of situation children become mute while simmering with anger at the unfairness of it all. Encourage the development of skills and talents. When children are stars in some area, prowess is likely to take precedence over racial differences. Teach behaviors related to competence in handling routine demands such as going to the store by oneself or traveling on the bus. Increasing independence and feelings of being in control enhance children's self-concepts. Heightened self-esteem is the off-shoot of these various accomplishments.

Sexual Harassment

Sexual harassment is defined as unwanted and unwelcome sexual behavior that interferes with an individual's life. It includes behaviors such as unwelcome sexual advances, demands for sexual favors, touching in a sexual way, and accusations of homosexuality and lesbianism. In the United States, sexual harassment is rampant in elementary and secondary schools (Cheevers, 1995; Colino, 1993; Stein, 1993). Unequivocal evidence of its extent comes from a 1993 survey sponsored by the American Association of University Women (AAUW, 1993) that documented the incidence of sexual harassment in eighth- through eleventh-grade students ($n = 1,632$) in 79 public schools across the continental United States.

The study was conducted in exemplary fashion. Classes were randomly selected, with no teacher participation in the data collection. The questionnaires were anonymous, with the questions referring only to school-related experiences during school hours. The respondents were asked how often, if ever, they had experienced 14 types of sexual harassment, half of which involved physical contact and half, no physical contact (see Figure 3.1). Also included were questions on when and where sexual harassment was first experienced; if they themselves engaged in it, why they did so, whom they told about it, if anyone; and what impact the sexual harassment had had on them educationally, behaviorally, and emotionally.

The results were staggering: Eighty-one percent of the respondents reported some experience of sexual harassment in school, most of which occurred in hallways and classrooms, and of this group, one in three girls and one in five boys had experienced it frequently. Peers were responsible for four out of five incidents, but adult school personnel sexually harassed one in four girls and one in 10 boys. Students usually did not report any incidents to adults, especially not to teachers, and boys were less likely than girls to tell anyone. On the issue of being called a lesbian or gay, girls felt that they would be very upset and boys rated it as the most disturbing form of sexual harassment. Suffering, in such forms as not wanting to go to school, being embarrassed and upset, and feeling a loss of confidence, was experienced by more girls, particularly white and African American girls, than boys. In the latter group, African Americans were subjected to an alarming amount of sexual harassment involving physical contact. Figure 3.1 shows the percentages by gender for each of the 14 kinds of sexual harassment experienced in school by

Figure 3.1 Types of Sexual Harassment Experienced in School.

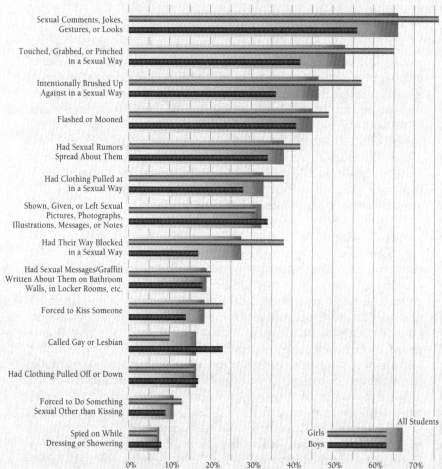

Source: AAUW Educational Foundation. (1993). *Hostile Hallways: The AAUW Survey on Sexual Harassment in America's Schools* (p. 9), Annapolis Junction, MD. Copyright 1993 by the AAUW Educational Foundation. Reprinted with permission from the American Association of University Women Educational Foundation, 1111 Sixteenth Street, NW, Washington, DC, (202) 785-7700.

the respondents (81% of the 1,632 students) who reported being harassed.

Sexual comments, jokes, looks, gestures, and touching in a sexual way are commonplace in school. A girl aged 15 wrote:

> When I was in the seventh grade, a boy on my bus said nasty, unrepeatable things to me and several times touched my breasts. Now I wish that I had broken his wrist or at least told someone about it. But back then I thought that if I said anything, everyone would get mad at me or make fun of me, because this boy was very popular. So I kept quiet about it. I realize now that if I had told someone, I probably would have freed myself of much stress. (Minton, 1994, p. 30)

Frequently, several boys will harass one or two girls. One girl described the following incident:

> the last week of January, they would put us in choke holds and they would trip us and they would fall down on top of us. And the last day, they would touch us in the private places of the body. And so we told our parents and they went in to talk with the school and the school said that it was taken care of. But then it got worse and on May 5th, two of my friends were sexually assaulted. They were pushed on the ground and their heads were hitting on the ground and they were throwing grass in the mouth to keep them from screaming and they would put their hand in their blouse. And they throwed one of my friends on the fence and they would throw their bodies on her and they would just touch them all over. And it was really hard. (Donahue, 1994, p. 3)

In 1992 a national scandal erupted over the behavior of aviators in the U.S. Navy and Marine Corps attending their annual convention of the Tailhook Association. An aide to Admiral Jack Snyder, Lieutenant Paula Coughlin, had gone to the Association party to deliver a message, been swept unwillingly into the mob of drunken aviators, and then had been sexually assaulted. Her attempts to report and complain about the experience were first brushed aside by the Admiral and then moved so slowly through the complaint hierarchy that in 1992 she took her case to the news media and then the courts. More than 80 women also stated that they were assaulted or molested. Lieutenant Coughlin won her court case, and 12 other lawsuits are pending. Some high-ranking officers were demoted and a number of promotions withheld (Zimmerman, 1995). This incident is mentioned here because it bears a chilling resemblance to the kinds of sexual harassment that a group of 13- and 14-year-old girls from a junior high school in Washington State described to the author as commonplace at their school. Table 3.1 contains their comments, along with quotes from Zimmerman's book (pp. 17, 18, 25) on the Tailhook scandal.

Table 3.1. Parallels Between Tailhook and Sexual Harassment in Junior
High School

Tailhook	Junior High School
Women were getting "zapped," having squadron stickers slapped on strategic parts of their bodies	Girls get "graded," the guys have stickers with letter grades and they put them on your breasts and butts and other private places.
Suddenly there were hands reaching out at her, a frenzy of groping, touching and feeling. She felt hands insert themselves under her blouse, hands up her skirt. She screamed, "Stop." Nobody stopped. "Here were 5 or 6 guys . . . grabbing my crotch from different angles."	"I dived off the highboard and when I came up the guys were all round me. Then they put their hands inside my top and others squeezed my butt and tried to tear my suit off and some were poking their fingers in my crotch. I yelled for help and their hands were all over me." No one helped.
"I told another aviator and he grinned and said. 'I guess you've just been through the gauntlet.'"	"When I told the man at the pool he just laughed, 'You just got caught in the whirlpool, baby.'"
. . . he had hold of her breasts as if he thought they were handles.	". . . . he grabbed my boobs and it was like he was steering a motorbike."

Homosexuality

Harassment accelerates if the students are thought to be gay or
lesbian, possibly because this belief may invoke an element of fear
mixed in with the rage that fuels the attack. In an investigation of
such harassment in Washington State schools, these victims

> were beaten, spit upon, followed, cornered, rubbed against or chased. . . .
> Name-calling, rumors and graffiti were reported. One girl was raped
> and forcibly kissed by three other girls who told her: "We don't want
> your kind, lesbian. Leave." ("Report details harassment," 1994)

Sexual harassment has a number of associated problems that are
specific to it and that differ from those related to bullying in general.
There are federal mandates that apply to it that school personnel
and parents should take the time to study. In addition, there is
information concerning prevention that should be transmitted to
students as well as their parents. Chapter 5 contains the specific
procedures that should be followed by school personnel and parents
when a child is sexually harassed, as well as general instructions on
how school personnel and parents should handle the problem of
bullying. This section presents school and parent action that should
be taken to protect children from sexual harassment and is followed
by a discussion of sexual harassment that occurs within and outside
of the school's jurisdiction. The section also contains dispiriting
accounts of some schools' reactions to parents' complaints of sexual
harassment of their children.

What Parents Can Do to Protect Their Children

A common theme in many of the children's accounts of being sexually harassed is an inability on the children's part to tell their parents about the problem. This failure in communication is the weak link in the complaint sequence: Parents cannot protect their children if they do not know that their well-being is threatened. From an early age, any complaints or problems that the children have should be treated with respect and discussed thoughtfully. The children's reasons for thinking that a problem exists should be explored even if, to the adult, the whole thing seems ridiculous. Establishing an atmosphere in which children feel free to reveal problems that they are having can be facilitated by sometimes having one parent bring up a problem and then following up with a discussion about it, with no recriminations or blame (Bandura, 1969).

In the specific case of sexual harassment, begin in the early preschool period with simple discussions about the private places on the children's bodies that no one touches (except in routine toilet and bath care). The "no one" includes preschool personnel, church officials, other children, neighbors, relatives, and baby-sitters. Emphasize how important it is to tell parents if anyone touches the children in their private places. Occasionally have a fictitious discussion of an incident that occurred when one parent was a child and how it was handled or an incident that occurred to a friend when the parent was young. Accompany all such discussions with practice in how to resist sternly and verbally: Give demonstrations using the exact rebuttal that the children could make, and have them practice in role-play sequences so that the responses become automatic.

When Sexual Harassment Occurs Within the School's Jurisdiction

When children complain to their parents about being sexually harassed, the parents should first establish that the complaint is a valid one. Obtain all possible information, including names of witnesses, where and when it happened, and other pertinent information. In theory, parents should be able to expect positive results when a legitimate complaint is lodged with the school administration through the channels of teacher, counselor, principal, and school board. In practice, rare is the school that will handle sexual harassment complaints with skill, fueled by a determination to create a positive learning environment that has no room for any kind of harassment. The large majority of schools, however, appear to tolerate such behaviors and take little or no action against the aggressors. What the schools and parents should do is described in the section in Chapter 5, The Special Case of Sexual Harassment: Procedures for Schools and Parents.

What Usually Happens When Parents Complain to the Schools?

Generally, little is done to correct the problem and school officials react with total indifference, although sometimes they go as far as to blame the victim while exonerating the aggressors. The following accounts are representative of these attitudes:

> After a boy in her elementary school planted a sexually explicit note in her desk, 9-year-old Jennifer . . . felt humiliated, confused and sick to her stomach. But after she complained to school authorities, she said, things got worse. Although the note contained language worthy of a pornographic movie, the vice principal told Jennifer to "respect" the boy and "give him his space". . . Jennifer's parents pleaded with school officials to expel the boy, but they merely suspended him for 2 1/2 days. The boy's mother said six other boys helped write the note, but none was disciplined. Two of those boys threatened to kill Jennifer. Fearing for her safety, her parents pulled Jennifer . . . out of school. . . . For the rest of the year she studied at home . . . her family is considering a move to another city. (Cheevers, 1995, p. A8)

In another account (Donahue, 1994), Eve and her friends in sixth grade were sexually harassed by a group of boys. When girls came into the classroom in the morning, and all throughout the day, the boys would snap the girls' bras, run their fingers up and down their backs, and snap the bras again. When the girls complained to the counselor, the boys called them bitches, dogs, and lesbians, and stepped up the harassment by punching one girl in the eye and pushing and shoving the girls. When Eve asked the teacher, a man, to do something, he merely told the boys, "Oh, stop it, guys." Next, Eve's mother met with the teacher, told him what had happened to Eve, and asked him to confront the perpetrator. The teacher's reply was that it was not his job, not his role. When the mother disagreed and said that it was his job, the teacher replied, "Guys are going to call Eve names throughout her life. She's just going to have to get used to it." He ended the meeting by saying, "Eve is so beautiful. What are you worried about? These guys are going to be all over her in a couple of years." The mother next contacted the assistant superintendent and then the vice-president of schools, but received no satisfaction from either. Eve switched schools and was then very happy.

In a similar vein a school counselor told a 10-year-old girl who had had sexual slurs shouted at her on the school bus and had had boys grab her crotch, that it was just how boys always acted and she should consider transferring to an all-girls school (Donahue, 1994).

A boy who was called names related to the anal/genital area in first and second grade, was then sexually assaulted by other boys in third grade. His father complained to the principal, only to be told that the boy should have psychiatric help in order to find out why other boys treated him that way (Donahue).

Sexual Harassment That Occurs Outside the School's Jurisdiction

When it is clear from the description of the incident that the complaints have grounds, the parents must pursue the case with diligence. Make a written report of all possible information about the incident. If there were witnesses, contact their parents for permission to talk to the children about the incident. If witnesses are willing to come forward, the victims' parents can threaten the aggressors' parents with police action. Although contacting the aggressors' parents and demanding that the harassment stop should precede mention of police action, the parents seldom believe that a problem exists or else blame the whole thing on the victims. Whatever the justification for inaction, it is often more effective to omit the step of reasoning with the aggressors' parents and go directly to the threat of police action. If at all possible, the parents should seek legal help.

Comment

The consensus among investigators (see, for example, Olweus, 1993a) is that bullying occurs more often and is significantly more serious and brutal than it was 10 to 15 years ago. In the United Kingdom the bloody noses and racial slurs of the early 1980s have escalated to savage beatings that all too often end in death (Klein, 1994). In Ottawa, Canada, high school students are "taxed"; they pay substantial fees for a variety of "privileges" such as sitting in specific areas at school basketball games or dating a girl of another race. If they fail to pay, they are beaten, their clothes are torn, and their books destroyed. Even if they do pay, they may still be beaten up (Fennell, 1993). Victims in the United States are sometimes reduced to such a state of helpless misery by long-term intensive bullying that they commit suicide. An eighth-grade honor student in Iowa endured 3 years of bullying and humiliation by other boys who routinely tripped him in the hallways, banged his head into a locker, stole his most valued books, vandalized his bicycle, and kicked the cast on his broken ankle. He blamed himself for the other boys disliking him and finally, became so upset that he killed himself (Marano, 1995).

What is particularly disturbing in the current literature in the United States is the extreme lack of remorse on the part of those who are bullies. When high school seniors in a Virginia school were asked why they had relentlessly persecuted some much younger boys, one of them said:

> "Pick on people? We do that all the time. . . . We pick on the little guys, because we think they're weaker than we are. . . . We don't leave them alone, we pick on them constantly." "Why do I do it?" he asked himself. "To have fun. To really have fun." (Priest, 1987)

The same theme was evident in high school seniors in a rural Midwestern town: A 17-year-old boy commenting on a bullying incident he had witnessed said, "There was no real reason why they picked on him. They just did it out of fun for themselves." (Hazler, Hoover, & Oliver, 1993, p. 18).

Even more disturbing is the fact that in adulthood men who bullied in their school years frequently brush aside accounts of their bullying as unimportant, of little consequence, and just what boys used to do. Their failure to regard their own behavior as reprehensible in any way and their casual indifference to their victims' suffering are glaringly apparent on television talk shows. The format on these shows routinely brings perpetrators and victims together. Even when confronted by their former victims, and on national television, these men appear to be genuinely perplexed that their bullying behavior in childhood (which they describe quite freely) could have caused any distress to their victims. The odds that the children of these men will continue in their footsteps are depressingly high (Eron & Huesmann, 1990).

A particularly sickening example of a total lack of remorse in an adult is contained in a feature ("Growing up nasty," 1993) about a memoir by an assistant editor of the *London Review of Books*, Andrew O'Hagan. According to this feature, watching television accounts of the two 10-year-old boys in Liverpool who kidnapped and killed two-year-old James Bulgur made O'Hagan think of his own preadolescent years:

> We were brimming with nastiness. . . . Torture . . . was fairly commonplace. . . . For many of us, bullying was a serious game. It involved strategies, points scored for or against, and . . . detailed planning.
> We walked to school with . . . a younger, fragile boy named David. . . . When he didn't walk straight . . . we'd slap him. . . . Over time, we started to hit the boy hard. Our way to school was dotted with new trees . . . bound with rubber belts. . . . We began to punish David with them whenever he'd "been bad" . . . when we were caught . . . we were beating his bare legs with the coiled-up straps . . . we were late,

having spent half an hour . . . practically skinning the screaming boy's legs.

It's not that any of us were evil. . . . Now and then it got out of hand . . . a game of rounders . . . would end up as a game of clubbing the neighbor's cat to death. A night of camping . . . could usually be turned to . . . killing people's pet rabbits. Mindless stuff . . . it was just the way most of the boys I knew used up their spare time. (pp. 13–15, emphasis added)

This account typifies the pitiless and detached attitude that has led Hammond (1989) and others (Pearce, 1991; Smith, 1991) to speculate that among this group of bullies there is a hard core with some deep-seated psychological problem of a pathological nature that is urgently in need of identification and psychiatric help.

HOW DO CHILDREN BECOME BULLIES?

A child becomes a bully through the interaction of a heterogeneous group of causative factors, rather than as the direct result of a single factor. From a preventive point of view it is important to identify these factors because some are modifiable and clearly justify intervention efforts, whereas others are not. There are three major factors associated with a predisposition to bullying.

Child-Rearing Influences

On the basis of his research with boys, Olweus (1980) has identified several child-rearing conditions that are conducive to the development of bullying. One is a pervasive negative attitude on the part of the parents, particularly the mother, toward parenting. This attitude is characterized by a lack of warmth and caring for the child and it has the potential for later difficulties. Parenting of this caliber often is associated with a failure on the child's part to bond with the parents or feel loved by them and the consequent development of an attachment disorder (Bowlby, 1969). The failure to bond in turn is likely to be associated with a lack of empathy for other children and a tendency to behave in an inappropriate and coercive manner toward them.

A second characteristic concerns the failure of the parents, particularly the mother, to set adequate limits for the child's behavior; an excessive tolerance is shown for inappropriate aggression toward siblings, other family members, and peers. The fact that the emphasis here is on maternal attitudes and child-rearing behaviors does not imply that the mother's parenting style has greater impact than that of the father. It simply reflects the fact that in most cases mothers care for their children for many more hours per day than do fathers.

The combination of the above two parenting styles results in an increased risk of the child developing a pattern of antisocial aggression and hostility toward others. Olweus (1993a, p. 39) refers to these child-rearing practices as providing "too little love and care and too much 'freedom' in childhood" and states that they make a major contribution to the development of the aggressive reaction pattern that characterizes the typical bully.

A third parenting procedure that is associated with a predisposition to bullying is the use by parents of power-assertive disciplinary methods that are geared toward control and coercion, for example, violent emotional outbursts and routinely administered severe corporal punishment. This parenting style often is characterized by inconsistency: Misbehavior that is punished one day may be ignored the next. Because the children are uncertain about the consequences, they come to expect the worst in interactions with powerful others. This expectancy often generalizes to interactions with peers, with ambiguous situations being interpreted with a paranoid eye (Dodge, in Greenbaum, 1989), thus leading to unjustified attacks on others. These children also learn that might is right. This cognition, in combination with exposure to parental aggressive behavior and the absence of any attempt to teach more appropriate behaviors (because of parental indifference or ignorance), is likely to further the development of the aggressive personality pattern characteristic of boys who bully.

It is not uncommon for such parents to teach their children to be aggressive. Of relevance here is a major study of adolescent aggression (Bandura & Walters, 1959) that focused on parental rather than community influences on aggression. The subjects were adolescent boys of average or above-average intelligence from middle-class, two-parent homes. Half of the boys were high aggressive and half were neither overly aggressive nor passive. This latter group formed the control group. Intensive interviews with all the parents and boys in each group showed marked differences in parenting style. The control group parents were not overly aggressive, encouraged their sons to assert themselves in socially acceptable ways, and generally discouraged physical aggression, especially in the form of provoking other children. By contrast, the parents of the high aggressive boys were often combative themselves, encouraged fighting in their sons, used physical punishment at home, and clearly admired aggression in others.

The following responses are representative of parents who openly demanded aggression in their sons:

MOTHER (Case 13): When Glen was about six or seven years all the kids were fighting and he would never fight. . . . So my husband . . . saw two little boys, really fighting him. So he took off his belt and he said, "Glen, I'm going to tell you something. You're going to whip these boys or else I'm going to whip you." So he made him stand up and fight both of them. (Bandura & Walters, 1959, p. 107).

INTERVIEWER: Have you ever encouraged Russell to use his fists to defend himself?

MOTHER: (Case 39): Yes, . . . in kindergarten. He came home every night for about three weeks; some little boy had picked on him and pounded on him and he'd come home all dusty, dirty and crying. So I told him . . . the next time he came home crying he was going to get a spanking. So the next night . . . this kid was still following him. He saw the house and decided he was pretty safe, so he turned on the other little boy and pounded him, and he felt pretty good about it after he stuck up for himself. (Bandura & Walters, 1959, p. 111)

Characteristics of the Child

Several factors may predispose a child to the antisocial aggression typical of bullies. These are constitutional factors, activity level, and temperament.

Constitutional Factors

There is strong research evidence, some of it cross-cultural, that simply being male predisposes a child to aggressive behavior (Maccoby & Jacklin, 1974). Another constitutional force that may be directly involved in aggressive behavior, or may work indirectly through the production of testosterone, is the Y chromosome. Increased aggression is associated with both an extra Y chromosome and high levels of testosterone in both boys and men, although the evidence for the testosterone effect is not unanimous. Olweus (Blanchard & Blanchard, 1988) has speculated that testosterone may be linked to characteristics that are *precursors* of aggression rather than to aggression itself. In a study of adolescent boys, he found that boys with high levels of testosterone tended to be more irritable and impatient as well as more easily frustrated than those boys with lower levels. All of these traits could increase the probability of the boys engaging in aggressive behavior such as bullying. Of particular interest are the findings of Tremblay (Marano, 1995) who is conducting longitudinal studies with bullies and other aggressive children. When Tremblay checked the testosterone levels of a group of boys who had reached puberty, he found that aggression was negatively correlated with testosterone level. Boys who had been rated by their teachers and peers as most physically aggressive in middle childhood had lower testosterone levels at age 13 than their peers rated as average on aggression, and the provocative bullies had the lowest testosterone levels of all. Tremblay has concluded that direct extrapolations to humans from animal studies of dominance, in which testosterone levels are an index of aggression are in error. Instead, he believes that in humans testosterone levels signify social success. For example, boys whom he describes as *tough leaders* score high on aggression, but they also have well-developed social skills. They do not assume leadership in new situations with tactics such as physical and verbal aggression. Instead, they establish dominance with verbal fluency. In Tremblay's studies these tough leaders were the most socially successful, the most popular, and they had the highest testosterone levels of all.

Activity Level

There is unequivocal evidence that as a group, boys are more often overactive (Askew, 1989) and hyperactive than girls (Ross & Ross, 1982). Increased activity is linked to the subsequent development of antisocial aggression (Richman, Stevenson, & Graham, 1982).

Temperament

The child's temperament represents the interaction between biologically anchored predispositions and environmental demands. A child's temperament in the early months of life is associated with his or her later behavior. Temperament characteristics that were subsequently found to be associated with a high level of difficult behavior, such as aggression and hotheadedness (temper outbursts, poor impulse control, irritability, easy to anger) were (1) difficulties adapting to new situations; (2) irregular eating and sleeping habits; (3) negative moods, strong moods; and (4) unpredictable behavior (Thomas & Chess, 1977). These findings were consistent with those of Graham, Rutter, and George (1973), who used the foregoing characteristics to identify a temperamental adversity index that could be used to predict which children would have problems a year later. A high score indicated that the child was three times as likely as the average child to be at risk for difficult or aggressive behavior at home, and eight times as likely to be at risk for problems at school.

Children who continue to exhibit the foregoing characteristics throughout the first years of life are reported to push, hit, and fight far more than average in nursery school (Billman & McDevitt, 1980; Pearce, 1991). However, Olweus (1993a) believes that the effect of the temperament factor on bullying tendencies is less potent than that of two of the child-rearing practices discussed earlier: negativism and a lack of warmth on the part of the parents, especially the mother, and too much freedom particularly in relation to aggressive behavior. A child's temperament sets limits on his responsivity to stressors, particularly stressors of an aggressive nature. Although temperament is not easy to modify, much could be achieved by teaching the child how to live with it.

Factors in the Environment

A number of environmental factors facilitate bullying, a major one being that negative consequences for bullying are generally rare in American homes and schools. The increasing number of single parents and parents who are both working full-time precludes attention to misbehaviors such as bullying that are often regarded as transient or inconsequential. In addition, many parents perceive reports of bullying in boys as evidence that the boy is "standing up for himself" or is "all boy." In school other misbehaviors are censured, but bullying often goes unnoticed or is ignored. Supervision in the school setting often is grossly inadequate both inside and outside, thus constituting an open invitation to the child with bullying tendencies. Crowded conditions, especially on the playground, also encourage bullying (Opie, 1988). On a more basic level, some norms in American school culture actually protect the bully, for example, the admonition not to tell tales.

Modeling influences (Bandura, 1977b) also facilitate bullying. Particularly at the elementary school level, bystanders who admire the exploits of bullies or who adhere to the widely accepted concept of survival of the fittest often reward bullying by being interested and may turn to it themselves. Even school personnel, particularly teachers, often bully children and, in doing so, serve as powerful models.

An unusually potent modeling influence can be found in television presentations in which bullying often goes unchecked and in many cases is rewarded in the course of the story with further approval signaled by dubbed-in laughter. Continued exposure to sequences of bullying desensitizes child viewers to the pain and misery of being bullied. With this deterrent removed, the way is further cleared for the child to engage in bullying others.

In Japan, bullying is widespread in the schools, but a different set of environmental factors are linked to the problem. According to the Monbusho, Japan's Ministry of Education, violence in Japanese schools is increasing: Many of the most worrying incidents have involved *ijime*, the excessive bullying of other pupils. The Japanese have been trying unsuccessfully for 10 years to contain *ijime* (Prewitt, 1988).

The bullying has been attributed to pressures in the Japanese schools, specifically the extreme demands for uniformity, iron discipline, and the highly competitive ethos of the schools (White, 1993). Suicides are common (Greenlees, 1993). Children are expected to conform to rules that dictate the number of pleats a girl can have in her skirt and the exact length a boy may grow his hair. In administering discipline, teachers provide many instances of modeling bullying behaviors. A teacher gave electric shocks to pupils who forgot to bring their textbooks to school; 40 high school students had their hair cropped (culturally, a real humiliation) as punishment for poor performance on an examination (White, 1987, 1993); and teachers in one school buried two terrified students in sand up to their necks for 20 minutes in an attempt to obtain information about an incident that had occurred in school. Although reform of the rigid severity of the school system clearly is indicated, the Monbusho is reluctant to modify one of the world's most admired educational systems (White, 1987). Instead, 14,000 adult advisors have been hired to keep in close contact with school children who are facing problems (Greenlees).

BULLYING ON THE BULLIES

Immediate Effects

By bullying others, bullies gain a sense of being in control. This feeling overrides any possibility of empathy for the victims or for anyone else and reduces any anxiety that they may be experiencing. In fact, bullies feel pleased with what they do to their victims (Batsche & Knoff, 1994). This need for control may explain why bullies appear to experience more satisfaction from using threats and other power-oriented statements to force other children to obey them than they obtain from the often substantial material gains. This imposed obedience frequently involves actions of an antisocial nature. An incident in a middle school in Seattle fits this pattern ("Pupils accused," 1992). Two sixth-grade girls and a boy put mechanical pencil lead into an apple and then tried to persuade their teacher to eat it. Their insistence aroused the teacher's suspicions and, when questioned, the three said that they acted out of fear of being beaten up by three other sixth-grade girls if they failed to get the teacher to eat the apple. In the early school years bullies are popular, admired by others, or accorded a certain deference stemming from fear, but these reactions lessen sharply by junior high school. Often they become the leaders of a group of willing accomplices who are subordinates rather than equals. At least for this group, the bully's word is law, which further reinforces the feeling of power and, in addition, eliminates the need for friendship with other children. Bullying allows children who are either bored with school or not doing well to be "good" at something, to prove their courage and dominance to their peers. It allows them to feel superior. A high school senior who had been subject to long-term bullying offered this explanation for why some boys are bullies: "If you don't feel like you can do anything else and you can beat up everyone in the school, at least you can do something" (Priest, 1987, p. 16).

Once solidly established with their henchmen, however, they are in a position of power with no opposition from within their group. Consequently, some activity is needed that will allow them to demonstrate their power and serve as an outlet for it. It is reasonable to think that the next phase in this sequence could be a shift from bullying and extortion and so on, with limited gains, to a more lucrative and reputation-enhancing level. Included here might be major shoplifting or confrontation with other ganglike groups to demonstrate dominance or superiority of some kind.

The groups affiliated with bullies should not be equated with the gangs that roam the streets of many major cities. Although the bully's group may show some ganglike behaviors, they are *not* a gang in the true sense. Gangs typically have a group name, and members often have guns, wear specific insignia, claim a neighborhood or a particular territory as theirs, and often defend it literally to the death. Gangs are not open to everyone. When new members are accepted, they are required to undergo initiation rites that may include being beaten up by gang members or, in the case of girls, gang rape.

Long-Term Effects

A common misconception about bullying is that it is a transient problem of childhood and early adolescence that disappears with increasing age. Nothing could be farther from the truth: Olweus (1979) has reported a remarkable persistence into adulthood of the aggressive behavior that manifests itself in childhood as bullying. Although some children who bully do outgrow this behavior (Olweus, 1993a), many do not, and for them the outlook is bleak. In his longitudinal study Olweus (1991) found that approximately 60% of the boys who were identified as bullies in grades 6 through 9 had, by the age of 24, at least one criminal conviction, and that 40% of them had had three or more arrests.

In 1960 Eron and Huessmann (1987) began a longitudinal study of an entire group of third-grade children (n = 870) in the Midwest. They have reported that children who bullied at age 8 had a 1 in 4 chance of ending up with a criminal record by age 30, as compared to the 1 in 20 chance that most children have. In addition, the childhood bullies were more likely to have been convicted of crimes including a higher number of more serious crimes, had more moving traffic violations, and more convictions for drunken driving. They had not achieved well educationally and were more often high school dropouts. They were below the nonbully group professionally and socially. They were more abusive to their wives and children and, perhaps most serious of all, their children were often bullies, so in effect, they were raising a whole new generation of bullies. Contrary to common expectations, the results were independent of the children's IQ and social class level at age 8. Further confirmation of this dispiriting prognosis has been reported by Beale (1993), Farrington (1993), Robins (1978), and Widom (1991).

The surprising thing about the problem of bullying is that despite its serious short- and long-term effects, there have been very few concerted attempts at intervention by the schools. The exceptions are a cluster of major programs in Europe and the United Kingdom (see, for example, Olweus, 1993a; Smith & Sharp, 1994; Tattum & Herbert, 1993). Whereas other antisocial behaviors such as disobedience, cheating, truancy, theft, and vandalism are routinely censured and often punished severely, only minimal action, if any, is taken against bullying. The reasons for the failure to take decisive, schoolwide action are diverse, and many are based on erroneous thinking. Despite the unequivocal evidence of the stability of childhood aggression (Eron & Huesmann, 1987; Olweus, 1978, 1980), bullying often is tolerated because it is incorrectly believed to be a transient problem of childhood and early adolescence. School administrators who prefer to believe that bullying is not a problem in their school often are concerned about the reputation of the school (as opposed to the welfare of the students). Others justify their dismissal of bullying as a problem by preferring to focus their efforts on "real problems," such as drug dealing and weapon-related violence. It is commonly believed that it is primarily the victims of bullying who suffer (Besag, 1989), a belief that seriously underestimates the breadth of effect that bullying episodes evoke. Reports of the prevalence of bullying mask the true extent of the damage because they give no indication of the effects of the bullying on bystanders and others who subsequently hear about it, usually in a distorted form. As Tattum (1989) has cogently noted, you cannot intimidate one child without making others afraid.

Despite the immediate and long-term negative effects of bullying, a survey of the literature shows that, for the most part, bullying goes unchecked in the school setting. Bullies rarely encounter organized opposition to their behavior from school personnel and parents (who often are unaware of the bullying), and individual action on the part of peers is sporadic at best. We briefly consider the attitudes and reactions of these three groups to bullying, beginning with peers.

REACTIONS TO BULLIES

Peers

Some of the findings are encouraging. Studies with English and Australian school children and adolescents (Boulton & Underwood, 1992; Rigby & Slee, 1991) showed that the majority were opposed to bullying and tended to be supportive of victims. Half of those in the Boulton and Underwood study tried to help those who were being bullied, and nearly one third expressed their regret about failing to help. On the negative side there was a trend toward diminishing sympathy for the victims with increasing age (Rigby & Slee) and in the Boulton and Underwood study one fifth of the children said that they did nothing because it was none of their business. Also discouraging was the finding that almost one third of the children said that they could understand why bullies did it. This reaction might indicate a tolerance for bullying, or it might reflect justifying the bullying of provocative victims. Victims are generally disliked by their peers, and within the victim group, provocative victims are the most disliked members of the peer group (Perry et al., 1988).

Taking a different tack, Perry et al. (1990) asked American children in grades 4 to 7 first to imagine acts of aggression against victims and nonvictims and then to state how much the respondents would care about hurting the victims. Hurting the victims caused significantly less upset than hurting the nonvictims, which suggests that the respondents also would be less likely to help a victim in a bullying episode.

What Holds Peers Back?

Because most peers are not friends with victims, they are not motivated to come to their assistance: Low sociometric status can deter peers of both genders from helping victims (Munsch & Kinchen, 1995). In the case of boys the reluctance to intervene could also be due to the fact that male macho stereotypes run counter to having empathy for any weakness. An interesting explanation for the failure of school children in general to help victims has been offered by Rigby and Slee (1991). They propose that some children and adults are reassured by the belief that the world is a just place and that bad things do not happen to people who are good (Lerner, 1980). Shaver (1975) has studied some of the prerequisites for applying the "just world" belief, and, in the case of bullying, he has suggested that when there is a moderate threat of harm, there is a strong motivation to adhere to this belief and to blame the victim for being a victim. When the victims are blamed for their problems, the implication is that the problems are controllable by the victims. Consequently, children are unlikely to offer help. Blaming the victims for being victims is unfortunately a prevalent attitude in many schools; it eases the conscience and justifies inaction.

Far more likely is the very real possibility of retribution for the child who intervenes in a bullying attack, particularly in those schools in which bullying appears to be condoned by the authorities because no attempts are made to prevent or halt it. Sometimes the individual child can successfully thwart bullies' attacks. A sixth-grade boy in a Canadian elementary school was outraged at the sight of boys 3 or 4 years older than their victims persecuting a small group of second-grade children daily on their way home. The boy arranged to escort the children home every day. The bullies became angry and challenged the boy to fight, but when he called their bluff, they left hastily and the bullying ended (H. H. Smith, personal communication, December 14, 1991).

Other attempts to intervene have been disastrous. In an English day school a 13-year-old boy was stabbed to death when he went to the assistance of others who were being bullied (Tattum, 1989). A 16-year-old English girl who went to the police and identified one of a group of 20 boys who had severely beaten a Pakistani student has since received favorable publicity and praise from some, but she has been vilified by others (Klein, 1995). In the year following the incident she received death threats, was verbally abused by total strangers, was bullied at school, and in a recent attack by another student sustained concussion and minor injuries.

The Potential of Group Peer Pressure

Clearly, individual peer pressure has a high risk potential, but group peer pressure could be another matter. Some experts in the field have proposed that peers could be a major force in combating bullying. Olweus (1993a), for example, has stated that "it is important to recognize that 60 to 70 percent of the students (in a given semester) are not involved in bullying at all . . . it is essential to make use of this group of students in efforts to counteract bully/victim problems at school" (pp. 17–18). Herbert (1989) strongly concurs with this view: "Perhaps the most important factor in combating bullying is the social pressure that can be brought to bear by the peer group rather than the condemnation of individual bullies by people in authority" (p. 80).

Some schools that have been genuinely interested in using peer pressure to combat bullying have set up programs that require a substantial number of peer participants. Two of these, the student watch and the conflict resolution programs, are described in Chapter 6.

Peer-initiated groups also have been effective, if somewhat unorthodox in their approach. Bullies attract physical retribution more often than other categories of juvenile offenders (Opie & Opie, 1959), so peer-initiated retribution usually involves a jungle justice approach of a physical nature. A 12-year-old boy gave the following description of how to deal with a bully (Opie & Opie, 1959):

> In S ____ (a village in Oxfordshire) there is a well-known bully usually named Stinker Maynard. He is always fighting younger boys so we tried our usual "bully bounce" on him. This is how it is done: the victim is captured and tied to an object consisting of two ashen poles. The bully is then dragged up a very bumpy hill to shake him about. He is then untied and hung upside down from a tree by his feet for a few minutes until he begs for mercy. The captors then hoist him down and fight him until he says he will leave us alone. This is done to every bully in our village. (p. 192)

Schools' Response to Bullying

Schools have given the problem of bullying a low priority and when asked, cite their focus on the "serious" problems of weapon-related violence and drug use. This either/or reasoning overlooks the fact that it is the school's responsibility to ensure the safety of all students within the school environment. It is not enough to select some problems and ignore others.

There are a number of reasons for the failure to take decisive action, and most of them reflect badly on the school. Often school personnel are largely unaware of the extent of the bullying problem in their school (Olweus, 1993a; Zarzour, 1994), particularly if supervision is inadequate or indifferent and pupil–teacher channels of communication are nonexistent. It is more difficult under the best of circumstances for teachers and other adults to detect bullying because it is often a covert activity well hidden from adult scrutiny.

Even when school personnel are aware that there is a bullying problem, they generally take no action. Sometimes they dismiss it as just a stage that children go through, an inevitable part of growing up; or they ignore it because they believe that the children involved should be left to find a solution. They believe that adult intervention would deprive the victim of an important social experience. These lines of thought have some validity, but not when a helpless child is being abused and terrorized with no relief in sight. Sometimes the victim is seen as a wimp whom school personnel secretly despise. This makes it hard for them to offer support or sympathy, an understandable reaction but not a justifiable one. When school administrators are reluctant to admit that a problem exists, they sometimes go to extraordinary lengths to hide it. One teacher (G. Walters, personal communication, January 24, 1995) told us that her principal "insisted that the term *bullying* not be used. Instead, it should be referred to as scuffling (physical aggression), joking (name-calling), and playing naughty tricks (taking, damaging other children's possessions)."

School personnel, including maintenance people, playground supervisors, and all others who work regularly in the school, often have inadequate or even no training in the management of bullying and little understanding of its effects on the climate of the school. Teacher training programs include no courses on the management of bullying. One teacher told us: "Bullying makes me furious. I see it and I stop it but I know that's only a stopgap at best. Of all the behavior problems, it's the one I feel least able to deal with effectively" (B. Miller, personal communication, January 25, 1995). However, the prime reason for the failure of the school to take action against bullying is the absence of organized parental pressure. Sporadic complaints by individual parents about specific bullying incidents are ineffective. The school will brush them aside as they did these parents who had grounds for complaining (Winfrey, 1994).

In the sixth grade, 11-year-old Megan transferred into a public school from a private school. Almost from the beginning a group of same-age girls bullied her (used name calling, hit her over the head, pushed her up against the lockers) and threatened to beat her up if she reported them. Her parents went immediately to the school only to be told that if they were frightened for their daughter's safety, perhaps they should send her to another school. Megan spent a whole day with the counselor who then, on finding that she had transferred from a private school, dismissed her with the advice that she had better get used to it because "this is the real world." When a member of the group of bullies was questioned, she could not remember doing most of the behaviors and denied the rest. The school took no further interest in the complaint.

Parents of Bullied Students

Two things are needed to make the schools take action to halt bullying. Parents need to form a large group to exert pressure en masse, including formal demands for action by the school, newspaper publicity, and letters to members of Congress: in short, a movement, rather than a scattering of isolated complaints, to build up awareness in the community along the lines of the activity of Mothers Against Drunk Driving (MADD) and the more recently formed group, Mothers Against Violence in America (MAVIA). It is clearly the responsibility of the school to intervene decisively in cases of bullying. Second, parents should work for legislation that requires the schools to report all incidents of a violent nature that occur within a school or on its grounds. As Orth (Winfrey, 1993) has pointed out, at the present time few schools voluntarily keep such a record because it reflects negatively on their school and on the administrative competence of the principal and staff.

The actions that the schools should take are spelled out in detail in Chapters 5 and 6. The final topic in the present chapter concerns the failure of many parents to take appropriate action when their child is accused of bullying.

Parents of Bullies

Often the bullies' parents are unaware of the bullying despite warning signs such as high aggressiveness to peers, low tolerance for frustration, impulsive reactions, easily aroused anger, and little empathy for others, particularly younger children. When told, a small minority of parents are genuinely appalled. They take decisive action: They cooperate fully with the school and the victims' parents, make reparation for any injury to the victims or damage to their possessions, and seek professional help to identify why their children bully others (Marks, 1993).

But these parents are a rarity. Far more often parents fail to see anything wrong with the bullying and interpret it as "standing up" for oneself. They clearly approve of their children's actions, regardless of gender and resent the school's involvement as "interference." All suggestions about procedures for modifying the bullying behaviors are rebuffed. One father said, "It's a mean world out there and he's gotta learn how to push back hard now." These parents also reject the possibility of any kind of change in their own behavior, such as curtailing corporal punishment in favor of other forms of deterrents, being less physically aggressive to spouses and children in everyday interactions, or limiting exposure to violent films and television programs. The actions that parents should take when their child is accused of bullying or complains of being bullied are described in Chapter 5.

Comment

Childhood bullying is a complex and serious problem that is not evenly distributed across gender or developmental periods. It has multiple determinants and develops as the result of transactional processes involving the parents, child, family, school, and often the community. Parents generally play a more important role than their children in the etiological equation, but the transactional framework suggests that the behavioral characteristics of the child may elicit power-assertive child-rearing of an inconsistent nature from the parents.

Most bullying involving children occurs in the school setting. As the various research surveys have shown, a substantial number of children are directly involved in bullying, with a significantly larger group, the silent majority of peers, being indirectly involved. The negative effects are pervasive. The short-term effects are destructive; the long-term ones have implications for abusiveness as parents and spouses as well as the potential for a cycle of inter-generational transmission of bullying behaviors. To halt this sequence and work toward the goal of long-term resolution of bullying and its associated problems, intervention becomes as essential for the bullies as it is for their victims.

4 Victims

BULLIES DO NOT attack all available targets; instead, they selectively focus on a stable subgroup of peers who serve in the role of victims. Victims are children who are exposed, usually repeatedly and over time, to negative actions on the part of one or more bullies (Olweus, 1991; Perry et al., 1990). They are a heterogeneous rather than a homogeneous group. Olweus (1993a) has distinguished between the bully-victim, mentioned in Chapter 3, the passive or submissive victim, and the provocative victim. These categories are of prime importance for planning intervention programs for victims and also for understanding the differences in the types of bullying that victims in each category elicit. The immediate and long-term effects for all categories of explanations why a bully selects a specific child as a target, namely the victim and difference hypotheses, are the subject of continuing controversy. The procedures that parents and schools should follow when a child is victimized are described. The chapter concludes with a brief discussion of some investigative approaches to the problem of victimization that either have expanded our knowledge of this problem or have the capacity to do so.

TYPOLOGY OF VICTIMS

Passive Victims

Most of the victims fall into the category of passive victims. A clear description has been provided by several investigators (see, for example, Björkqvist et al., 1982; Farrington, 1993; Olweus, 1978; Perry et al., 1988). Although less is known about girls (Olweus, 1993a), the following composite picture applies to victims of both genders unless otherwise stated.

Passive victims tend to be more anxious and insecure than children in general. In the case of boys, the anxious personality pattern often is combined with less physical strength than boys in general. This combination does occur in some girls but less often than it does in boys. Passive victims often are cautious, sensitive, and quiet, and their self-esteem is low so that they may see themselves as unattractive, stupid, and failures. They often are depressed (Neary & Joseph, 1994). Many of the victims who contacted the Bullying Line (La Fontaine, 1991) emphasized the negative effects of being bullied. They described it as conveying a message of rejection and hostility that showed the victims that they had no friends and were powerless.

In a Kidscape study (Elliott, 1991), victims were described as intelligent and creative, but lacking in those qualities that ease everyday social interactions. They often have no sense of humor, for example, and their demeanor is serious, which is a real handicap. Children who are capable of the timely and effective use of humor in peer interactions tend to be more popular and make new friends easily (McGhee, 1989). Victims are generally incapable of the relaxed give and take of informal peer interactions. There is evidence that this inability may exist from an early age, prior to the child's assuming the victim role. In an observational study (Schwartz, Dodge, & Coie, 1993) of boys in contrived play group settings, those who later became victimized were more submissive in their interactions with peers. Comparisons with boys who did not subsequently become victimized showed that the more submissive boys were notably nonassertive in that they did not initiate assertive behaviors such as social conversation; they also were socially incompetent and consequently spent more time in passive play rather than in interactions with peers. Intervention at that point might have halted the trend toward victimization.

One result of this combination of characteristics is that passive victims probably have received many rebuffs in informal play, further lowering their confidence in peer interactions. They have difficulty making friends and often lack a single good friend in their class, in effect often becoming social isolates in the school setting. A 15-year-old girl said, "The bullied person is always sad and depressed and doesn't have any popular friends" (Hazler et al., 1993, p. 19). Because they lack friends and, in fact, are often actively rejected or ignored by many of their peers (Perry et al., 1988), they are deprived of the social support that could offer them protection from bullying as well as the peer interactions that are critical for the development of the requisite social skills of middle childhood and early adolescence. These assorted factors set them on a downward spiral of decreasing social competence. Their whole demeanor signals to children with bullying tendencies that they would be unlikely to retaliate if bullied. Their initial response to exploratory bullying is helplessness, futile anger, crying, and withdrawal in the lower grades and heightened upset and avoidance (in the form of different routes to school, for example) in the upper grades. Rarely do they strike back physically or psychologically, although there is evidence that passive boy victims are more likely to bring guns to school than boys in general (Greenbaum, 1989). This might indicate an intention to strike back or it could make them feel safer. In the absence of any attempt to help the passive victims cope more competently with their social inadequacies and the related bullying problems, the bullying increases their anxiety and fear, leading to further social withdrawal, so that the downward spiral continues unchecked.

Implications of Lazarus's Theory for Intervention

The bully-related problems that confront passive victims must seem insurmountable to them. Typically, their initial appraisal of the bully goes far beyond threatening to the point where the bully is seen as omnipotent. Boys who bully are generally physically much stronger and more able than their victims and bullies of both genders are justifiably very confident and psychologically intimidating. Despite these formidable differences, the victims may make a brave, but futile, effort at self-defense. As Perry et al. (1988) have pointed out, passive victims often differ markedly from bullies in physical aggressive skills, so it is usually unrealistic to expect them to counterattack successfully. When self-defense fails, the victim's only other option is to seek social support; for a variety of realistic and unrealistic reasons, they are often very reluctant to take this step. At this point they may engage in reappraisal (emotion-focused coping) and see themselves as worthless and deserving of the punishment meted out by the bully. Strangely enough, blaming themselves may result in their feeling that they have some control of the problem, and this in turn has an element of comfort.

The critical flaw in attempts by victims to cope is their failure to seek social support. If intervention is to succeed, it is essential to provide them with some form of social support: Parents and family are the optimum source because they are of vital importance to successful intervention. What the passive victims desperately need are reasons for some confidence in themselves. To this end it would be imperative to improve their self-esteem and strive to equip them with the social skills, including assertiveness, that are prerequisites to a beginning acceptance by the peer group.

The fact that passive victims often are described as intelligent and creative (Elliott, 1991) suggests that if school cooperation is available, these assets could be used to their advantage in the classroom. Consideration should be given to identifying the behaviors or qualities in the victims that invite attacks and then initiating changes where possible. An outside, objective opinion would be invaluable here: In many cases professional help in designing an intervention program would be mandatory.

Provocative Victims

Within the victim pool, Olweus (1978) and others (Pikas, 1989; Stephenson & Smith, 1989) have found that one in five to seven, the provocative victims, form a distinct group; Perry et al. (1988), however, found that the chances of a victim being provocative or passive were approximately equal. In any case, these children, who are variously described as reactive bullies and ineffectual aggressors (Marano, 1995), are more active, assertive, and confident than other victims. The anxiety is there, but it is combined with aggressive reaction patterns. The common excuse of bullies, "He asked for it," has some validity here: The provocative victims behave in ways that create tension and irritation in their peers. They tease and taunt and are hot-tempered. When peers retaliate, they fight back, often ineffectively. David Perry, who is widely acknowledged to be the leading expert on victims of bullying, has stated (Marano, 1995) that provocative victims prolong the fight even when they are losing. He attributes their illogical behavior to their being easily aroused emotionally but unable to handle the ensuing conflict because they get "invested" in their fights. Their high level of arousal prevents them from stopping fighting, and their behavior serves the function of providing the bully with sought-after rewards, for example, the demonstration of his superior power and a level of overt upset in the victim that Marano (p. 64) describes as "lots of theatrical value." Sometimes they force themselves on the bully in an effort to join the group (Stephenson & Smith), thus eliciting the label, "too pushy."

Olweus (1978, 1993a) has described these victims as the least popular of all bullies and victims. Despite their unpopularity, they do not appear to have low self-esteem (Smith & Boulton, 1991). However, because of the disturbed nature of many of these children, Smith, Bowers, Binney, and Cowie (1993) have speculated that their responses on self-esteem inventories may be defensive rather than accurate.

In marked contrast to the passive victims who at school are very little trouble, provocative victims often create considerable management problems. They have difficulty attending to one task for long because they suffer from poor concentration. Often their distractive behavior provokes other students and the teacher so that everyone reacts negatively to their antics. This reaction serves only to incite them further. It is possible that they may be attention-deficit-disordered or learning disabled, and are therefore in need of special education class placement. Such placement would be beneficial in many respects, but the bullying problem would likely increase: Special education children are bullied and teased more than students in the regular classes (Whitney, Nabuzoka, & Smith, 1992; Whitney, Smith, & Thompson, 1994).

Implications of Lazarus's Theory for Intervention

The focus of intervention for these rather puzzling victims should be on teaching them not to pick fights. One facet of this task would be to determine how the provocative victims see the adversaries that they select and then use this information to develop an intervention program to change their perceptions. The victims' assessment of their own social status and their motivation to effect changes in it should be considered. They may need a special program to improve or eliminate their academic and cognitive shortcomings and to develop social skills. The management problems that they create in the classroom often repel peers and antagonize teachers. These victims often are more active, assertive, and confident than other categories of victims. It would be important to consider how these positive attributes could be used to the provocative victims' advantage, who although often exasperating, are at the same time the most interesting of all the bullies and victims.

Bully-Victims

One small group of children, the bully-victims, overlaps both categories. Olweus (1985) reported that 6% of those who were seriously bullied in turn bullied others, a finding that was confirmed in a 1988 survey by Stephenson and Smith (1989). Bully-victims often are physically weaker than those who bully them, but are almost always physically stronger than their victims. They have some of the characteristics of the provocative victims in that they frequently provoke others and are easily aroused themselves (Stephenson & Smith). Typically, the bully-victims are not popular with their peers. Their behavior pattern is reminiscent of the Freudian mechanism of displacement as is evident in the following account:

I was the smallest kid in the whole third grade, even smaller than the girls, and the big guys beat up on me all the time and called me Teeny. They said it was my fault I got beat up but I didn't know why. Whenever they did it, I'd turn right round and really let some little kid have it and I told myself he asked for it. Then in fourth grade I grew a lot and I was really good at baseball and they stopped the bullying and so did I. (T. Bradford, personal communication, October 13, 1995)

Intervention

The appropriate intervention for the bully-victim is problematic. If a careful assessment of the home environment rules out bully- and victim-related etiological factors, an individual treatment protocol should be devised. Treatment should focus first on the behaviors of the child that resemble those of the provocative victim.

Other Categories of Victims

Vicarious Victims

In terms of the negative impact of bullying on a school or neighborhood, a seriously affected group are the vicarious victims (sometimes called surrogate victims). These are children who witness bullying incidents or who hear reports, often exaggerated, of bullying incidents. They become victims of the climate of fear in the school. They perceive their own vulnerability as potential targets and, consequently, suppress any impulse to try to help the victim or to speak out about the incident. They may feel very sympathetic but at the same time they are wary of a contagion effect or of direct retribution; although they often feel guilty, they ward off the urge to support the victim in any way (Greenbaum, 1989). The combination of awareness of their own vulnerability and guilt over their failure to help creates a high-stress situation and considerable upset in the vicarious victim.

False Victims

Besag (1989) has hypothesized that there is a group of false victims who complain frequently and without justification about being bullied by their classmates. We would interpret this not as victim behavior, but rather as a dependency bid for teacher attention and/or sympathy. In any case, this pattern of behavior should be firmly stopped not only for the child's benefit, but also because teachers who are unsympathetic to the problems of bullying victims are handed an alibi for ignoring genuine complaints about bullying.

Some empirical support for this category comes from Perry et al. (1988). In developing their Modified Peer Nomination Inventory for the purpose of identifying victimized children, they discovered a small group who reported that they were "extremely victimized," that is, in the top 10% of the sample. However, these children were not perceived as victims by either their teachers or their same-gender peers. Perry et al. commented that the lack of correlation between their self-reports and the peer and teacher nominations raises questions about relying solely on self-report measures of victimization.

Perpetual Victims

Elliott (1993a) has proposed this category to encompass those victims who are bullied throughout their lifetime. Because it is likely that some passive and provocative victims may continue to be victimized in adulthood (Smith & Thompson, 1991) and that the term *perpetual* refers to the duration of bullying rather than to a separate group, this category should be eliminated. It is included here because in the discussion relevant to it, Elliott mentions a very interesting idea that has considerable potential. She suggests that such a victim might have developed a *victim mentality*, that the victim role could have become a permanent part of the child's psyche as a result of reward in the form of attention from others when the child was bullied or from a tendency to brood and constantly replay the script. A child or adult with this attitude needs therapeutic help.

Colluding Victims

These are children who take on the role of victim as a means to an end: social acceptance, popularity, and possibly protection. They go to great lengths to be accepted, for example, they play the part of the class clown, join in disruptive behavior, and often mask their true academic ability, if it is high. In addition to their problems in the school setting, they often are the least popular and most rejected children in the peer group. This combination puts them at risk of developing the externalizing problems that characterize many bullies, as well as the internalizing problems that often develop in victims.

THE MODIFIED PEER NOMINATION INVENTORY

In 1988 Perry et al. developed a modified version of the Peer Nomination Inventory (Wiggins & Winder, 1961) to assess children's victimization and aggressive bullying behavior. The Modified Peer Nomination Inventory (see Table 4.1) requires children to nominate classmates who fit specific behavioral descriptors, for example,

Table 4.1 Items on the Modified Peer Nomination Inventory (Boys' Form)

1. He's always losing things. (F)
2. He's a fast runner. (F)
3. Kids make fun of him. (V)
4. He is the kind of kid I like. (F)
5. When he doesn't get his way he gets real mad. (A)
6. He gets beat up. (V)
7. He has lots of friends. (F)
8. He's just plain mean. (A)
9. He shares his things with others. (F)
10. He gets called names by other kids. (V)
11. He's a real smart kid. (F)
12. He makes fun of people. (A)
13. He says he can beat everybody up. (A)
14. He's a good-looking kid. (F)
15. Kids do mean things to him. (V)
16. He tries to get other people in trouble. (A)
17. He's a good friend of mine. (F)
18. He hits and pushes others around. (A)
19. He likes to help the teacher. (F)
20. He gets picked on by other kids. (V)
21. He's good at sports. (F)
22. He gets hit and pushed by other kids. (V)
23. All the kids like him. (F)
24. He tries to pick fights with people. (A)
25. Kids try to hurt his feelings. (V)
26. He's a real nice kid. (F)

Note: F = filler item; V = victimization item; A = aggression item.
Source: Reproduced with permission of the authors and publisher from Perry, D. G., Kusel, S. J., & Perry, L. C. (1988). Victims of peer aggression. *Developmental Psychology*, *24*, 807–814. © American Psychological Association, Inc.

"Kids do mean things to him." It contains 26 items, of which seven describe victimization (V), seven describe aggressive behavior that bullies commonly exhibit ("He hits and pushes others around." [A]), and the remaining 12 are filler items ("He's a good-looking kid" [F]) to mask the purpose of the inventory. The 26 items are listed down the left-hand margin of a legal-size sheet of paper and the names of all the same-gender children in the class are listed across the top at right angles to the test items. Boys' forms have only boys' names and girls' forms only girls' names. Each child's task is to place an *X* beneath the name of any classmate(s) whose behavior fits an item. Any number of nominations can be made for each item. The children are asked to cross their own names off the list in order to prevent them from nominating themselves.

The victim score is determined by calculating the percent of same-gender classmates who checked the child's name for each victim item and then totaling these percentages. The same procedure is used to determine the aggressive bullying score. Because there are seven items on each scale, a child's score could range from zero to 700.

Methodologically sound investigations of the Inventory established its reliability and validity. It is a scale that children find interesting and enjoyable to complete. As would be expected with a statistically sound instrument, the participating children's victim scores did not correlate with their aggression scores, were positively correlated with peer rejection, and negatively correlated with peer acceptance (Perry et al., 1988).

Why Is Victimization So Common?

Children in our society generally have little control over their environment. As Finkelhor and Dziuba-Leatherman (1994) have noted, they probably have less choice about their surroundings than any other segment of the population with the exception of prison inmates. They are limited in their choice of whom they will associate with at home, school, and in their neighborhood. They are not free to leave abusive parents. If their school is overpopulated with bullies and other delinquents, it would be difficult to transfer to another school, and, in any case, they would still have to traverse the same neighborhood. These restrictions increase vulnerability to victimization by bullies.

Adults within the children's environment often have an extraordinary tolerance for the bully–victim interaction. Until recently school personnel and many parents accepted it as an inevitable hurdle of school life, with some from both groups even regarding it as beneficial for the victims. A classic double standard exists here: Adults tolerate forms of bullying, such as theft and unprovoked bodily assault with resultant injuries, as relatively inconsequential when the victim is a child, but in the case of adult victims, these abuses are regarded as grounds for criminal complaint.

Within this framework of few choices and dubious support, children who have potential victim attributes such as small physical stature, poor coordination, a lack of confidence, unassertiveness, and the lack of social support that friends would provide, are terribly vulnerable to attack by those who are bigger, stronger, aggressive, and on the alert for opportunities to demonstrate their power at little risk to themselves.

When Does Victimization Start?

Victimization starts early in the preschool years when 2- and 3-year-old children neither resist nor complain when others snatch a toy away from them, push them off play equipment, or elbow in ahead of them in the juice lineup. These children reward the bullies by giving in to their demands, crying and cowering away from them, and not protecting their rights (Patterson, Littman, & Bricker, 1967). If children continue in this pattern of submissiveness, they are headed toward the victim role (Schwartz et al., 1993).

Victimization is common in day-care and preschool settings. Although in some there is an emphasis on taking turns on play equipment, having temporary ownership of toys until they are voluntarily given up, and discouraging inappropriate pushing and shoving, in other care settings it is a case of survival of the fittest (Chazan, 1990). In this latter group, a dominance hierarchy is established quickly and accepted by those who are least assertive. Even at this early age dominant children appear to be able to identify those who will not offer much opposition. One explanation for their ability to judge other children has been provided by Troy and Sroufe (1987). They found that preschoolers who were victims often had a history of anxious or resistant attachment that resulted in visible anxiety identifying them as vulnerable to their aggressive peers.

Three studies of kindergarten children by Kochenderfer and Ladd (1995, in press a, b) showed that victimization was well established in this age group. Of particular importance to the topic of early victimization were their findings (in press b) on the prevalence and types of victimization by 5- and 6-year-old children. Four types of victimization were assessed: physical victimization (being hit), direct verbal (mean comments to child), indirect verbal (mean comments about the child, made to other children), and general (picking on one child). (This latter category creates problems of overlap with the physical and direct verbal categories.) About half of the children had experienced victimization to some extent, most often in the form of direct verbal and general. Direct verbal victimization also has proven to be more common than physical attack with older age groups (Boulton & Underwood, 1992; Perry et al., 1988). However, gender differences were less specific than those reported in older children (see, for example, Olweus, 1993a; Smith & Sharp, 1994). Boys and girls were equally at risk for victimization in general and for the four types. The latter were related to reported loneliness at school and school avoidance, but only the direct and indirect verbal types were related to disliking school.

The Stability of Early Victimization

In a study of 200 kindergarten children by Kochenderfer and Ladd (in press a) victimization was not a stable experience for all the subjects. Over half of the sample were victimized only in the fall.

This finding led to an investigation of what behaviors would result in continued victimization and what strategies, if any, did the children use in trying to stop being victimized. Early in the school year Kochenderfer and Ladd (1995) used self- and peer reports to identify children with victim characteristics. (A methodological finding of importance here was that the use of self-reports was a more valid method than peer reports for identifying peer-victimized children.) On the basis of findings from a study of preschool children by Patterson et al. (1967), it was hypothesized that crying and giving up possessions (acquiescing without resistance to the aggressor's demands) would result in continued victimization, whereas taking direct action (fighting back) and seeking social support (having a friend help, telling the teacher) or just walking away from the aggressor would be successful coping strategies for stopping victimization. The relationship between response strategies and their effect on victimization was significant only for boys, but not as predicted. Fighting back was related to continued victimization, whereas having a friend help was associated with reduced victimization. The important point, however, is that the victims tried to stop the victimization themselves. As Kochenderfer and Ladd have noted, other factors such as increased popularity could have contributed to ending the victimization.

How Some Children Become Victims

Attempts to explain the genesis of victimization have focused on maternal behavior and relationships as well as the behavioral characteristics of the child. A common assertion in the victimization literature is that maternal overprotection, particularly of boys, spawns victims (Olweus, 1978). The rationale for this belief centers on the effects of a deficit in early social experience. The preschool or early school child who has been sheltered from the social contacts and play experiences that most young children routinely experience is ill equipped to cope with the public school situation. Children who are overprotected often exhibit a cluster of inappropriate behaviors that deviate from the norm and establish them as different in a negative way from their peers; as a consequence, they become targets for exploratory bullying and teasing. They tend to seek adult help and protection when conflicts with peers arise and react to minor slights by showing upset. They cry easily. Because they have been deprived of peer interaction experiences, they lack the social skills that are habitual in children with more experience: For example, in games they often are unwilling to take turns and they react badly to losing. That maternal overprotection has the potential to seriously disrupt the young child's social development is evident in the following example of maternal infantilization and discouragement of autonomy in a young boy:

> We have a grandson who is probably two or three years behind his peers. This child is not retarded or brain-damaged. The problem is that "Terry's" mother refuses to allow him to interact with other children. She would not allow him to start school until the age of 6 because she believed he would not be able to handle it. He used a pacifier until he was 5 years old.
> Terry is afraid of his own shadow. . . . Terry's mother is crippling him in a way that could impact the rest of his life. His father thinks he is a sissy and a mama's boy and has little contact with him. . . . Terry's mother is setting up her son for victimization, bullying, and dependency. (Landers, 1995, p. 35)

Recent research by Finnegan and Perry (1995) has considerably refined the role of maternal overprotection in the victimization of the child. In it, two sets of mother–child interactions were examined: The first focused on the mother's behavior toward the child, particularly during control and conflict episodes; the second set was concerned with the child's responses during these interactions. The subjects were 184 fourth- through seventh-grade boys and girls who provided verbal reports about their mothers' and their own behavior at home during conflict and control episodes. Peer nominations were used to assess victimization, physical strength, internalizing behaviors such as withdrawal, anxiety, and depression, and externalizing behaviors, including aggression and disruptiveness in the school setting.

The results showed gender differences in the patterns of mother–child interaction associated with victimization. Maternal overprotectiveness was associated with victimization only for boys who reported that they felt afraid and compelled to submit to their mothers during conflicts. In the case of girls, victimization was predicted by maternal hostility, especially for those girls who were assessed by their peers as lacking in physical strength. Finnegan and Perry (1995) have suggested that hostility in the mother could create anxiety or depression in the daughter that is evident in peer interactions and attracts attacks from aggressive peers. Despite the divergent results for boys and girls, Finnegan and Perry suggest that they may be assimilated into a single principle of the influence of maternal behavior on victimization: Peer victimization may occur when maternal behavior impedes the child's progress toward the developmental goals and tasks that are salient for the child's gender. For boys, what is impeded is their progress toward autonomy and self-assertion, whereas for girls, maternal hostility may threaten their sense of connectedness in their primary relationship.

Another maternal-related behavior that has been associated with victimization in preschool (Troy & Sroufe, 1987) and school-age children (Finnegan, Hodges, & Perry, in press) is an anxious/resistant attachment to the caregiver, usually the mother. Children with such an attachment typically have a marked need for a parent to be with them in new situations and exhibit an unusual degree of distress when the parent leaves. On the first day of school or on being admitted to hospital, these children have great difficulty coping: They tend to be visibly anxious, cry much more easily than most other children of their age, and have poor self-esteem (Bowlby, 1973). In peer group settings these behavior patterns mark these children as potential targets for bullying. Because they are notably incompetent in managing aggression from peers, their inept attempts to fend off exploratory bullying are dismal failures that facilitate their assumption of the victim role.

Behavioral Characteristics of the Child

Children who are clumsy and lacking in the motor skills that most children of their age have acquired, or those who have difficulties with academic work and who elicit amusement, contempt, or other negative peer reactions also are at risk for victimization *if* they do not know how to handle the comments that result from these inadequacies. The child who can brush these shortcomings aside with a matter-of-fact acceptance or with humor is unlikely to be harassed. The problem here is that few children of any age can handle the quick retort in the face of personal attack, at least without some preliminary training.

Children who are physically or psychologically abused at home by their parents or older siblings and as a result suffer a loss of confidence and self-esteem sometimes fall into the victim role. For these children there may be some comfort to be derived from thinking that there is no solution other than to give up. Although a victim at home is sometimes a bully at school, more often the victim demeanor generalizes to the school setting and labels the child as a possible target for teasing and bullying.

One of the best statements on becoming a victim comes from Thompson and Smith (1991):

> some children and adolescents find themselves pushed into playing the role of victim in the emerging social pattern. Like the children who . . . learn to behave in a bullying manner in social groups, so many victims

enter social life as children with a lesser tendency to behave aggressively or even assertively and what seems to be a slightly greater difficulty in making effective social relationships with peers . . . and find that the patterns of social interaction leave them on the margins of groups, waiting to be "picked on" by children interested in demonstrating dominance at very little cost to themselves. (p. 141)

Other children find themselves pushed into the role of victim by their teachers. In *Children First*, Penelope Leach (1994) writes about the child's unremitting experience of adult power. Teachers have extraordinary power over children and in most cases use it appropriately (Rogers, 1993). However, when they abuse their power, the consequences can be exceedingly painful for the child. Consider the following example of misuse of teacher power (D. M. Ross, Case study, University of California Medical Center, San Francisco, 1977–1979).

Peter was a bright 6-year-old who was very small for his age. Right from the start his teacher drew unfavorable attention to his height ("You're the smallest first-grader I've ever seen," "Someone get little Peter that book, he can't reach it"). His classmates soon picked this up and derogatory names about his height ("Teeny," "Midget") were followed shortly by pushing and shoving, then hiding his books out of reach. The final indignity came when Peter's birthday coincided with that of the tallest boy in the class. The teacher had the two boys stand side by side and said, "Would you *believe* they're both *seven*?"

For the first time, Peter complained bitterly to his parents, who were furious but took no immediate action against the school. Instead, his father, who was aware that Peter was an unusually fast runner began preparing him for the Sports Day events. Peter became extremely proficient and won the first- and second-grade events with ease and came second in two of the third-grade races. His status at school soared. At the same time his parents warned his teacher that if she made any reference to his height again, they would file a complaint against her.

A question of critical importance in preventing and controlling bullying is *Why does the bully select one child rather than another as a target?* One view is that the potential victim is picked by chance and that it is a matter of being in the wrong place at the wrong time. Another idea is that it is certain qualities in the victim that invite and sustain bullying. The two most commonly cited explanations favor the latter. One of these, the *victim hypothesis* (Olweus, 1978), attributes the bully's choice to a victimlike demeanor that conveys that the child is a likely target. An anxious expression or body language that suggests fear, for example, are cues that guide the bully's choice. In preschool children this demeanor has been described (Troy & Sroufe, 1987) as radiating anxious vulnerability; in elementary school children it appears as an appeasing shrinking posture (Ginsburg, Pollman, & Wauson, 1977). The other explanation, the *difference hypothesis*, has been proposed as often by victims as by investigators (Pearce, 1989; Phillips, 1989). Here the bullying is attributed to external negative deviations such as obesity, extremes of stature, unusual clumsiness, physical defects such as protruding teeth or ears or poor eyesight, and speech problems such as stuttering. Social status is also a factor, according to some high school students in a survey by Hazler et al. (1993). One 15-year-old girl attributed being bullied to not being in "the in-group." The victim and difference hypotheses have generally been accepted in the literature despite the fact there is little evidence to suggest that either one is the exclusive causal link that identifies the child as a victim.

Valid objections have been raised against both hypotheses. Concerning the victim hypothesis, La Fontaine (1991) has contended that, unless victims are observed or tested before the onset of the bullying, it is impossible to determine whether the characteristic demeanor of the victim has preceded or followed the bullying. If it occurs or develops after the bullying, then it has no causal relationship to the bullying.

La Fontaine (1991) has also questioned the difference hypothesis on the grounds that references to the victim's features and behaviorial deviations are the *means* of causing distress, but are not necessarily the *cause* of the bullying. Data from an early study by Olweus (1978) with two different groups of boys showed that victims were no more externally deviant than a group of control boys who were not bullied. The only external deviation occurred in physical strength: The victims were weaker than boys in general, and this difference was greater when victims and bullies were compared (Olweus, 1993a).

The major fallacy in pursuing either the victim or difference hypothesis is the failure to consider the well-documented complexity of bullying (Besag, 1989; Olweus, 1993a; P. Smith, 1991). Clearly, multiple contributors to the selection of victims should be sought along with intensive study of the various motivations of the bullies and their interaction with the characteristics of the victims. If outcome is highly valued by the bully, for example, if he wants to enhance his status with his peers, then the basis for selecting a victim may be availability and a spur-of-the-moment decision.

Still on the complexity issue, there is the failure to consider the contributions of the various subgroups of victims to the bully's decision as to whom to select. If payoff is the desired outcome, the bully might choose a passive target who is known to have "enough" money and is also of a submissive nature. If the motive is a desire to show that the bully is in the power spot, then he might select a provocative victim, that is, one who is noted for irritating others and when attacked, for fighting back ineffectually. As Bandura (1986) has pointed out, in cognitive social learning theory outcome expectations are considered to be causal influences on behavior.

Another important omission in the search for the factors that contribute to the bully's choice of victims is the failure to consider factors that might be operative in the victim's social environment rather than in the victim alone. Following this line of thought, Perry and his associates (Hodges, Malone, & Perry, 1995) started from the fact that some or all of the triad of externalizing, internalizing, and physical weakness are likely to be implicated in victimization *but* not all children who are vulnerable (who have some or all of these behavioral attributes) are victimized. They speculated that certain social factors, when present, might decrease the risk of victimization in vulnerable children and, when absent, might increase that risk. The vulnerability of children with the foregoing cluster of behavior problems would likely increase if these children were also at social risk, that is, if they lacked supportive friends and were rejected by their peers. To test this hypothesis, 229 children in third through seventh grade were selected, an age group for whom social support from peers usually is of prime importance. There was strong support for the hypothesis that social risk conditions increased the probability of victimization of vulnerable children, whereas the absence of social risk served a protective function. These findings underline the need for early intervention designed to facilitate entry into the peer group and the acquisition of the social skills required for subsequent peer acceptance.

EFFECTS OF BULLYING

Short-Term Effects of Bullying on Victims

Repeated bullying is a serious problem because of the adverse effects it has on the victims. Fear becomes so ingrained a response in their everyday life that victims adopt fugitivelike routines to avoid areas in and around the school likely to be frequented by the bully. Avoidance is the most common tactic, its effect being to deprive them of essential formal and informal social experiences so critical to social development. Many victims experience active rejection (Perry et al., 1988) by peers who formerly were friends or at least friendly toward them. Some are intimidated by fear of being bullied if they associate with the victims; others despise them for not being able to cope with the bullies. Whatever the cause, the effect is to deprive the victims of further much-needed interaction and social support. A study of 200 five- and six-year-old kindergarten children (Kochenderfer & Ladd, in press a) focused on victimization and its relationship to two indices of school adjustment, feelings of loneliness, and school avoidance. Some were victimized only in the fall or spring of the school year, but for 8.5% of them victimization persisted throughout the school year, a finding consistent with that of Boulton and Underwood (1992) with 8- and 9-year-old children. Those victimized only in the fall experienced immediate effects in the form of loneliness and delayed effects in school avoidance. Although these children were less lonely in the spring, feelings of loneliness persisted after victimization had stopped.

In commenting on the plight of the victim, Floyd (1987) said: ". . .not only is the victim scorned, humiliated or attacked by the bully, but he also often is rejected by others as a sort of pariah, one damaged, tainted, infected. The stigma of being victimized casts a long shadow and leaves a dark pall" (p. 24).

As the bullying continues, often intensifying, the victims begin to see themselves as unworthy and inferior and, in some cases, as deserving of the punishment. This latter reaction has a surprising parallel in cases of abused wives, in which the wife comes to feel unworthy and consequently believes the abuse to be justified (Douglas, 1987). The damaged feeling of self-worth that results from bullying makes it impossible for the victims to reach their academic and social potential. Some school personnel describe victims as less intelligent and point to their poor grades as evidence, but they fail to consider that children do not perform well in the climate of fear that chronic bullying, terrorizing, and intimidation create in the victims' lives (Turkel & Eth, 1990). The negative effect of bullying on school performance often has been noted by clinicians and parents. Empirical evidence of this effect comes from Hazler et al. (1993) who reported a significant drop in grades for 90% of the victims of bullying in their study. Many victims are caught in a downward spiral leading to low morale and acute despair that manifest itself in truancy (Reid, 1990), chronic illnesses such as recurrent abdominal pain of unknown origin (Ross & Ross, 1988), running away, and in extreme cases, suicide (Beck, 1986; Besag, 1989; Elliott, 1991).

Long-Term Effects of Bullying on Victims

Besag (1989) believes that bullying may be character building for some victims but that for others the erosion of self-confidence and self-esteem is so severe that even in adulthood their social interactions are adversely affected. Some support for this view comes from Gilmartin (1987), who reported that 80% of heterosexual men who had great difficulty in progressing beyond casual contact and interaction with the opposite sex had experienced bullying at school. Parker and Asher (1987) also felt that the peer rejection that often accompanies victimization is a strong predictor of disturbances in adulthood.

Further evidence of the serious consequences of intense bullying in the school years is contained in the following accounts. The first is from a 28-year-old woman engaged to be married, whose bullying experiences had left her with long-term anxiety about having children:

> . . . they were older than me, they took a dislike to me . . . various things happened . . . they would take my cardigan and kick it around as a football, and they would kick me out of the way and carry on . . . one boy pulled my hair so hard that some came out, he dropped it in front of me . . . I was pushed off the climbing-frame, I didn't realise I had concussion but that's what it was . . . I remember feeling very alone—no one would help me . . . I dreaded going to school. (Smith & Sharp, 1994, p. 1)
>
> To the question: "Do you feel that's left a residue with you . . . what do you feel the effects are?" the above respondent continued:
>
> I'm quite insecure, even now . . . I won't believe that people like me . . . and also I'm frightened of children . . . and this is a problem. He (fiancé) would like a family, I would not and I don't want a family because I'm frightened of children and suppose they don't like me? . . . those are things that have stayed with me. It's a very unreasonable fear but it is there and it's very real. (Smith & Thompson, 1991, p. 7)

The second quote is from a 21-year-old college student whose bullying experiences had apparently isolated her from the outside world. She felt as if she were totally removed from her peers and complained that she could not seem to get into conversation with anyone. Her difficulties appeared to stem from the cruel bullying that she had been subjected to in high school when she became the prime target of a constant barrage of cruelty by a school clique of both boys and girls:

> Maybe it was my appearance of naiveté or vulnerability that attracted them . . . but their sights were set on me especially because they could see me crumble before their very eyes. Each day I would have my books stolen or scribbled on, or the john locked while I was inside, or my locker painted with insults. I was even pushed and shoved in the hallways, and more than once chased down darkening winter streets after school. Worst of all, though, was the barrage of comments about my appearance. I had . . . acne then and my breasts were late in flowering. Each

morning I was greeted as "pimple puss," or "tiny tits." There was no way for me to stem the tide. This was a powerful and influential group that was attacking me, and I had no friends to take up my defense, or to whom I could turn. I was isolated. I still am. (Segel & Yahraes, 1978, pp. 248–249)

In a follow-up study of two groups of Swedish boys who were or were not victimized by their peers during the period from sixth to ninth grade, Olweus (1993b) found that at age 23 the former victims were "normal" in many respects. This finding was attributed to the fact that as adults, they had considerably more freedom to choose their social and physical environments than is the case for most children. However, they had poorer self-esteem and were more likely to be depressed than their nonvictimized peers.

Effects on Other Children

Bystanders can be deeply affected. In one school a child reported feeling anger and helplessness at not knowing how to help the victim. Some felt guilt at not intervening: "I don't like it that Gill is bullied but I can't do anything about it or they will turn on me, too" (Elliott, 1993a, p. 9). Others had nightmares and worried that they might be the next target of the bully. Bystanders' accounts to others often are exaggerations designed to justify their failing to help the victim or possibly to be the focus of attention by telling a good story. Whatever the motivation, the result is to create anxiety about bullying. Students entering a new school are particularly vulnerable. The transition from one school to a higher level school can be stressful (Davies, 1986), and if the children are also anxious, they will not be as discriminating about lurid accounts as they might otherwise be.

A valid reason for considerable concern is that when bullying is witnessed by others and goes unpunished, it can create a climate of fear with widespread effects. It inhibits learning and distracts minds. Many students do not enjoy free-time periods such as recess and lunch time, are afraid to go to certain areas of the school, including the bathrooms, and feel vulnerable to attack on the way to and from school. An atmosphere of this sort encourages absenteeism, truancy, and early school dropout (Olweus, 1993a; Zinsmeister, 1990).

Responsibility for failing to take action against bullies is not entirely due to indifference on the part of school officials. Bullies are to a surprising extent protected by their victims, peers, parents of both bullies and victims, teachers, and in some instances, the legal system. In short, many of those in a position to take decisive action fail to do so. The contention that bullies often are given the protection that is normally accorded to an endangered species is not an exaggeration.

THE ISOLATION OF VICTIMS

Parents of Victims

Although some victims are reluctant to tell their parents (or other adults) about the bullying attacks, there is very little excuse for parents who are unaware that *some* problem exists. When no significance is attached to the obvious warning signs of bullying, such as lumps and bruises, torn clothing, "lost" possessions, and an unusual number of requests for money, the parents are either completely indifferent to their children's welfare or, to put it kindly, very naive.

When parents have been told about the bullying problem by their children, failure to investigate and follow through on the complaint, that is, to do nothing, is seen by children as the worst response to the problem that a parent can make (La Fontaine, 1991). Parents may do nothing because they are afraid that it will go on the child's cumulative school record and ultimately prove to discredit the child. If they have been bullied themselves as children, they may foresee that action on their part could lead to teacher scorn and peer contempt. Or they simply might not know what would be the best way of handling the problem and so do nothing. Whatever the reason, a total lack of social support from an adult who could reasonably be expected to offer help results in additional misery for victims without solving their bullying problems (Lazarus, 1966).

Why Victims Do Not Complain

The single most important contributor to bullying going undetected in school or elsewhere is the code of silence that is operative in most peer groups. Being identified as an informer is the ultimate disgrace. Some victims do not tell anyone because they know on the basis of experience or observation that neither parents nor school personnel will handle the problem effectively: Telling may lead to far more severe physical and psychological suffering if the adults fail to ensure the victim's anonymity. In one case reported to the Bullying Line, ". . . the headmaster made an announcement about bullying in assembly in such a way that the bullies were able to identify the caller as the source of his information and the bullying then intensified." (La Fontaine, 1991, p. 28). Although seeking social support should be a viable option for the victim, many children do not report bullying because their initial attempts at talking about the problem were brushed aside by impatient or unsympathetic adults:

> When a friend told the teacher I was being bullied he said I was old enough to deal with it myself (Girl, 14). (Mellor, 1991, p. 90)
>
> All I can remember is being hit and called names and never getting a chance to learn anything. When I told the teachers, they just told me to stand up for myself. (O'Moore & Hillery, 1991, p. 56)

Victims are sometimes described as "reluctant communicators," but in many instances the problem is one of "indifferent listeners." With older children embarrassment about their inability to handle the bullying problem themselves may prevent them from seeking help. An example of this predicament came from a boy age 14 ". . . who called the Bullying Line. James was being shouted at in the street by class mates who ran at him and grabbed his sandwiches, throwing them around and stamping on them. He said he would like to talk to his parents but he would be too embarrassed to tell them about it" (La Fontaine, 1991, p. 11). It reflects badly on the parents when a child who needs help cannot tell them about the problem. The expectation that the child should be able to handle problems independently clearly has been conveyed to the child and effectively cuts off the parents as a source of help.

Sometimes the bullying goes on for so long and all attempts at direct action fail that finally the victims reappraise the situation and decide that they deserve the punishment that they have endured for such a long time (Lazarus & Folkman, 1984). Under these circumstances the victims will not report the bullying and will feel that complaints are unjustified.

Children who are bullied are in a no-win situation. If they identify the bullies the reprisals could be very severe. Often they will be harder to detect by adults because the bullying is continued in a more subtle form. If the victims do not report the bullying, it may intensify as the bullies feel increasingly secure, and the ensuing misery will increase, probably sharply. It is no wonder that bullying has been described as "the silent nightmare" (P. K. Smith, 1991, p. 243).

It is interesting to speculate how adults would feel about bullying if their expectations concerning their children's handling of bullying episodes were applied to themselves. Consider the scenario in which a man on his way to work is regularly accosted by others who snatch his briefcase, destroy its contents, tear at his clothes, and tell him that there will be more of the same on his way home. At that point they demand money in return for letting him go. He knows that if he leaves the office after work they will be waiting for him, so he tries different routes, to no avail. If he can bring himself to report these incidents to the authorities, he is told that he should be able to handle the problem himself, if indeed it is a problem and not merely "boys being boys."

Comment

There is no question that from the first signs of concern in the 1970s about childhood bullying, investigative interest in the United States and elsewhere has focused more on bullies than on their victims. However, several quite diverse approaches to the problem of victimization have markedly expanded our knowledge of this phenomenon or clearly have the potential to do so. The first of these is an impressive body of empirical data on victimization in middle childhood and preadolescence from the Perry Victimization Project under the creative leadership of David Perry, who is without question the leading authority on this problem. His early research in the 1970s and 1980s established a solid base of information about the victims of bullying. Since the mid-1980s he has branched out in investigations that have altered and refined some of the basic premises about victimization and in so doing has strongly influenced the focus of intervention.

Gary Ladd and his associates at the University of Illinois, focusing on victimization in kindergarten children, have noted that these children typically offer the advantage of being a relatively unacquainted group with few established patterns of aggression or victimization (Ladd & Price, 1987). Kochenderfer and Ladd (1995, in press a, b) have extended our knowledge with their findings on such topics as the effects of victimization on school adjustment and how children cope with victimization. A major contribution here has been the insight concerning the content and directions that prevention programs might take in working with children identified as potential victims.

At a step removed from the specific problem of victims of bullying is the body of research on peer rejection by John Coie and Antonius Cillessen of Duke University (see, for example, Coie and Cillessen, 1993, and Cillessen, van Ijzendoorn, & van Lieshout, 1992). The long-term correlates of early peer rejection have significant implications for the kinds of intervention needed for the primary prevention of the victimization caused by bullying.

Taking a completely different tack is the recent research of David Finkelhor at the University of New Hampshire (Finkelhor, 1995;

Finkelhor & Dziuba-Leatherman, 1994). Finkelhor's interest in victimization is not confined to the bullying situation; he is, in fact, deeply concerned about the tendency of investigators to focus on specific types of victimization, such as child abuse, rather than to consider these sequences as falling within the broad spectrum of childhood victimization. He contends that the fragmentary nature of investigative interest to date has been detrimental. It has impeded the development of a general victimology of childhood that would emphasize the vulnerability of children in general to victimization, the areas of overlap in different types of victimization, and the commonality of risk factors and effects. Finkelhor is working toward a victimology of childhood that takes a developmental approach to understanding the vulnerability of children to different victimization experiences and their effects. Such an approach is likely to add to our understanding of victims and the misery they experience at the hands of bullies.

Victimization starts in the preschool years and, in the absence of effective intervention, may continue to blight the life of the individual through adulthood. Although many factors may be involved in a child becoming a victim, there is no one essential cause. Even the short-term effects of victimization can be serious if the victim is unable to take control. The failure to cope makes victims of either gender and any age vulnerable to feelings of shame, unworthiness, and helplessness, all of which make it more difficult than it should be to engage in age-appropriate peer interaction. These damaging effects underline the urgency for early intervention to stop ongoing bullying.

There is continuing controversy about why one child rather than another is targeted for victimization. Often neither the bullies nor those who join in are able to explain the basis for the choice. Typically the reasons given are singularly lacking in causative content, for example, "There wasn't anything wrong with her, we just did it." It is our opinion that childhood victims are ostensibly the victims of bullying, but in reality they are the victims of the value that 20th-century society places on conformity to the group norm. Current texts on bullying often focus on the ways in which the victim is "different" or does not "fit in." Providing remedial intervention to remedy these "faults" is essential for the well-being of the victim, who urgently needs entrée into the peer group, but it should not divert attention and effort from the real problem: changing the behavior of the bully and the groups that allow bullying to continue.

5 School and Parent Interventions for Bullying

THE NORWEGIAN CAMPAIGN Against Bullying (Olweus, 1983) activated widespread concern in other Westernized countries including the United Kingdom (Smith & Sharp, 1994) and Canada (Pepler et al., 1993), as well as Japan (Greenlees, 1993). This concern has led to determined attempts to combat bullying, the focus being the school setting. A description of a plan of action for a whole school campaign against bullying (Olweus, 1993a) and its prerequisite, a school code of conduct, is followed in Chapter 6 by a group of specific intervention procedures that could be incorporated into the plan. The whole school campaign must be operative and functioning smoothly before any of the specific interventions are included.

INTRODUCING A CODE OF CONDUCT

Bullying in the school setting does not exist in isolation: It is always one of many forms of antisocial behavior characteristic of a school out of control. To introduce an anti-bullying campaign into such a setting is doomed to failure. Instead, a general code of conduct must first become an established facet of school life, after which specific problems, such as bullying, can be dealt with within the framework provided by the code of conduct.

Definition

A code of conduct is a whole school disciplinary policy with a clearly spelled out set of rules and regulations that should make it possible for all school personnel (teachers, students, administrators, and service staff) to work together safely and productively. It states clearly, with examples, what is good and bad behavior along with their respective rewards and sanctions. In the latter case, only nonphysical sanctions, such as community service or suspension, should be used.

Development of a Code of Conduct

Ideally, work on the code should begin far enough ahead that its introduction will coincide with the start of the new term or semester, or the new school year. A 3-month preparation time would be realistic in view of the fact that input must be obtained from all interested parties, that is, students, teachers, administrators, service personnel, and parents. All students in the school should first be asked to contribute ideas and suggestions in writing, anonymous or signed (respondent's option). These, along with input from the school staff, would form a pool from which a preliminary code would be developed by a designated staff member. This version would then be distributed to the whole school community and mailed to all parents, with an accompanying request for comments and suggestions. A final code would then be drawn up, subject to approval by the school principal.

Introduction of the Code

First, a copy of the code should be mailed to all parents, their responsibility being to read it, go over it with their children, and return it signed to the school. Next, there should be a whole school assembly in which the principal goes over the code of conduct and introduces the idea that the school will be from now on a *telling school*. It will be every student's responsibility to report students who engage in activities that harm others or damage property, that is, antisocial activities that in most cases in adults would be regarded as criminal behavior: arson, vandalism, bullying, theft, extortion, destruction of another child's belongings and actions, such as throwing stones, that threaten the well-being of another child. The distinction must be clearly stated between these actions and others that are *not* reportable, that are in the tattle-tale category because they do not meet the criteria of harming others or damaging property. These include chewing gum in class, passing notes in class, being in off-limit areas of the school, and so on. The telling accounts should be reported to a designated teacher with complete confidentiality assured. Immediately after the assembly, all homeroom teachers should go over the code with their classes and answer questions. Simplified lists of rules would then be posted in every classroom and on notice boards in the halls. In other words, ignorance of the code would be no excuse. A more detailed account of the telling school can be found in Chapter 6.

Unequivocal Enforcement

To bring about any long-term change in behavior, the system of reward and punishment must be consistently enforced, without exception. Enforced rules can make the difference between law and order for all and the reign of terror that exists in many schools (Besag, 1989; Prothrow-Stith, 1991). If rules vary from one teacher or one setting to another, the students can, with some justification, challenge them: Variations provide an alibi for rule infringements. Consistent enforcement of the code of conduct requires active vigilant supervision and is one of the most effective and economical preventive strategies (Besag). An important supervisory contribution can be made by the nonteaching personnel (custodians, school secretaries, lunch ladies, safety crossing guards, and parent volunteers), many of whom know some of the children well. Here, too, the procedure would be to report punishable incidents to the designated teacher.

A WHOLE SCHOOL APPROACH TO BULLYING

When the school has settled into the code of conduct routine, a whole school approach can be mounted to tackle the problem of bullying. A number of whole school approaches have been reported in the literature, the two best known being those of Olweus (1993a) and Smith and Sharp (1994), who also published a companion volume (Sharp & Smith, 1994). Other relevant reports are by Pepler et al. (1993), Tattum and Herbert (1993), and Thompson and Arora (1991).

Establishing Awareness of the Bullying Problem

An essential prerequisite to a whole school approach is to establish awareness of the bullying problem at the staff level. School personnel, starting with the principal and filtering downward, often are reluctant or unwilling to admit that there are enough bullying incidents to make an issue of the problem. Although they may genuinely be unaware of the amount of bullying (a lack of awareness that casts doubt on their administrative competence), it is far more likely that they are concerned about the school's reputation as well as their own failure in handling the problem. A second deterrent to action is the downgrading of any bullying problem to the status of a minor fuss. Proponents of this view see bullying as part of growing up, a need to fight one's own battles, or as one of a cluster of behaviors within the general catch-all of "boys will be boys." Media accounts of the serious short- and long-term effects of bullying on both bullies and victims, plus the formidable statistics concerning the latter effects, should have some motivating influence on garnering teacher support. Just the practical aspects of dealing with bullying incidents and outraged parents takes up a considerable amount of teacher time. Also time-consuming and costly are parents' lawsuits when faced with the schools' indifference to their children's plight, a tactic that is gaining increasing momentum (Croall, 1993; Greenbaum, 1989). Apart from these parents, cooperation from other parents is limited by indifference, unavailability, and denial that a problem exists. All in all, responsibility for an anti-bullying campaign lies within the school's jurisdiction.

Prevalence

The school community must first be aware of the magnitude of the bullying problem *and* admit that it is a major problem. Start by establishing prevalence, using teacher questionnaires that include teacher nominations of bullies and victims, student questionnaires completed anonymously, and, if feasible, a parent survey, also handled anonymously. Disseminate the names of all bullies and victims privately to the appropriate staff, and the prevalence data on bullying to the entire staff and student body in an assembly period followed by classroom discussion. Ideally, a similar assembly for parents should occur, but realistically all parents would receive a mailed summary of the prevalence findings only.

In the discussions with the students it should be made clear that the goal of this interest in bullying is to make school a safer place: Eliminating or sharply reducing the problem of bullying is one way to achieve this. It also helps to create a school ethos that does not tolerate or condone the oppression of one person by another. Remind the students that this is now a *telling school*: Bullying thrives on secrecy and the code of silence, which protects bullies, was invented by people like bullies for their own protection. Declaring the school to be a telling school legitimizes peer support for victims and peer pressure against bullies. Discuss the short- and long-term effects of bullying in terms of its cost to both the victims and the bullies. Longitudinal research (Eron & Huessmann, 1987) has shown that young bullies are five times as likely as other children to end up in adulthood with a number of serious problems, including a criminal record. As one principal told the children, "Tell and help keep a bully out of jail."

Is the School Bully-Friendly?

The school personnel must look critically at the school in terms of what opportunities exist that stimulate bullying. When bullying incidents are ignored by the school, even following specific complaints from victims and parents, bullies accurately interpret the school's reaction as condoning or giving tacit approval to the bullying. The message received by the victims is that not only are they on their own with no school backup, but also they are worse off for having made the complaint. It is not uncommon for a teacher to tell a victim that it was something the victim did to deserve the bullying. On the playground those who complain about bullying are likely to be told not to tell tales. There are other signs when a school is bully-friendly: Gangs (as opposed to groups of bullies) exist in the school, and no effort is made to break them up; the school ethos is competitive and cut-throat; and classes are sometimes unsupervised, which puts vulnerable children at risk. Inadequacies in the physical plant can be contributing factors, for example, crowded halls when classes change, with unchecked pushing and shoving. Failure to supervise or regularly check lavatories and out-of-the-way places in the school also can provide fertile ground in which bullying will flourish.

The school playground should be one of the most enjoyable areas of the school, but all too often this is not the case (Besag, 1993; Tattum & Herbert, 1993). Three-quarters of the bullying that occurs in school is centered in the playground, with children of 12 and under being the most frequent offenders (Boulton, 1995). Many young children are reluctant to go out to play at recess and in the lunch hour in the bully-friendly atmosphere. Although this unhappy state of affairs is often attributed to insufficient or indifferent supervision, there are other important and remediable reasons. These became apparent in the United Kingdom in the 1980s during a campaign to improve school playgrounds that involved seeking input from children (Smith & Sharp, 1994). The result was an unprecedented outburst of negative comments all the more surprising because up to that time children had never complained about their playgrounds. Among the major complaints were the lack of play materials, the domination by older boys of the available space and their use of threats and force to maintain their foothold, the indifference of supervisors to justifiable complaints, and the lack of quiet places (due to overcrowding) where children could have some privacy.

According to Iona Opie (Opie & Opie, 1959; Opie, 1993), the importance of such places has considerable relevance to the problem of bullying. Opie is probably the world's foremost authority on playground behavior and in a fascinating piece in the *New Yorker* ("Playgrounds," 1988, p. 39) she is referred to as "the Marie Curie of hopscotch and jumprope." She says that

> I really believe that it's a function of the geography of playing. In playgrounds, if there's a place apart, a kind of refuge, where people can get away from bullies, then on the whole there is no bullying. Everyone in a playground knows that the best thing to do about a bully is just to go away.... There's one playground in Leeds, for example, that's a nightmare. It's rather like a bullring—a big pit with high buildings all around. I'd hate to base a theory of good and evil on what one saw children do *there*! So often psychological problems have architectural solutions. Is there a place for people to play in quiet? Is there somewhere else to go?

The response to the stream of complaints was strongly positive and in many instances community support was also impressive (Kelly, 1993). The playgrounds were cleaned up. Play materials, some such as tires and jumpropes being quite inexpensive, were produced and class teachers taught the children traditional team games and jumprope rhymes. Hopscotch and four-square courts were painted on the tarmac. Where space permitted, small gardens were built, sometimes with ponds. The space available for the older boys' games was assigned on different days to different classes, and this was strictly enforced. The supervisors were also given intensive training in how to make the children's free time count. In one of the Sheffield Bullying Project schools, where these and similar changes were introduced, there was an encouraging reduction in playground bullying in a relatively short time (note, though, that this school had an ongoing whole school campaign against bullying). In addition, the children clearly enjoyed their free time (Smith & Sharp, 1994).

Introducing Changes to Reduce Bullying Opportunities

The school personnel should decide what actions to take and must commit themselves to a wholehearted effort to ensure the efficacy of the changes. They must act as a bloc in conveying their determination to accomplish this goal. As Zinsmeister (1990) has pointed out, it is the school's responsibility to keep children safe, to make sure that the school is a welcoming place where they can be comfortable enough to take advantage of the educational, recreational, and social opportunities offered. Those who are bullied are fearful and miserable (Besag, 1989; Elliott, 1991), with dread being the tenor of their days. Bullying affects everyone, not just the victims: The schools in which bullies go unchecked become stressful and unwelcoming, with an atmosphere of tension, fear, and isolation. Children do not have the options available to adults (Finkelhor & Dziuba-Leatherman, 1994): If adults are bullied in the workplace they can file a complaint or leave. Children cannot do this.

Problems for School Personnel in Developing a Whole School Approach

Staff time is a major element. It is clear from the descriptions of the various steps involved that there will be extra demands on teachers' time and energy. Someone in the school, for example, must assume leadership of the project and responsibility for it. However, much of the preparation of evaluation materials, their administration, and analysis could be handled by graduate students if a college or university is in the area. As a thesis or research project, much of the supervision of the college student would be the faculty sponsor's responsibility. It is possible, too, that the children would be more frank and outspoken about the bullying problem with nonschool interviewers' asking the questions. In-service training would likely be needed for the staff and this would have to be arranged. Often the staff are defensive about public reaction to the admission by the school that bullying is a sufficient problem that a campaign is needed.

The biggest problem is likely to be the active maintenance of the bullying campaign over time. Having handled all the preliminaries successfully and initiated the campaign there is a disastrous tendency to feel that the job is done. But unless it is pursued with energy and enthusiasm, the campaign is almost certain to falter. A good example of this effect can be found in the Nationwide Campaign Against Bullying in Norway. Olweus (1991, 1993a) conducted careful assessments involving a variety of measures in his project and reported encouraging results. Over the 2 years of the project, the rate of reported bullying fell for boys and girls by about 50%. In a different group of schools, after a 3-year project using Olweus's program, Roland's (1989a) postintervention assessment showed *no* clear decrease in bullying. What he did find was that not all the schools had made consistent use of the intervention materials. Those who had used the program more actively achieved a modest decrease in bullying. The difference between the findings by Olweus and Roland appeared to be due to differences in investigator support:

Olweus had provided continuing fairly intensive support over the 2-year period to the schools in his study, whereas Roland apparently did little more than provide the materials before leaving the schools on their own for 3 years. Further support for the necessity for continued effort in maintaining an anti-bullying campaign comes from Foster, Arora, and Thompson (1990), who also showed that consistent effort over time resulted in positive gains.

Other Procedures to Be Specified

Selecting Sanctions Against Bullies

The consequences of bullying acts should be spelled out in plain terms. These would likely include replacement of damaged property, monetary damages where appropriate, formal apologies to the victims, community service in the school, and loss of certain privileges. No exceptions should be made for bullying infractions and sanctions should be administered in a detached, objective way (Foster & Thompson, 1991).

Evaluating the Anti-Bullying Campaign

Near the end of the school year, repeat the questionnaire surveys used previously. In addition, randomly select 50 students from the pool of children who are known as neither bullies nor victims, and have someone from outside the school interview them using open-end questions such as, Has the anti-bullying program helped? The interviews should be taped and confidential. The interviewer should start each session with the following identification: "This interview is with a (boy/girl) who is (age) years old and in (x grade)" and emphasize that no one will know who the child is.

Following the analysis of the questionnaire and interview data, a schoolwide assembly should be set up to disseminate the results to the students. The results would then form the basis for modifying the campaign for its use the following year. Note that the focus on bullying, combined with making the school a telling school, is likely to result in a sharp increase in complaints about bullying in the first few months of the program. This does not reflect an increase in bullying, it only means that the kinds of bullying incidents that previously went unreported are now coming to light. We turn now to the procedures that schools should follow in handling bullying incidents and parents' complaints.

Procedure for Handling a Specific Bullying Incident

This procedure is for bullying incidents that are either witnessed by school personnel or are reported as ongoing to them:

1. Be sure that it is bullying. One push or shove, or accidental collision is not bullying. Immediate action when bullying occurs is crucial. It shows those directly involved, both bullies and victims, as well as onlookers, that bullying is regarded as a serious matter.

2. Remove the victim from the scene and have a second teacher (or other school personnel) talk to the victim because talking takes the heat out of the situation. Have the victim fill out an official school report form, writing down exactly what happened and why the victim thinks the bully did it, then signing and dating it. Review it for errors and omissions, keeping in mind that the victim is upset and may exaggerate. If the victim is visibly hurt, for example, has cuts or bruises, or if his or her possessions or clothing have been damaged, take color Polaroids for the record. Emphasize that the victim must not expect instant action or retribution. There is a procedure to follow and this is not a real emergency (unless the victim's injuries require immediate medical attention).

3. Remove the bully at the same time as the victim. Send him or her to a supervised place such as the secretary's office. *Never* challenge the bully in front of peers: Such action may enhance the bully's status and could lead to aggression against the adult. Tell the bully that he or she will be dealt with later, without specifying what action will be taken. As Pearce (1991) has noted, the bully is likely to worry about what may happen and will have a chance to reflect on what has happened.

4. Detain any witnesses, interview them, and have them fill out a report form. Their input is useful because it may be more accurate than the reports of the bully and victim. Ensure confidentiality, and that you just want to know what happened.

5. Talk to the bully the same day, and use a tape recorder throughout. Make it clear that bullying is unacceptable and will not be tolerated. One way to do this is to review the section in the school's Code of Conduct that specifies what will happen if bullying occurs. Have the bully write an account of what happened. Review it and have the bully correct inaccuracies. In an excellent discussion of practical considerations in dealing with a bully, Jones (1991) has offered some quick tests to counteract the excuses that bullies often make that may fool gullible adults; "It was only a joke": It is only a joke if everyone is genuinely amused—keep in mind that victims sometimes laugh out of desperation. "We were just playing": If the child who was hit or knocked down was clearly not playing although in the group or is the same child who was knocked down yesterday, the "game" is a cover for bullying. "It was only an accident," but the victim ended up clearly hurt and/or

with damaged clothes or possessions. In a real accident the child causing it could be expected to help the victim up and give any necessary assistance. Bullies rarely do this. Note that the most common words and phrases in their accounts are "only," "just," and "all I was doing," all of which are intended to lessen the seriousness of the bullying incident.

6. Punish the bully. The bully must make reparation for any damage and distress he or she has caused. These should be nonviolent sanctions and preferably ones that the victim and onlookers can *witness* or *know about*, such as picking up litter on yard duty or cafeteria duty. If personnel is available, isolate the bully in the school so that he or she works alone in a room supervised by an adult, eats lunch alone, and everyone knows about it.

Note that corporal punishment should not be used because it is modeling physical aggression by a more powerful person over a less powerful one: If you bully the bully, it gives credibility to his or her behavior. Punishment should go by the school rules. Noncorporal punishment such as deprivation of privileges and community service is far better. Also, keep in mind that the bully rarely sees the bullying episode as negatively as the victim and onlookers do (Besag, 1989; Greenbaum, 1989), so *any* punishment will be seen as unfair, overly harsh, or completely wrong. Bullies often have genuine difficulty in understanding the viewpoints of others and consequently are unable to empathize with the distress of their victims.

7. Mail the bully's written account of the bullying episode to the parents and ask them to respond in writing.

8. Set up a meeting with at least one of the bully's and victim's parents and the victim and bully, and a senior school official such as the vice-principal or head counselor. The bully sees that the victim will repeat the accusations in public, thus removing his or her best defense, the silent victim. The victim may see a bully with at least some of the bravado gone.

9. The parents of the bully must take responsibility for his or her behavior in the form of financial reparation and/or supervisory control. Issue a stern warning: Point out that assault, theft, and intimidation can be police matters.

10. The victim should not see the outcome as a victory over the bully but instead should feel that he or she has been given school support and need no longer fear the bully (Jones, 1991). The bully and his or her parents should feel that the school has dealt strictly but fairly with the bully. When the punishment has been completed, the bully should be received back with no further recrimination, no grudges.

Procedures for School Personnel Regarding a Parent's Complaints About a Child Being Bullied at School

1. The teacher should tape the complaint discussion, have the tape typed up, and have the parent make any changes and additions relevant to an accurate account, then sign and date it.

2. Make it clear that the school takes such complaints seriously, that it will be investigated, and the parents informed of the findings.

3. In individual sessions following closely on the complaint, talk to the bully, victim, and any witnesses who will talk.

4. If it is clear that the complaint is justified, call in the bully's parents. They may be very unpleasant and totally unwilling to acknowledge that their child is in the wrong. Go over the bully's alleged actions and supporting evidence. State the consequences (reparation for damage caused and community service at the school). Be blunt about what could happen if there is further bullying, for example, police involvement. Point out that the laws of assault, threatening behavior, and extortion, or whatever tactics the bully used, apply to their child as they do to others.

5. Have the victim's parent(s) come to the school. Go over the steps followed and the decision made. If the complaint is justified, describe the punishment. If it is not, explain the reasoning behind this decision. Suggest that the victim come to school with other children because bullying beyond the school grounds is outside the school's jurisdiction. If the attacks continue outside of school, the school will support the parents should they decide to seek police help or legal aid.

Throughout this discussion avoid any suggestion that the victim is to blame for the bullying. No matter what shortcomings the victim has, such as shyness, lack of athletic skill, or physical defects, they do not justify bullying and should not be offered as reasons for the bullying. In addition, express the school's appreciation of the parent taking the time to pursue the problem and inform the school of it. Reiterate that the school's goal is to provide a safe environment in order for students to make maximum progress without fear for their safety.

The school can only do so much: It can halt the immediate bullying and administer sanctions. If the school counselor or psychologist has the requisite time, there are small-group programs that are designed to teach bullies more acceptable ways of interacting with peers than the use of force. Lochman (1993), for example, has developed an 18-session small-group program that can be used to teach bullies to substitute assertiveness for aggression in solving problems. A 3-year follow-up of the program demonstrated long-term benefits. If the school has instituted any of the interventions described in Chapter 6, the bully should benefit. But in the main it is the parents' responsibility to take further action about their child's behavior.

What the Bully's Parents Can Do

1. When the school complains that your child is bullying others the whole idea may come as a complete surprise. Instead of lashing out at the school, listen to what they have to say. Start by getting all possible information about the child's social and academic behavior in school, including a description of the bullying incidents that led to the complaint.

2. Although the bullying that prompted the complaint may be over, the problem will not be solved. The bullying is a *symptom* and what is needed now is to determine the *cause* of it. It is essential to see that assessment of the cause of bullying and subsequent treatment are as important for the bully's welfare as they are for the victim's protection.

3. Professional help is essential. Possible sources for such help include the school counselor or psychologist, professionals in the community, or local social services departments. Parents are rarely equipped to identify the cause of the bullying and develop an intervention plan, but they play a vital part in the change program. If they do not support it wholeheartedly, its chances of success are seriously undermined.

4. Before the first appointment, all possible helpful information should be assembled. Parents could begin by independently writing descriptions of what the bully is like at home and how the school describes the child's behavior and ability. Honesty here is essential, however painful.

5. The professional will want to know if the home is bully-friendly, that is, what conditions in the home encourage bullying tendencies. Do the parents use power-assertive-child-rearing practices such as severe but inconsistent corporal punishment coupled with violent emotional outbursts? Do they condone or even demand aggression against peers when the child is in conflict situations? Does the child have unrestricted access to televised and film presentations regardless of their aggressive content? If so, this combination is likely to increase antisocial aggressive behavior and result in passive acceptance of real-life aggression and indifference to it (Bandura, 1977b; Bandura & Walters, 1959). Is the home a hotbed of conflict, including parental fighting, a constant threat of violence, and an atmosphere of negative instability? The important feature of

all of these social and environmental influences is that they are potentially alterable.

If there is any suggestion of family dysfunction, the professional, who is often a family counselor, is likely to be interested not only in the parents' statements about the home, but also in how the bully and any other children in the family view their parents. Of relevance here is a study by members of the Sheffield Bullying Project (Bowers, Smith, & Binney, 1992). They selected two dimensions, power and cohesion, that have proven to be useful in describing family systems, the goal being to determine how these dimensions related to the bully–victim status of their subjects at school. Four groups of 20 children aged 8 to 11 participated: bullies, victims, bully–victims, and controls. All children completed a version of the Family System Test (FAST) (Gehring & Wyler, 1986), a figure placement technique that can be used to elicit a child's perceptions of intrafamilial cohesion between different family members and power structures within the family. In this test, which children like taking, they are asked to place wooden figures on a checker board so as to show "how close people in the family feel to each other" and to elevate figures on blocks to represent the relative power of members of the family.

Bullies portrayed their families as low cohesive, their fathers as more powerful than their mothers, and their siblings and others as much more powerful than themselves. By contrast, victims generally showed no separation of figures, which suggests overly cohesive families, and although they tended to have more powerful fathers than mothers, they did not see their siblings and others as particularly powerful. Bully–victims had low cohesion scores, but these were not as low as the bullies' scores, and fathers were seen as much more powerful than mothers. This group tended to allot the highest power scores to themselves. Control children generally saw their families as moderately cohesive, their parents as equally powerful, and their siblings and others as low on power.

In discussing initial counseling strategies related to family dynamics, Oliver, Oaks, and Hoover (1994) suggest that the troublesome family dynamics typical of many bullies' families indicate two directions. The first of these, increasing intrafamilial cohesiveness, sometimes occurs in the process of establishing an effective working relationship between the counselor and each member of the family. In such a relationship, the counselor finds out how each member perceives the family and how he or she would like the family to be. The second direction is designed to increase structure within the family by specifying rules and limits and emphasizing the need for consistency. Agreement between the parents concerning the rules is of prime importance: If it cannot be reached amicably, marital counseling may be needed before the family counseling process can profitably be continued.

A Case Study

The following case study (Marks, 1993) is a good example of how far removed the cause may be from the immediate bullying problem and why we recommend professional help for the bully and, indirectly, the parents.

Eric, aged 9, was normally a friendly, likable child in fourth grade who had never exhibited any real problems in peer relations. Consequently, his parents were astonished and distressed when the teacher notified them that Eric was picking on vulnerable children, taunting them, and calling them names, apparently without provocation.

Eric denied the charge. But then a neighbor told his parents that her son, Will, who lisped, had come home from school crying. A group of boys, one of whom was Eric, had teased him mercilessly, called him a girl, and thrown his jacket in a puddle. Eric's parents spoke severely to Eric, then punished him, but he contended that no one liked Will. Nothing worked. Eric was nice to Will when no one else was around but behaved in a beastly way when he was with his new "cool" friends, the big three who were clearly a force in the school and were also very popular. Punishment had no effect.

In desperation they consulted a child psychiatrist. It soon became apparent that Eric was willing to do almost anything to keep his cool friends. Over several sessions Eric's opinion of the big three's behavior and their bullying of other children gradually became more negative. At the same time, the psychiatrist noticed that Eric quickly became embarrassed if he dropped the ball in a simple game of catch. This led the psychiatrist to focus on embarrassing moments that Eric might have experienced. However, even when his parents, in a joint session with him, recounted their own very embarrassing childhood experiences, Eric would not open up.

Finally, in the next session, the last piece of the puzzle about Eric's behavior fell into place. By this time Eric had come to think of the big three as jerks and to acknowledge that he felt bad about their teasing Will, but he did not want to become a target, either. When the psychiatrist asked why anyone would make fun of him Eric's face got red. "Because in nursery school I used to play in the doll corner. Steven (one of the big three) was there! He'll tell and I'll be teased" (Marks, 1993, p. 306).

The psychiatrist convinced Eric that if he broke with the big three and was teased there were ways to handle it, for example, indifference, acting cool. During the following weeks Eric gradually broke away from the big three and became his own person—more assured and no longer relying on mean behavior to maintain his social position.

What Parents Can Do When a Child Complains of Being Bullied

1. If there are any cuts or bruises, attend to them first. If the injury merits it, or if there is damage to clothing or other possessions, take color Polaroid photographs.

2. Without overreacting, convey to the child that you are angry about the bullying, sympathetic about the problem, and will take appropriate action. *Never* blame the victim or suggest that you cannot help. That such behavior is demoralizing is evident in this 11-year-old girl's account of more than a year of being terrorized by other girls:

> "You don't have to play with them," my mother says. . . . "You have to learn to stand up for yourself. . . . Don't be spineless. You have to have more backbone."
>
> I think of sardines and their backbones. . . . The bones crumble between your teeth. . . . This must be what my own backbone is like: hardly there at all. What is happening is my own fault, for not having more backbone.
>
> My mother puts her arms around me. "I wish I knew what to do," she says. . . . Now I know . . . as far as this thing is concerned, she is powerless.
>
> I can't afford the distraction of comfort. If I give in to it, what little backbone I have left will crumble away to nothing.
>
> I pull away from her. (Atwood, 1989, pp. 166–167)

3. Do not promise to keep the bullying a secret. Explain that this protects the bully, who is counting on the child to remain silent.

4. Find out exactly what, when, and where it happened, who was involved, and if there were witnesses. Ask what response your child made, and whether this incident was one of a series.

5. Make an appointment with the school principal or the staff member who handles parents' complaints. Give them a written report of the bullying incident. Make detailed notes of the reaction by school personnel to your complaint. Include names, staff position, and date (Lawson, 1994).

6. Contact the parents of the bully. Some will react in a concerned and cooperative way and will make reparation for damaged possessions, but many will not. In the latter case, point out that what has happened is *assault*, you are reporting the bullying to the school, and it could become a matter for the police.

7. If neither the parents nor school personnel show appropriate concern followed up by action, go higher in the school administration. If this proves unsuccessful, send a copy of the report of all events to date to the police *for their files* and advise them that you are seeing a lawyer. If money is a problem, low-cost legal help is available in most cities.

8. Under Title IX of the Education Amendments of 1992, schools have a legal responsibility to ensure that a nonhostile environment is available to all students. So parents can sue the school under federal law. A Title IX complaint goes to the Office of Civil Rights, where a decision is made as to whether the school is in compliance with Title IX or a hostile environment does exist (Cheevers, 1995).

Filing suits against school boards has met with mixed success in this country and the United Kingdom. The stronger the evidence that bullying has occurred, the greater the chance of a successful suit, but even here there are no guarantees that the suit will be won. However, it is an option to be given serious consideration. The parents of a boy in Minnesota, exasperated after months of futile complaints to the school administration, finally "wired" their son and with that concrete evidence sued the school board and won (Van Buren, 1995).

Assuming that the bullying has stopped, the parents' next concern should be to determine why the child is being bullied. Start by getting all possible information about the child's social behavior (and academic behavior if it seems relevant) from the school. Tap other sources such as friends, church personnel, and leaders of any groups to which the child belongs, without letting the child know of your investigation.

In most cases the parents should seek professional help, not only to get at the cause of the child's victim status, but also to develop an intervention plan, a change program that the parents can follow. Before the first appointment assemble all relevant information about the child. Consider carefully if the household is victim-friendly, that is whether there are conditions in the family/home that might encourage victim tendencies: Do older siblings bully the child? Are others in the family far superior on all fronts so that the victim feels hopelessly second-rate (and possibly deserving of the bullying abuse)? Are the adults overprotective (Lawson, 1994)?

The consensus among professionals with expertise in school counseling (see, for example, Oliver, Oaks, & Hoover, 1994) and researchers (Bowers et al., 1992; Olweus, 1993a) is that the families of victims often are overly involved or enmeshed. Whether the victims' unusually close relations with their parents are the causes or consequences of victimization remains to be determined. Such closeness could have its genesis in early parent–child relations that impeded the shift from dependence to independence in the early preschool years; or it could have evolved later as the victimized child, lonely and isolated from peers found comfort at home. When parental overinvolvement clearly is a problem, the counselor must strive to increase the psychological space not only between the victim and parents but also between members of the family. Sometimes this can be accomplished by involving the victim in outside activities of a somewhat structured kind so that the lack of experience in peer interactions is not immediately obvious to others. It is particularly important to discourage the parents from making routine decisions and speaking for the victim, for example, "Steve would like to join a drama club, wouldn't you, Steve?"

In seeking help, some parents for all practical purposes stay within the jurisdiction of the school. Those who choose this course of action may be in for a long period of frustration with doubtful outcome. Consider the following case. In his first 3 weeks in kindergarten Kevin was beaten up several times by two older boys and left with injuries such as a cut lip and bruised face. His mother worked through the school hierarchy to no effect. His teacher said that other boys picked on Kevin because he was the smallest boy in the class and he could not even throw a ball. The school counselor believed that Kevin invited attacks with his body language, described him as too passive and polite, said that he could only hit back with ineffectual little jabs when pushed, and blamed the mother by saying that "a parent must teach a child to function in his environment. It's a tough, aggressive world out there, and . . . you have made your son weak" ("My son was being bullied at school" 1989, p. 38). The school principal said he could do nothing because no adult had witnessed any of the attacks. The mother's brother-in-law, a clinical psychologist, advocated a do-nothing policy and eventually the problem would go away. Her husband said that she was overprotecting the boy. Meanwhile, Kevin continued to come home bruised and beaten and developed stomach pains and other stress-related problems. When the mother sought help from the chairman of the child development department at a major university medical center, she was told to teach Kevin things that would toughen him up.

Throughout this sequence the family had been trying to avoid overprotecting Kevin, which he unfortunately had interpreted as "not caring for him." When this misconception was cleared up, the family dealt more effectively with the problem by providing an unusual amount of social support, for example, his older siblings went out of their way to help him, and his mother encouraged him to join a drama group in which he performed exceptionally well.

Comment

Kevin's case is the norm rather than the exception as far as the school's willingness to accept some responsibility for halting bullying attacks. Although the proper procedures for lodging complaints and seeking help were followed, ultimately the family was on its own. Until a workable solution was arrived at Kevin endured a long period of torment. Parents should not be willing to submit their children to this kind of treatment in what should be a relatively safe environment. After hearing about numerous cases in which legitimate concerns were brushed aside, we have come to believe that parents should attempt only briefly to deal with the school, if at all, and instead should plan some direct action of their own. One father, whose daughter was bullied mercilessly by two older boys at the same school, handled the problem by meeting the boys as they got off the school bus and having a severe talk about what he would personally do if they continued to bother his daughter. The girl had no further trouble with the boys. Another father pursued the problem of older boys beating up his son by first sending registered letters about the problem to the school and the boys' parents. The school's response was a "boys will be boys" attitude and took no action at all; the boys' parents were totally disinterested. Next, he notified the police and asked them to acknowledge his complaint in writing, but to refrain from acting on it until he requested their help. Armed with his folder of correspondence (and a small tape recorder for recording the conversation), he confronted the boys. In a tone of quiet but menacing intimidation he warned them that if they ever bothered his son again, they would be in juvenile court and that the police department already knew about their behavior. His son had no further trouble.

If this route is chosen, some cautionary comments are in order. Under no circumstances, ever, should any attempt be made to buy off the bully with money, goods, or favors. Apart from the fact that bullying should not be rewarded in any way, such actions often are interpreted by the victim as "going over to the enemy." The bully should never be given any grounds for lodging a countercomplaint against the victim's family. This means that great care must be taken not to touch the bully, while at the same time talking in a very stern fashion about what will happen should the bullying continue. Action taken on behalf of the victim should be played down somewhat when discussing the problem with the victim. The father might say, for example, "I don't want you to be bothered anymore with X so

I am going to speak to him about it." It is enough that the victim knows the family is concerned about the problem and is doing something about it (Lawson, 1994).

The Special Case of Sexual Harassment: Procedures for Schools and Parents

In addition to the previously discussed general instructions on how the school should handle ongoing bullying and what parents can do if their child is bullied, there are specific procedures that school personnel and parents should follow when a child is sexually harassed. It is particularly important that both groups be aware of the special laws that apply to sexual harassment.

What the Schools Should Do

As a first step, a list of unacceptable behaviors should be worked up: The 14 kinds of sexual harassment shown in Figure 3.1 could be used. Next, an information sheet about sexual harassment should be given to all students, citing the procedure for complaints and the consequences for engaging in unacceptable behaviors. In conjunction with this step, in-service training for teachers should be set up focusing on how to handle children's complaints and how to talk to parents about such complaints. Teachers have to accept that handling sexual harassment is their job, as is handling other forms of misbehavior. All students should attend an auditorium period in which the principal spells out the problem and the procedures set up for handling complaints. A similar meeting should be set up for parents. In both, the consequences of infringements should be emphasized. When the first justifiable complaint is lodged, the consequences should be enforced visibly beginning in the aggressor's class with a serious discussion of the decisive action taken. This should be followed up by a brief summary in an announcement made to the school, preferably in an auditorium period. It is absolutely essential that the previously spelled-out consequences be imposed, with *no* exceptions. For some unknown reason, when punishment for specific behaviors is promised, the first transgressors are sometimes students with otherwise impeccable records. The school administration must resist pleas from these students' parents to modify the punishment. It cannot be reiterated too often that the success of the anti-harassment campaign depends on a no-exceptions policy for administering promised consequences.

Obstacles in the Way of Responsible School Action

There are no firm standards for drawing the line between acceptable behavior and behavior that constitutes sexual harassment, especially between adolescents who are beginning to be interested in the opposite sex but are not sure how to express their feelings (Cheevers, 1995). An expert on gender equity, Harper (Colino, 1993), believes that the line is crossed when one child's words and other behaviors intimidate and interfere with another child's feeling of security in the school. If this standard were adhered to, all complaints from students that are accompanied by reasonable supporting evidence would be treated seriously by school personnel. In reality, however, teachers and other school personnel often disagree strongly over what behaviors are unacceptable, and students are quick to read and take advantage of any signs of ambivalence leaning toward implicit approval of their own basically unacceptable behaviors.

Under the provisions of Title IX of the Education Amendments of 1992, schools failing to handle sexual harassment complaints properly are vulnerable to civil rights investigations jeopardizing millions of dollars in federal funds. This big stick should elicit terror and compliance, but a search of the literature reveals that nothing much happens to nonconforming schools beyond a mild reprimand and instructions to establish proper sexual harassment procedures. There is no loss of federal funds and, consequently, no incentive to change.

What Parents Should Do

If a child complains of sexual harassment and after some parent–child discussion the complaint appears to be a valid one, the parent(s) should contact school personnel immediately to lodge a formal complaint. It is essential that a log be kept of all actions taken on the child's behalf, for example, dates, times, names, and summary of discussions with all school officials contacted. A written account of the child's experiences, with as many names as possible, would also be helpful.

Under federal law, districts must have a written policy on harassment that includes information on how to lodge a complaint, but schools often omit important details such as whom to contact with a complaint and how to appeal school district decisions to federal authorities. Find out whether the school does have the information required, and, if they do not, include this omission in the case against the district. Under Title IX, school districts are required to appoint a coordinator to handle such complaints and most districts have complied. However, according to a review of school compliance with antiharassment laws conducted for the California Department of Education, appointees often are personnel directors with other duties and little or no experience with sexual harassment and the laws concerning it (Cheevers, 1995). The Supreme Court has ruled that students who can prove that they have been sexually harassed can sue school officials under Title IX of the Education Amendments of 1992.

If the school is unwilling to take action in a specific case, if at all possible, the parents should obtain the help of a lawyer. In addition they should call the U.S. Office of Education's Office of Civil Rights, the State Department of Education's Department of Human Rights, and write to the NOW Legal Defense and Education Fund, 11 Hudson Street, New York, NY 10013, for advice. These steps take time. Within the realities of their financial circumstances, the parents should give thought to how they can best help the children in the interim. Some have removed their children from the schools and begun home schooling, others have had the children transferred to another school or have moved to another district.

Comment

Many schools do not have a formal code of conduct; and some of those that do have one have, for all practical purposes, shelved it. Yet an operative code of conduct is important for the protection that it provides school personnel, pupils, and parents. Establishing awareness of bullying in a school by assessing prevalence is of critical importance for justifying a whole school campaign against bullying. If the data show that bullying is a frequent occurrence, it is impossible for school personnel to deny that a problem exists. In cases that are all too rare, the data can support those who claim that there is virtually no bullying in their school. The concept of bully-friendly has important implications for the school and home environments, as do the specific procedures for handling bullying incidents. With the exception of bullying that is stimulated by the actions of the provocative victim, it is essential that victims not be explicitly or implicitly blamed for bullying incidents. Although immediate intervention in bullying incidents is the responsibility of school personnel, action directed to changing the behavior of the bully is a task that parents must handle, usually with professional help.

6 Specific Interventions for Bullying

A NUMBER OF specific interventions are available that could be incorporated into the whole school campaign against bullying. These include those that legitimize reporting bullying, such as the student watch program, several that provide victims with social support, some that require direct problem solving by students, and two sets in which the absence of negative consequences is a distinguishing feature. The whole school campaign must be functioning well before any specific interventions are added to the program. The only exception is the Big Brother Program, which, like the whole school campaign, is best introduced at the beginning of the school year. To avoid overload, use discretion in adding one or possibly two of the specific interventions. Note that the telling school intervention already is a part of the whole school campaign. We regard this as particularly important because children who are ardent supporters of the code of silence also may willingly conform to sex molesters' demands for secrecy.

CATCHING ONGOING BULLYING: VIDEO MONITORING

At Lyndon Comprehensive School in Solihull, England, cameras that were installed for theft prevention proved invaluable in the school's campaign against bullying (O'Malley, 1993). The cameras, which record 24 hours a day, were installed as a crime prevention measure after a series of thefts had occurred while the school was open for evening activities. Two cameras were positioned to cover the main entrance to the school, the playground and rear entrance, and the changing room corridor.

It soon became apparent to the camera maintenance staff that problems other than theft, such as bullying, could be detected and, more important, documented for later use. The head of the video maintenance staff said:

> You'd get pushing and shoving, maybe with three or four kids on to one youngster . . . or in the playground you'd spot a lump of kids gathering and you would want to know what was going on. . . . They sometimes stand there waiting outside the back door for someone they want to get. (O'Malley, 1993, p. 15)

The procedure was to have the staff member monitoring the four-way split screen in the video office zoom in at the first signs of trouble to see exactly what was going on and then to notify the teacher on duty.

Having a record of actual instances of bullying has proven to be highly effective. The school has grounds for accusing the student of bullying and can rebut denial or attempts to minimize the bullying interaction as "just a bit of fun" by confronting the bully with a replay of the recording. Further, if parents question the bullying accusation, as they often do, they can be shown the recording. The tape can also be used to force the bully to examine the antisocial behavior by requiring that the tape be watched and the consequences for the victim be considered. The taped record of bullying events can also help in increasing awareness among pupils, teachers, and parents, that bullying *is* a problem in the school. In classroom discussions of the problem, showing a video of an actual bullying incident by a student that others in the school know provides an excellent starting point. It also puts the bully in an unfavorable light and at the same time removes the secrecy element that bullying thrives on. In addition to picking up instances of bullying, some schools are installing video cameras as security measures against violence and other misdemeanors. In a Toronto suburb, where intimidation and extortion at school had reached epidemic proportions, the school board has authorized the installation of closed-circuit TV cameras in isolated sections of the high schools (Fennell, 1993).

The use of video cameras in the school setting raises the question of whether the students are being subjected to unreasonable surveillance. Such concerns are not justifiable in view of the fact that videos and similar devices are commonplace in our society, for example, video surveillance in stores, electronic gates in public libraries, and metal detectors in airports. In schools with good anti-bullying programs already in effect, several kinds of monitoring are usually involved, such as student watch or a telling school, with the video cameras seen as a legitimate feature of the campaign against harassment. Certainly, at Lyndon Comprehensive School the potential for video recordings was immediately apparent to a group of senior students. They produced a video aptly titled, *I Can't Take It Any More*, in which pupils reenacted actual bullying sequences that had occurred in the school and in the video interspersed these sequences with short discussions about what could be done to stop bullying at the school (O'Malley, 1993).

BULLYING REPORTED BY STUDENTS

The Telling School

A telling school is one in which any child who is bullied by another child or adult, or who sees another child being bullied, is urged to report the incident to designated school personnel. Children who report such incidents are promised anonymity. It is the responsibility of *everyone* in a telling school to help to stop bullying. There are no bystanders. There is a designated teacher or other administrator to report to, along with a comprehensive reporting routine that records all the details of bullying incidents. The promise of anonymity to students who report bullying must be ironclad. It is essential to establish what is legitimate telling (for behaviors that injure others or damage property) as distinct from telling tales (for rule breaking that causes no injuries to self or others and no damage to property), for example, chewing gum or reading a book in math class. Traditionally, "telling on" someone is viewed as bad behavior, with the "sneak" being a standard villain in school fiction. To overcome this ingrained belief, the following rationale could be used in presenting the idea to students.

Children have rights, one of which is the right to feel safe in school in an atmosphere conducive to learning. Bullying is a violation of children's rights: Children who are bullied or who witness bullying incidents generally do not feel safe. Consequently, they neither benefit from school as they should nor enjoy it. One head teacher of a telling school in England tells her pupils that the code of silence was invented by bullies for *their* protection (Besag, 1989) because it renders their victims defenseless. As long as other children (victims, bystanders, and those who hear about the bullying) continue to protect bullies by remaining silent, bullying will flourish.

Adults who assault others, steal from them, or extort payment for protection are not protected. Instead, their victims report them to the police who make determined efforts to apprehend them and have them prosecuted. When bullying occurs in the workplace adults have some recourse: They can file a complaint with the company and action should then follow against the wrongdoer. In a telling school, children have the same rights and they must report a child or teacher who bullies them.

Although unreported bullies appear to go unpunished, the long-term outlook for bullies in elementary school who keep on being bullies is extraordinarily bleak (Eron & Huessmann, 1987; Olweus, 1993a). It is a well-documented finding that those who are bullies at age 8 will end up in all kinds of trouble in adulthood. So anyone who reports young bullies is helping to deter behavior that ultimately will cause many problems for the child.

In setting up a telling school, considerable effort must be expended to avoid or overcome various pitfalls. Most serious is the possibility of retaliation. The guarantee of anonymity can be difficult to maintain if the one telling clearly is associated with the bullying incident. In this case, sanctions must be extremely powerful to deter retaliation when adults are absent. In other cases, for example when the one telling is an observer who is merely passing by, preserving anonymity should not be a problem. Clumsy or ineffective handling of any bullying incident by the school personnel will make it abundantly clear to the children that the whole idea of "telling on" is a completely foolhardy one that should be abandoned at all cost, thus sabotaging any attempt to make the school a telling school.

Several factors act as deterrents to bystanders reporting instances of bullying, one of these being dislike of the victim. Research by Perry and his associates (Perry et al., 1988, 1990) has shown that as a group victims are disliked and consequently, children have less concern for a victim experiencing a painful assault than they do for other classmates in general. With these negative feelings, the bystander might disregard instructions to report the incident. Apathy or unwillingness to get involved must also be overcome. In the Boulton and Underwood (1992) study, 20% of the respondents said that they would not help a victim of bullying because it was none of their business. It would be interesting to know what effect, if any, discussions of the rationale for making the school a telling school would have on this belief. Boulton and Underwood also reported that one third of the respondents said that they could see why bullying happens, a reaction that seems to imply acceptance and condoning. In fact some children (Elliott, 1991, p. 35) see bullying as endemic, like the common cold, an inevitable part of growing up. Such beliefs, if left unchallenged, are highly unlikely to lead to any decrease in the incidence of bullying.

Student Watch Programs

Students who are not involved in bullying (neither bullies nor victims) can help with the problem by participating in Student

Watch Programs. The goal of these programs is to improve the school by making it a safer and more pleasant place for students in general. To accomplish this goal, trained student volunteers patrol the school buildings and grounds and report instances of bullying and other antisocial activities, such as drug dealing and vandalism, to designated staff members. *Except in emergencies they take no action themselves.*

An example of the effective use of the Student Watch Program concept comes from Lakeland Senior High School in suburban Shrub Oak, New York. The program was set up by assistant principal Robert Maher (1987) when he became aware that problems such as vandalism, bullying, low morale, and apathy were prevalent at the school. In addition to regularly patrolling the buildings and grounds, the volunteers must also enroll in a yearlong student leadership class in which commitment to self, school, and community are emphasized through leadership activities and participation in selected volunteer activities. The course is a difficult one, with no guarantee of a passing grade.

The main task for these students is an observational one: They note instances of antisocial activity and report them to a designated staff member. They are expected to avoid physical confrontation except under dire emergencies, to be reasonable in their expectations for others' behavior, and to behave like concerned fellow students rather than policemen. Particularly noteworthy is the fact that input from the participating students is *not* used as proof of antisocial behaviors. Instead, it functions as a means for the staff to secure proof of guilt by making their own observations of those identified by the Student Watch volunteers. The information provided by the volunteers remains confidential: Only the administration and volunteers know why particular students or groups of students are under observation by staff members.

Although the potential for retribution or reprisals against the Student Watch members logically would appear quite high, Maher (1987) reports that this has not been the case. Participation in the program is presented as a high-status activity open to a broad section of the student body: Among the participants are football players, tough kids, straight-A students, jocks, and students who are not turned on by school. Although the participants often are called derogatory names, for example, Rat Pack, squealers, and spies, the sheer range of status makes the barbs lose their punch. The breadth of target greatly diminishes the impact of name calling, which would not be the case if the target group were homogeneous, for example, all straight-A students.

Student Watch members who report an incident are guaranteed anonymity even when the actions reported are criminal ones. Only staff members would testify in court because the student information is used solely as a guide. No action is taken until the staff witnesses the wrongdoing. According to Maher (1987), those who are caught are more angry about being caught than about how they were caught, a reaction that further removes the volunteers from the outcome.

At Lakewood, Maher reports that antisocial behavior has decreased, with a concomitant improvement in the quality of the school environment. The program draws on the fact that students in a school typically are more knowledgeable about what is going on than are most staff members. The presence of a Student Watch group helps to break the code of silence that protects the antisocial, by presenting "telling on" in a positive light. Unlike special-activity school groups, the program is open to any student willing to make a commitment to improving the school environment. Maher states that

> In addition, I believe many of the students who become involved in this program will achieve great success throughout their private and professional lives, at least in part because of their involvement in this program. They have learned to care, to step forward and do something to make their school a better place to be. That is a lesson worth teaching all students, and the Student Watch program helps set them on the correct path. (1987, p. 27)

EMOTIONAL SUPPORT

Big Brother Programs

One source of stress for children entering kindergarten is fear of what might happen to them in their new school (Besag, 1989; Maccoby, 1980), a fear that is magnified if they have no friends entering at the same time. This fear is a rational one: The children are making the transition from being the oldest in a small preschool group to the youngest in a large school. Their classmates will be more critical, demands will be greater, and restraints will increase. To ease the transition, some schools, particularly Roman Catholic schools for boys, pair all those entering kindergarten, as well as first-grade boys who are new to the school, with a Big Brother, a student from an upper grade. The Big Brother meets the boy assigned to him on registration day, makes him feel welcome, and explains that they will see a lot of each other. At least once a day he checks with the new boy to see how he is getting along (but without ever suggesting that school is a problem-laden experience). He also shows the boy the room where the boy can contact him. Often the pair will team up with other Big Brothers and their charges to set up a game or other group activity at recess or during the noon hour. Occasionally the Big Brother will eat lunch with the child or drop by his table for a short visit.

The Big Brother program has many advantages, not only for the child but also for others concerned with the child's welfare. It is good experience for the Big Brother, particularly if he has no younger siblings, to be partially responsible for another child. He is a good source of information for the kindergarten teacher because he is in a position to spot potential problems and act on solutions. His presence is a deterrent to bullying and teasing. He may also be a help to the child's mother: Usually he contacts her by phone when he is first assigned the child and may occasionally call her thereafter. In coeducational schools the program is expanded to include Big Sisters, with similar functions and objectives.

Sometimes, older children will "adopt" a younger child spontaneously. The teacher of a bright fourth grade (S. Wood, personal communication, April, 1994) told the author that early in the school year some children in her class became angry when they saw a second-grade child (Rebecca) with facial disfigurement and cerebral palsy being cruelly teased about her affliction by her classmates. They called a meeting of the whole class and the decision was made to see that no one teased Rebecca again. Different children, either singly or in pairs, were with her or nearby at all free play times: before and after school, during recess, and at lunch hour. They set about teaching her games, being careful to select only those games that Rebecca could manage fairly successfully. Soon other children in her class, motivated by a desire to play with the "big kids," wanted to join in. The class' commitment to this project was taken very seriously: One day there was a much anticipated field trip for some of the class; when the teacher was checking to see that all of those chosen were going to go, one boy declined because he "was on Rebecca duty."

Telephone Hotlines: Childline

Childline is the toll-free national helpline set up in England in 1986 for children who need any kind of help. Trained professional counselors are available 24 hours a day, every day, to listen to the child's problem and help in any way possible. A child who calls Childline need not provide any identification and is assured of complete confidentiality. Childline has received a large number of calls about bullying and teasing: Anonymity clearly appeals to children who are deeply troubled about being bullied but for some reason are deterred from complaining to parents or teachers.

An unexpected major benefit from these services has been information of great value to researchers and others who are concerned about understanding bullying. Unlike questionnaire surveys and other standard procedures for eliciting information, the hotline generates information that is direct, spontaneous, and unsolicited. Furthermore, it is uncontaminated by adult preconceptions of the bullying problem, so the data obtained are that elusive phenomenon, the child's view of bullying (La Fontaine, 1991). More recently, Olweus (1993a) has suggested having a contact telephone but has not reported whether any Norwegian schools have implemented such a service.

The following account (Townsend-Wise & Harrison, 1991) is an example of how a Childline counselor helped an adolescent girl who was being stressed beyond the limit of her endurance to take effective action against a group of bullies. Sandra, a shy, not very sociable 14-year-old, had been an accepted member of a group of girls as long as her best friend, Jess, was in the group. When Jess moved away, the group first ignored Sandra and then began to bully her, sometimes subtly by undermining her performance in class, and at other times with crude attacks. These attacks were often of a sexual nature whose purpose was to humiliate and embarrass. On one occasion they glued a sanitary towel to her school blazer; on another they soaked tampons in ketchup and put them in her desk. Sandra tried ignoring the girls and avoiding them by hiding to no effect. As the bullying escalated, she felt more and more isolated and depressed, to the point where she considered suicide. Burdened by the code of silence, compounded by a bad home situation and the conviction that no one would help her, she never considered telling her parents or teachers to be an option. Finally, one day the bullies destroyed her school books, ruined her school uniform with make-up, and brutally assaulted her. For several days she played truant, then, in desperation, she called Childline. The following excerpts are from her account of her experience with Childline:

> I was surprised that I told him (the counselor) all those things. A lot of it was embarrassing. . . . He made it easy for me to tell him . . . he encouraged me to talk about it and sounded like he believed me. I was half expecting him to tell me to pull myself together, or to fight back . . . but he didn't say anything like that. . . . I found that at the end of the call (that had lasted nearly an hour) I had a lot to think about. . . .
>
> I phoned Childline back a few days later . . . I got to talk to the same counselor. . . . I found it was even easier telling him about things this time, because I was beginning to feel like I could trust him . . . and I knew he wouldn't start preaching . . . he helped me sort things out.

As a result of the counselor's help Sandra got up the courage to go to a teacher and tell her the whole sordid tale. The principal investigated the problem and the bullies were first put on litter duty during break times so that they could not bother Sandra; they were then suspended for 2 weeks. Things improved markedly at school.

SUPPORT GROUPS

Support groups for children and adolescents have existed in the United States since World War II (Katz, 1993). They are usually formed by parents and/or professionals for children with specific problems whose needs are not being met by existing organizations. The adults involved believe that the children could achieve some gains by meeting regularly with other children who have the same problem. Most problems involve discomfort: Often it is psychological, such as dealing with divorce, a recent death in the family, social stigma, or social isolation; but sometimes it is physical, such as disablement through illness or accident.

These groups have proliferated in the last two decades, with good reason. They satisfy a wide range of needs, such as the need for gaining peer acceptance, belonging to same-age group and having positive status in it, and being like others (Maccoby, 1980). Before joining a support group many children feel unique because of their problem and alone in their misery: Interacting with those with similar problems markedly lessens these feelings of isolation. Being with others who understand what it is like to have the particular problem is a great comfort to a child. These groups also fill the gap once occupied by the extended family units of grandparents, uncles, cousins, and so on, as well as very close neighbors. As our society has become increasingly mobile, urbanized family units that once could have provided the child with social support have become smaller and more isolated. Consider, for example, the number of single-parent families in which that parent is employed full-time, with no relatives in the area and little or no contact with neighbors. The support group fills the void, sometimes to a considerable extent: One 9-year-old girl with terminal leukemia lovingly described her support group as "my very own little family."

Characteristics of a Support Group

The group consists of a leader and a maximum of 12 adolescents, 10 children at the middle elementary school level, or 6 at the primary school level. The leader must be a person who is experienced in small-group work and has a genuine interest in the problem as well as a sound knowledge of and healthy respect for its complexities.

The number of regular group meetings varies, depending on the type of problem. The interval between meetings also is determined by the type and urgency of the problem, with shorter intervals for acute problems, longer ones for chronic cases. Help needs to be available over a specified time at the end of which some form of evaluation is conducted, with a subsequent follow-up check. Attendance is voluntary.

SUPPORT GROUPS FOR VICTIMS OF BULLYING

Forming the Group

Sometimes there are so many parents asking for help and children who want help for bullying problems that forming a group in the school presents no difficulty. But if active soliciting is required in order to fill up the group, be alert to some of the obstacles. A significant number of victims, especially boys, are reluctant to admit to any adult that they are being bullied. Assuming that this hurdle can be bypassed, the children's teachers must be notified and their parents' permission obtained, all subject to the children's approval. In discussing the advantages of participation with reluctant victims of bullying, it is essential to stress that, although the children have a serious problem, it can be changed and the purpose of the group is to effect such a change.

Should the group be a mixed or same-gender group? The latter is preferable for two reasons. Many boys would be embarrassed about describing their failure to cope with bullying episodes and their feelings of despair, even to a sympathetic mixed group. Furthermore, boys generally engage in direct bullying and tend to be more physically aggressive, for example, kicking, punching, and tearing the books and clothes of the victim. In contrast, girls' bullying is more indirect and subtle, although equally cruel: It takes the form of whisper campaigns, social exclusion, and rumor spreading (Olweus, 1993a), with less emphasis on physical attacks. Because the purpose of the group is to have the victims become proficient in coping with the type of bullying that they are experiencing, same-gender groups would be more conducive to achieving this goal.

During the initial discussion with potential members of the group, a measure of self-esteem should be obtained before the first session (to be repeated at the end of the course and used as an indication of the participants' progress). There are a number of instruments available for the assessment of self-esteem in children. We recommend that the inventory in use in the school district be selected in order to provide a base for comparisons with previous and subsequent measures of self-esteem.

Meetings

The group should meet on a regular schedule, weekly meetings probably being the most feasible. A minimum of 12 sessions would be acceptable, but 20 would be far better. Each session would likely be 60 to 75 minutes, but duration depends on many factors such as staff availability and group members' after-school commitments. As is the case with support groups in general, attendance is voluntary (Arora, 1991; Katz, 1993).

Content of the Sessions

From the beginning, a major function of the group sessions is to provide reassurance that the victims are not alone and that help is available. This reassurance is implicit from the first session, when often each victim briefly describes specific attacks. Frequently the children are surprised to find themselves disclosing events, feelings, and other information that they normally would not reveal to anyone. This willingness to speak about the formerly unspeakable will occur with a good group leader, one who is matter-of-fact, encouraging, and rewarding. Such candor is further enhanced by the assurance of confidentiality that what is discussed in the meeting will never be repeated outside of it, as well as by the feeling of empathy and sharing of the problem that the discussion evokes. Sometimes a child will begin to cry when first describing being bullied. With the help of the group leader, the other children let the child know that they understand how awful the bullying problem is because they share the same feeling.

In addition to providing emotional support for the victims, the purpose of the group is to begin to change their behaviors in order to decrease the probability of their being bullied. The amount of change that can be expected depends on human resources and the number of sessions that can be scheduled. Ideally, the victims should acquire *protective strategies*, such as how not to look like a victim and become more competent socially (Lowenstein, 1978). They should learn how to use *non-victim body language*: to stand up straight, look the bully in the eye, and walk confidently, with no defensive cowering (Goffman, 1963). By teaching the victims how to react to bullies, the bullies are deprived of the easy rewards that they generally experience in bullying encounters (Arora, 1991). Group members should become verbally more assertive and improve their ability to stand up against verbal bullying. They should also begin to acquire the requisite social skills that are important for acceptance by the peer group: Apart from the general benefits from such acceptance, membership in the peer group provides some protection against bullying.

Methods

Some support group leaders mainly use discussion procedures. It is our opinion, however, that a variety of teaching procedures best serves the needs of the group. Role play, symbolic modeling using videos and fictional accounts of bullying, all combined with discussion and debate, make for very productive sessions. Using the victims' actual bullying interactions as problem situations in which the victims describe what happened and what they did allows for comparisons with how the victim would behave now. The following is a brief outline of how some of these teaching procedures might be used in the first session.

Because the first task in the support group course is for the victims to learn how to behave so that they do not present an inviting demeanor to bullies, start with nonvictim body language. A teaching procedure that should be used here is role play: The group leader first demonstrates the demeanors and behaviors that are likely to signal to a bully that the child is an easy victim, then the leader takes the role of a victim being confronted by a bully, played by one of the group members. Having a group member play this role, to see the bullying episode from the bully's viewpoint, is beneficial. A second procedure involves reading stories, preferably illustrated, that demonstrate right and wrong behavior in bullying situations. This is symbolic modeling (Bandura, 1969), which increases the potential for improving the victims' attitudes and behaviors. Sometimes a story results in a cognitive restructuring by changing the victims' understanding and perception of the bullying problem. Such a change may influence the victims' subsequent behavior. In the third procedure, the leader asks for a volunteer to be interviewed about an actual bullying or teasing incident that the child has experienced. Then the child and the group leader enact the incident and the "audience" discuss how it could have been handled more effectively by the victim.

After several sessions, the introduction of a role model is strongly recommended. The model should be a same-gender, same-age peer who, as a result of some intervention, has progressed to a more advanced stage of coping with bullying. This is a *coping* model (Meichenbaum, 1971), defined as someone who is managing bullying better, can talk about being a victim, but is still not really skilled. Benefits should accrue for the victims from the coping model's presence: They will likely acquire new coping techniques and improved attitudes toward the problem of victimization. Choosing a less than perfect model, that is, a coping model, increases the model's influence because the victims can see a similarity between the model and themselves: It becomes quite realistic to think that if the model can do it, then the victim can, too.

Evaluation

In addition to administering the self-esteem measure used in the pre-course interview, ask all participants what they learned, and what changes, additions, and omissions they would recommend. Did they enjoy the course? Would they recommend it to others with the same problem? Teachers and parents also should be questioned about possible changes they have noted in the victims' behavior. Have the frequency and intensity of the bullying diminished? If the support group effort is part of a whole school campaign to halt bullying, it is possible that the victims would no longer be bothered by bullies. Without such a campaign, the potential of the support group would be lowered, while still having some positive effects. The participants may make some real friends within the group and, perhaps for the first time, be a valued member of a group. The group facilitates the release of emotions and feelings in a constructive atmosphere of action, a cathartic effect that reduces the tensions associated with the bullying problem.

Follow-up checks should be made 1 month later and again 3 months later to find out from the victims, their teachers, and parents how the situation stands.

USING STORIES AND DRAMA TO INCREASE AWARENESS OF BULLYING

One of the most popular activities that can be used in the classroom to combat bullying and teasing is the use of stories and drama. Teachers have access to many books that can be used to enhance awareness of the cruelty inherent in forms of bullying, such as social exclusion, extortion, and sexual harassment, and that encourage open discussion of these topics as well as of reports of bullying that the children have actually experienced.

Consider racism. A teacher who is genuinely interested in combating racism could begin by having a class discussion of fictional and nonfictional accounts of children of the same race as the majority of the class who are rejected or actively tormented because they are different in some nonracial way, such as clothing, or academic and athletic skills, then move on to cases where the difference is racial.

In England, a book called *The Heartstone Odyssey* has been widely and successfully used as a way of combating racial bullying. Intended for children 6 years and up, it enables them to be confronted with the nastiness of racism, such as how frighteningly impersonal it is. Being attacked for what you are, rather than who you are, is dehumanizing, and the story conveys this message clearly and honestly. At the same time, it sounds a positive note by emphasizing that such behaviors can be challenged and changed (see Horton, 1991, for a detailed description).

There is a sparse, but encouraging, number of diverse programs aimed at counteracting racist beliefs and behaviors (Troyna & Hatcher, 1992). Representative of these is an American course developed by two junior high school teachers in Brookline, Maine, called *Facing History* (Strom & Parsons, 1982), that explores the question of why people embrace racism and its often violent consequences (as in Nazi Germany). It also focuses on the individual's responsibility when confronted with racial injustice. The course is frequently used in schools that have a history of racial conflict, and it has proven to be highly successful.

Drama and role play can be used to help children gain an understanding of their own behavior and increase their capacity for empathy. Children feel safe in the role-play situation because it is one step removed from the real thing. In addition, they can go further than they would in real-life interactions. Drama can be particularly useful in helping children to deal with bullying and teasing.

There have been a number of excellent television programs on bullying. Two outstanding ones were produced by the BBC Educational Program in England and by PBS in the United States. The first of these, "The Soldier" (Holmes, 1993), was the prize-winning play in a Young Playwrights Competition, written by an English schoolgirl, Sarah Holmes. It depicts the cruel bullying of adolescents with impressive skill. The other, a PBS documentary, "Not in Our Town," was a heartening account of the supportive actions taken by the residents of Billings, Montana, after some white supremacists had attacked African American, Native American, and Jewish families. The Billings citizens not only supported the victims of the racist attacks, but also helped bring the bigots to justice. Television programs such as these often are available for educational purposes, especially from PBS. The script for "The Soldier" is available free from the BBC (see Holmes, 1993).

COMMENT: THE ISSUE OF PEER COUNSELING

Peer counselors usually are secondary school students who are carefully selected from the student body, given training in communication and listening skills, and opportunities to practice these skills under the supervision of an experienced professional counselor. The assumptions are that children will find peer counselors more approachable than they would adults and that, with training, peer counselors can be trusted with confidential information, will make good decisions, and will offer appropriate advice. The quality of the training and supervision varies in different programs. Carr (1988), for example, reported a 10-day training program that included 30 hours of basic communication skills, 30 hours of training in special issues, and 45 hours of supervised, in-school work experience.

Generally, the reports on peer counseling have been favorable (see, for example, Carr, 1988; Sharp, Sellars, & Cowie, 1994; Thompson, 1986). However, others have raised serious criticisms. De Rosenroll (1986) contends that peer counseling services may diminish access to professional support services and questions whether the outcome is in fact a broader base of support for those needing help rather than an inexpensive way of using students in adult roles. Brown (1994), a former teacher, believes that the responsibilities assumed by peer counselors are dangerous for all concerned. Referring to an account in the *Times Educational Supplement* (Neustatter, 1994) of a peer counselor working with bullies, would-be suicides, and other problems, Brown says:

> Surely this is a professional job, with the need for years of maturity and training? As with any such process—or, indeed, no process—there will be cases where the counseling seems to work, and the bully stops. But the problem might have resolved itself anyway.
>
> Without control the bully would, in any case, go on operating while awaiting the cure. Who would be responsible if real damage were done to another pupil at this stage? How would the adolescent counselor deal with her feelings if a victim of one of her caseload committed suicide? How would she handle a case of a would-be suicide who decided to go ahead anyway after counseling?
>
> Where would the responsibility lie, personally and in law, for such an event, especially if it were suggested that a line of counseling had been wrongly chosen for the case or a proper treatment not given for a real disorder?
>
> Pupils need protecting from too much responsibility. The responsibility belongs with the head or staff. If they need help, or feel unable to cope with a pupil's problem, they need to seek out the relevant expertise, not push the matter on to a pupil. (1994, p. 2)

We are in complete agreement with Brown. Peer counselors are given responsibilities far beyond their capabilities and should not be permitted to assume the functions of adult professionals.

PROBLEM-SOLVING APPROACHES

Conflict

Conflict is an inevitable part of school life. Although it can follow a constructive or a destructive course, much of the conflict occurring in the generally competitive school environment is of a destructive nature. Children tend to view conflict narrowly as a win-lose situation, with verbal and/or physical aggression being the appropriate responses (Deutsch, 1993). This viewpoint is formed largely through family interactions and television. In most children's conflicts, however, there are other alternatives: The antagonists could both win or both lose. Conflict resolution programs help children to see conflict situations as potentially win-win, thus making them more amenable to constructive, cooperative, problem-solving approaches with disagreements seen as joint problems to be solved in a mutually beneficial way.

Conflict Resolution Training

Conflict resolution programs are in progress all over the United States (Bowman, in Dullea, 1987), Canada (Zarzour, 1994), the United Kingdom (Haigh, 1994), and other countries, their goal being to teach children how to manage conflict situations constructively. Although the content varies with the age and background of the students, most programs strive to instill the attitudes, knowledge, and skills conducive to effective, cooperative problem-solving and to discourage response patterns associated with win-lose struggles (Deutsch, 1993).

There is no room for passivity in conflict resolution. The children are taught that conflict should be faced, not avoided, and that there are alternatives to aggression. Emphasis is on being a good listener because being able to see the other person's point of view is a vital component in conflict resolution. Practice is provided in keeping emotions separate from issues.

Although there is virtually no empirical evidence of the minimum age at which children can benefit from learning how to resolve conflict constructively, Prothrow-Stith (1991) has reported that conflict resolution training can benefit children in the primary grades. In general, participants show improved self-esteem, possibly because the skills learned enhance leadership performance and increase the probability of having harmonious interpersonal relationships (one result of the emphasis on seeing others' viewpoints). Becoming proficient at resolving their own conflicts in the primary grades gives children a strong base to build on in the elementary grades. At the latter level they may wish to enroll in the Conflict Management course and possibly be chosen to act as mediators in other children's disagreements. S. J. Smith (1992) believes that all elementary school children could benefit from conflict resolution training but cautions that they may not be ready for the conflict management role. In her school 75% of the children enjoyed being conflict managers and thought that they had benefited from the experience, but 15% considered it to be "scary."

How Are Students Selected for Conflict Manager Positions?

Some conflict management teachers decide on the basis of their own assessment along with peer nominations, the rationale being that 20 opinions are better than one. In these instances, however, the teacher makes the final decision. Iwasaki (1992) has reported that teachers working with upper elementary school children chose students of average ability on the grounds that these children seldom qualify for any rewards and so need some kind of special activity in order to maintain interest in school. When conflict managers are elected by their fellow students, Prothrow-Stith (1991) found that, according to some teachers, it is the popular children and the bullies who are chosen. The former are presumably popular at least in part because they have good interpersonal skills, but the latter are unquestionably a dubious choice. In the teachers' opinion, however, the choice of bullies is a good one because bullies like power and acting as conflict managers gives them power legitimately. This reasoning fails to distinguish between leadership and domination. Most children in a school know who the bullies are and would be intimidated if a bully was mediating a dispute. Intimidation negates the whole idea of conflict resolution as a constructive, cooperative, mutually beneficial problem-solving experience.

Conflict Management

Conflict management can best be described as a refereed communication process, with the child trained in management being the referee. The referees are not concerned with deciding which of the disputants is right or wrong, nor do they reprimand, pass judgments, make demands, or force their services on others. They are peacemakers rather than policemen, with none of the authority usually accorded to teachers and other school personnel. Their goal is to provide an opportunity for direct communication between the disputants, making them responsible for finding their own solutions to their disagreements through negotiation and mediation.

Candidates for the conflict management role are given anywhere from 15 to 30 hours of training. Course content includes learning how to use conflict resolution skills to help settle disputes between other children; practice in active listening to disputants' complaints; constructive communication; learning the steps of the mediation process, managing the situation and controlling the disputants in an unaggressive way, and helping them to work out peaceful solutions. Although some of the training consists of lecture-type sessions, usually a substantial part of the course provides the students with well-planned opportunities to practice the conflict resolution skills in a supportive atmosphere (Haigh, 1994). Role play demonstrations of conflict situations by "trained actors" are produced so that the students have an opportunity to demonstrate their level of skill in conflict management. During the sessions the students are observed and given critiques in the classroom. When they are judged to be competent, they are sent out on trial and then required to report back in detail to the teacher. Follow-up training is then given as needed.

Once trained, the conflict managers work in teams of two. Usually they wear brightly colored T shirts, crests, and special hats so that they are easily identifiable. They patrol the hallways, playground, and sometimes the school buses, looking for ongoing conflict that is not serious (tough problems are under the aegis of school personnel). When a conflict management team sees ongoing conflict, they first ask whether the disputants would like help. If they accept, the conflict managers offer them the alternative of solving the problem themselves, with the conflict managers acting as mediators or going to a designated teacher for help. Conflict resolution has a set of rules that disputants must agree to abide by while the conflict is being resolved. These include no interrupting while a disputant is telling the conflict manager what happened; promising to tell the whole truth, no name-calling or insults, working to solve the problem, and avoiding any physical aggression.

The Conflict Resolution Procedure

1. The problem or disagreement is identified and both sides describe what has happened and what each wants. The conflict manager restates it and both sides agree that the restatement is accurate.

2. Both sides explain how they feel about the issue and suggest solutions that they would like. There is an element of brainstorming here with no limit on the number of solutions offered. Sometimes the solution is very practical, particularly in bullying cases ("Just stay away from me.").

3. One conflict manager writes down all the suggested solutions no matter how unrealistic and then the pair of managers help both sides to reconsider each idea and choose the one that is closest to best for both, as a mutually beneficial choice is not always possible. Note that the managers do not tell either side what to do.

4. The conflict managers help the sides to work out a balanced settlement that each agrees on and accepts as fair. If appropriate, both sides agree when, where, and how the solution will be carried out. Sometimes this agreement is written up in the form of a contract and signed by both. The whole incident is entered in the school record book and is treated as confidential.

5. The conflict managers then are responsible for following up the incident to see that both sides abide by the decision.

Evaluation of Conflict Resolution Programs

What Teachers and School Personnel Say

Many schools across North America are reporting benefits that they attribute to ongoing conflict resolution programs. Conflict and aggression in the schools have decreased, with a concomitant reduction in the frequency of punishment, suspensions, and expulsions. Conflict resolution brings children closer together: Teachers see more caring behavior among students, and tensions in free-play situations are eased as a result of providing a way for children to help each other (Iwasaki, 1992). Conflict managers (like most children) usually know what is going on in the school, so sometimes they are able to intervene early in the genesis of a conflict and convince the antagonists to submit their dispute to mediation by a conflict management pair, the result often being a peaceful solution (Prothrow-Stith, 1991). Conflict resolution is best carried out as speedily as possible: Teachers have been impressed by the speed with which conflict managers can work through the mediation process. One teacher commented that children have the ability to compress things down to the essentials in a way that adults do not.

What Other Professionals and Investigators Say

Researchers have shown that children who learn to assert themselves without attacking others either verbally or physically, are not only less likely to become bullies, they are also less likely to become the victims of bullies (Prothrow-Stith, 1991). The potential for long-term benefits is considerable: "To encounter it (conflict) naturally, to work out a solution amicably, and to learn to see the situation from the perspective of another, could be one of the most valuable experiences we can offer our young people" (Besag, 1989, p. 106).

The Quality Circle

The concept of the Quality Circle (QC) originated in Japanese industry in the 1950s and now is used worldwide by major companies (Juran, 1967). The QC consists of small groups of interested individuals in work settings who identify problems that they believe reduce work productivity either directly or indirectly through lowering morale. With the help of a trained QC leader they develop practical solutions to the problems and present them to management for their consideration. The QC leader's task is to work with the participants to foster group cohesion as well as acquainting them with the requisite skills and strategies for problem solving, generating ideas with brainstorming, interviewing, and other data collection procedures, and communication among the QC members and the upper levels of management (Cowie & Sharp, 1992).

Although the QC procedure originated in industry, it is clearly applicable to other work environments. It has proven successful with staff development in educational settings (Fox, Pratt, & Roberts, 1991) and recently has been adapted for use with school children (Cowie & Sharp, 1992; Mellor Smith, 1992). The following discussion shows how a group of concerned students can form a QC to address the problem of improving some aspect of their school. A specific sequence of events is involved here :

1. A group leader who is experienced in the QC method forms a group of five to seven school children all of whom have an intrinsic interest in a problem that affects them all. The group leader's responsibilities are to help the participants become a cohesive group, encourage them, teach some decision-making skills, and teach some systematic problem-solving techniques, such as the use of a series of *why* and *how* questions in pursuit of solutions to the problem.

2. A brainstorming session is used to decide on a specific problem. Lots are drawn for the order in which group members will present their ideas. In the QC no member of the group is in charge and no one is ignored or excluded. Ideas are thrown out freely and all ideas are considered, however briefly. By group consensus bullying is selected as the problem to focus on.

3. Priorities are assigned to different bullying-related problems in terms of feasibility of investigation and potential benefit to the school. Note that the group leader avoids being in charge as much as possible, but helps the group to anticipate the obstacles and consequences associated with different problems. The group chooses *bullying on the school bus* as the problem to focus on because it lends itself to pupil action (in the form of observation, interviews, and data collection) to establish whether the problem does exist and determine its severity.

4. A *why-why analysis* is used in trying to identify some of the causes of the problem, such as, "Why is there bullying on the school bus?" Some of the answers will come from the data-collection phase: "Because nothing happens to kids who bully others on the bus." "Why doesn't anything happen to them?" "Because there are no teachers or monitors to do something." The leader puts the questions and answers in a diagram on the chalk board. (See Figure 6.1 for an example of the type of diagram used in why-why and how-how analyses.) This visual breakdown of the problem allows contributing factors to be identified. The group then moves on to the how-how analysis depicted in Figure 6.1.

5. By working together, a plan is formulated to develop a possible solution to the problem. Feasibility is emphasized by the leader: School personnel may reject the plan if the group's best ideas are too impractical and/or costly. To forestall such an event, the group leader should veto the presentation of the plan but encourage the group to keep working on the problem. If the plan does have merit, then the leader helps the group prepare the verbal and visual (bar charts, handouts) presentation. It is essential to have timed rehearsal of the presentation so that the written request to present will specify the length of time needed.

6. School personnel will then discuss the problem and proposed solution among themselves in a private session followed by an evaluation of it in a joint meeting with the QC members. Note that it is essential that the school personnel, particularly the principal, show that they are clearly committed to allowing the children to participate in some aspects of the school management. If the QC group comes up with a feasible solution to this particular bullying problem, the principal must be willing to acknowledge publicly the group's contribution.

7. Should the plan be accepted, the QC group would then (with the principal's approval) assist in implementing it in any reasonable way. They could, for example, give short talks to classes about the new school bus regulations or act as a contact for children to lodge initial complaints about further harassment on the busses.

Figure 6.1 A How-How Analysis by 10-Year-Old Children of How to Stop Bullying on the School Bus

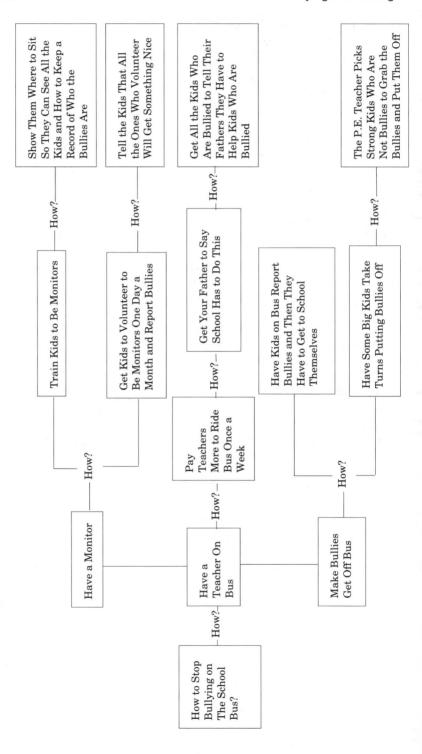

An evaluation of the efficacy of the QC procedure as a school project has been reported by Mellor Smith (1992, in Smith & Sharp, 1994, pp. 93–94). Three classes of 9- to 11-year-old children (n = 57) took part in the data collection, which involved observation, interviews with pupils and teachers, and a questionnaire. The purpose of the latter two was to determine how the children responded to the QC process: Did they like using it? What had they learned about themselves and about working with a group? What effect, if any, had the QC approach had on their attitudes to bullying and to their own behavior? In the study by Cowie and Sharp (1992), the responses of both groups were strongly positive. The teachers were pleased and sometimes surprised with the children's responses to QCs and what they had gained. The children were uniformly enthusiastic about the experience and reported that it had made them more aware of bullying, more likely to try to stop ongoing bullying, and more careful about their own behavior to others.

Although there is no evidence that the QC method alone will stop bullying, the data support its use in making children give careful consideration to the problem of bullying, as well as teaching interpersonal skills, such as communication, cooperation, and problem solving, that are critical elements for nonviolent behavior. In addition, it makes them aware of the complexity of the bullying problem and the fact that there are no easy solutions to it.

For the QC to be effective, several conditions must be met. The problem selected must have real meaning to the children: It must be a problem that they face directly or indirectly in the school environment. The QC group must be treated as serious contributors to the well-being of the school, involved in an activity of importance. Recommendations that are clearly valid and feasible deserve thoughtful consideration: If, for some reason, it is not possible to incorporate them into school procedures, a formal explanation should be provided. The prerequisites for these conditions are school personnel who are supportive and enthusiastic about the QC procedure.

Quite apart from the potential contribution that the QC group can make to the school environment (not the least of which may be the identification of problems previously unknown to the administration), the participants themselves benefit considerably. The QC procedure shows them how constructively children can work together when all members of a group are equal in terms of opportunity to participate. They begin to acquire improved communication skills along with skills that facilitate a problem-solving approach to social interactions as opposed to other approaches such as aggression or withdrawal. The procedure allows them to play an active part in improving the quality of the school experience instead of taking the passive route of just complaining, avoiding any involvement, and waiting for others to make decisions.

CENSURE VERSUS NO CENSURE

Bully Courts

In schools with bully courts, children who have been accused of bullying are required to appear before a panel of peers who listen to statements by the victim, accused bully, and witnesses, questioning them as necessary. If the bully is found guilty, the panel decides on punishment that, when appropriate, may involve reparation and restitution. An adult, usually a teacher, is present to monitor the hearing, including the punishment, but otherwise interferes as little as possible.

The idea of a children's court originated with Wills (1945, 1960), who was principal of a residential school for maladjusted children. Wills contended that children with low self-esteem, who were seldom entrusted with any responsibility or consulted about decisions affecting their lives, would benefit from sharing with school personnel some responsibility for helping individual children to be aware of their behavior problems. Building on this idea, Laslett (1980), who had worked with Wills, set up a children's court focused on bullying, in a day school for maladjusted children. More recently, Kidscape, under the leadership of Elliott (1991, 1993b), established bully courts as part of a whole school attack on bullying in 30 primary and secondary English schools.

Bully courts vary in organization from the more formal to less formal and in the extent to which their procedures and personnel resemble standard courts of law. Regardless of structural variations, however, the purpose is always the same: To confront the bully or bullies with the victim's account of the alleged misbehavior, have peers judge the seriousness of the allegations, and then decide on appropriate punishment. We briefly describe three bully courts representing a range in formality.

A Formal Court

The most ambitious bully court was one set up by Brier (Brier & Ahmad, 1991) in a short pilot study with three classes in which bullying was a serious problem. During the course of the study two cases came before the court. With commendable intent, Brier tried to adapt the basic principles of the British judicial system to the constraints and limitations of the school routine.

In addition to two teachers, nine representatives, three from each class, were elected to the Bench. The criteria were that they be honest, fair, and not easily influenced by others. To provide this group with a picture of the court situation, they went on a field trip to the Crown Court before hearing the first school case.

Simple complaint and summons forms were designed and complaint procedures were agreed on. These included first submitting the complaint to the victim's class teacher (in order to eliminate trivial disputes), having the victim and bully fill out complaint forms to be submitted to the Court Officer (a teacher), setting a date for the hearing and notifying the parents of the children involved. The hearings were closed to other students and parents. To ensure a well-conducted hearing the members of the Bench discussed possible questions in advance and did some role play.

At the hearing, the complainant(s) gave evidence and answered questions from the Bench, with the same procedure then followed by the defendant(s). The Bench discussed the case in private and announced their conclusions. The elected students proved to be competent: The teachers on the Bench were impressed with the detailed, fair, and objective closing discussion of the first case.

However, initially, the punishments and sanctions imposed were very harsh, but with adult help they became more moderate. Examples of acceptable punishments were picking up all the trash on the playground for one week or forfeiting a place on the next school field trip. Although these punishments appear to be rather mild, Brier (Brier & Ahmad, 1991) noted that the court experience itself served as a real deterrent to further bullying. Furthermore, the possibility of the punishment becoming a vendetta (a bullying of the bully) was to be avoided at all costs.

The results of the study, in the form of data collected in a survey, demonstrated a drop in bullying in the three participating classes. However, other factors such as a series of sessions on social development, could also have contributed to the improvement. The children believed that the court had reduced the bullying incidents with some children reporting that merely threatening to take bullies to court had an effect. However others stated that bullying in the neighborhood beyond the school's jurisdiction had increased.

Comment

Brier reportedly tried to make the court experience an authentic one. With this goal in mind it is surprising that she did not have the bully or victim each represented by a "lawyer," and that the court sessions were closed. Small groups of children should have been present as observers, with the understanding that if any talking or other disruption occurred they would be told to leave the court. Just observing a court hearing could be a sobering experience and valuable lesson in taking responsibility for one another, not to speak of the powerful modeling effect (Bandura, 1969) that hearing the accusation and the resultant punishment could have. Also puzzling is the fact that apart from the immediate punishment no sanctions were imposed that might result in long-term deterrence. For example, bullies could be required to sign contracts that they would not engage in bullying for the next month: they could be put on probation for the contract period with further punishment imposed should they fail to conform to the contract conditions. In this way, the pattern of bullying might be at least temporarily disrupted.

A Structured but Less Formal Court

Laslett (1980) ran a day school for maladjusted boys and girls, 7 to 12 years of age, some of whom were hostile and aggressive and bullied the younger children. He started a children's court as a way to put the bullies in a position of experiencing the disapproval by the student body of the bullying behavior. Laslett reasoned that the effect of peer pressure would be to make the bullies confront their behavior and see it as undesirable:

> I believed that the bullies needed opportunities to learn some things about their behavior from their victims who could say what they thought without fear of retaliation, that the whole group of children should have opportunities to express their feelings about bullying, and have opportunities to help in stopping it. (p. 393)

When Laslett discussed the idea of setting up a bully court with the students, they were very enthusiastic. They wanted teachers who bullied taken to court as well as children, and this was agreed to.

There were two justices and a court runner elected by students and staff, with Laslett to be present in court as clerk to the justices. The court would meet for 40 minutes twice a week, and anyone, including teachers, could attend. The justices would submit for the approval of Laslett and the staff the punishment to be meted out for bullying. The punishments set by the justices included apology for the bullying, restitution and reparation where appropriate plus doing something nice for the victim, and play restrictions for a specified number of days.

The court procedure began with the clerk entering the complaint in the court book and the runner locating the children involved and bringing them into court. Both the victim and the bully were heard and questioned, along with the witnesses. The justices then considered the offense and announced their decision of guilty or not guilty and the punishment, if any. These were then entered in the court book. The justices were required to submit for the approval of Laslett and the staff the punishment for the bullying. Should the bully not meet the requirements, the court reconvened and took further action.

The court was a great success. Laslett (1980) stated that he was amazed at the keen sense of justice and acumen exhibited by the children. There was clear evidence that the children often knew the accused better than the staff did, for example, the children knew who were formidable bullies and who were temporary bullies who were acting out because they were going through a bad spell for reasons unrelated to the school. Perhaps more important, the children distinguished between those who were victims in the real sense of the word and those who invited bullying (provocative victims). The latter were reprimanded by the court. The whole school benefited: The prestige of being elected a justice was great for the self-esteem of children who otherwise experienced very little success in school activities, and staff who observed the court in action learned a lot about the children that they previously had not known.

The bully court continued to sit twice a week for the next 10 years of Laslett's tenure as principal and continued with his successor. Although bullying was not totally eliminated (not surprising in view of the continually changing school population), it did decrease significantly.

The Least Formal Court: The Classroom Court

Classroom courts meet several times a week in some elementary schools. Students are invited to voice their concerns about any school-related problems, rather than focusing exclusively on bullying-related ones. They and the others in the class suggest solutions to the problem, then vote on a decision. The problems are relatively minor ones, with major problems being handled by other school personnel.

The rationale underlying classroom courts is called positive discipline (Nelsen, 1985). Advocates of the positive discipline approach say that when it is used correctly it helps children get along better with each other and learn to express, analyze, and solve problems on their own. Yoshikawa-Cogley (1995) reported the following sequence that she observed in a fourth-grade class:

> On this day Adrien claims Andy "pumped up" his shoe (today's high-tech sneakers have air pumps to create a snugger fit). Everyone comments, from Andy who says he didn't do it to students who observe inconsistencies in Adrien's or Andy's statements. The discussion continues for 15 minutes, and it appears Andy is responsible.
> Hunt (teacher) asks the class: "What is the appropriate consequence?" Someone suggests Andy should miss two recesses. Another suggests he shouldn't play four-square for the rest of the week. A third says he should miss computer time. As classmates talk, tears begin flowing from Andy's eyes.
> The teacher decides Andy should miss two recesses and write a letter of apology.
> Andy wipes the tears from his eyes and kicks his legs in apparent frustration.

Sometimes the problems cut across grade levels or involve same-age children from other classes. When this is the case, the class teacher sends a note requesting the child's presence.

Comment

When children come to the classroom court from another room, they are all alone and, in a sense, face a hostile audience. They should be allowed to have someone come with them, possibly a witness or at least a friend. In addition, if they are called with no prior warning, they have no time to marshal the facts and prepare their own defense.

NO BLAME OR PUNISHMENT METHODS

The programs of Maines and Robinson (1992) and Pikas (1989) are unique in that they advocate no negative consequences for bullying. Instead, the adult in charge conveys confidence that the bullies will know how to handle the problem so that the victim has no more trouble with bullying. We briefly describe each procedure, reports of their efficacy, their differences, and criticisms that have been leveled at them.

The No Blame Approach to Bullying

In 1988 Maines and Robinson (1992) developed a counseling-type procedure that rests on the assumption that bullying is an interaction that demonstrates dominance and status at the expense of others; a change to more positive values on the part of the bullies is essential if the bullies are to abandon their antisocial behavior and coexist peacefully with the victim(s). The critical elements in effecting this change in the bullies are no blame or punishment of the perpetrators and no policing of the environment. No lasting change in the bullies' behavior will occur if either of the foregoing is operative. The No Blame procedure can be summarized as follows:

1. Sit down with the victim (Peter) and listen carefully to his story. Take notes and use prompts as necessary. Be sure to get the facts about the bullying incident so that when you talk to the bullies you can consider the discrepancies in the two accounts.

2. Pay particular attention to Peter's account of the effects of the bullying on him. Note these down in detail, encourage him to provide details, either in writing or by drawing pictures.

3. Set up a meeting of those involved in the bullying. The optimum number is six or eight students. If there are only one or two perpetrators, try to include some students who saw the bullying and did not intervene.

4. Explain to the group that Peter has a problem. Tell his story clearly and in enough detail so that the group understands why Peter is upset.

5. Do not blame anyone. Merely state firmly that the members of the group are responsible and can do something about the problem. If some of the group were witnesses, suggest that they must have some ideas about what can be done even though they were not directly involved.

6. Arrange to meet with each member of the group in about a week to find out how things are going. Convey a certainty that action will be taken by the group to help Peter.

7. Throughout this procedure try to convey that those involved are basically good people, if somewhat misguided in this instance, and that they will be kind to Peter.

Support for the efficacy of the No Blame Approach comes from a report (Maines & Robinson, 1992) of 100% success with this method with primary school children and 97% success with secondary school students.

The Method of Shared Concern

Pikas (1989) has developed a somewhat complex counseling procedure for bullying problems involving children of 9 or over. The goal is to find a solution to the bullying problem that results in peaceful coexistence between the bullies and victim(s). In pursuing this goal, no attempt is made to determine blame or to administer punishment to any of the participants. Underlying this method is the assumption that in a bullying incident the bullies tend to think and act as one. It is essential, then, to get the group thinking as individuals and being willing to take responsibility for their own actions so that a feeling of shared concern can be established by the teacher about the plight of the victim(s) and what can be done about the problem.

The intervention procedure consists of three meetings, a week apart, with a mandatory follow-up check by the teacher 4 to 6 weeks later to determine if a further group meeting should occur.

The First Meeting

In order to minimize communication between members of the bully group, the teacher talks for 10 to 15 minutes individually with each of the bullies in a consecutive series, beginning with the group leader and ending with the victim.

1. The purpose is to establish that the victim is having a hard time. The teacher says in a matter-of-fact way, "I would like to talk to you because I've heard that you have been mean to Barbara."
2. "What do you know about it?" The teacher wants each member to say what form the bullying has taken and to concede that the victim must be unhappy.
3. Once the bully concedes that bullying may have occurred, the teacher shows approval, establishes that they are partners sharing concern about the victim, and that it is time to move on: "Allright. We've talked about it long enough."
4. The teacher and bully focus on solutions to the victim's dilemma: "What to do?" "What do you suggest?" A possible solution is agreed on.
5. The teacher asks the bully to put the proposed solution into use over the next week and conveys confidence: "That's good. We shall meet again in a week and you can tell me how you have been getting on."

The teacher next meets with the victim(s) individually to decide whether the victim is a passive or provocative participant in the bullying. With passive victims the teacher is supportive, making suggestions about what they could do to improve relations with the bullies. With provocative victims the teacher discusses the situation as a real problem. The victim slowly realizes that the persecution is not entirely the bullies' fault and gradually becomes interested in hearing of behaviors that are unacceptable. A plan of action and change is arrived at. A meeting for each victim is set up for the following week.

The Follow-Up Meeting

One week later the teacher conducts individual follow-up discussions with the bullies and the victim(s) to determine what progress has been made. Usually there will be some evidence of improvement in bully–victim relations, but typically some problems remain. The teacher decides whether it is time to schedule the next meeting as one for both bullies and victim(s). The victim must be ready and willing to meet with the bullies. Usually, the third meeting is a group one.

The Group Meeting

The teacher meets with the bullies first. Each one is asked to think of some positive comments about Barbara that can be made when she comes into the meeting. She is brought in and the group now discusses the improvements that the bullies have made in her predicament and considers how these could be maintained over time.

Follow-Up Check

It is essential that the teacher conduct a follow-up check a month or 6 weeks later to determine if further meetings with the group are necessary.

What Evidence Is There of Efficacy?

Pikas (1989) claims great success for his method on the basis of a small number of case studies. He has stated that his "shared concern method has only failed once in hundreds of documented cases throughout Scandinavia. . . . It is now used in 90 percent of Swedish schools" (in Dore, 1993, p. 9).

Smith and Sharp (1994) have reports of its use from some schools in the Sheffield Bullying Project. They conclude that "It appears it can be a powerful short-term tool for combating bullying; long-term change may depend on additional action where very persistent bullying is concerned" (p. 200). Herbert (in Dore, 1992) reported that after using the Pikas method for a year, it had proven completely successful in six outbreaks of group bullying.

How Do the Two Procedures Differ?

Pikas (1989) talks to the bullies first to protect the victim from reprisal for "telling." Maines and Robinson (1988) contend that their speaking for the victim will have a powerful influence on the group. Pikas speaks individually to each bully, whereas Maines and Robinson argue that the group process is likely to enhance the impact of the victim's story. Pikas's comments about the victim's plight are limited to hearing that the bully has been mean to the victim and asking the bully what he or she knows about it. Maines and Robinson tell the bully in some detail how the victim feels.

What Criticisms Have Been Raised?

Some criticisms apply to both procedures. Children, including bullies, often find that they are unable to talk candidly to teachers. Some way would have to be found to reassure them that candor is expected and confidentiality assured. Teacher time, for both the initial training and the subsequent meetings, would be a consideration. No mention is made of concrete retribution in the form of replacing damaged possessions or paying for their loss. Yet in many cases of bullying, considerable damage to the victim's clothes and school supplies occurs as part of the attack, along with theft of lunch money and bus fares. One reason for the bullies' apparent cooperation in stopping the attacks may be that they are elated at avoiding punishment, rather than being sincerely concerned about the plight of the victim. The children's parents are neither informed about the intervention process nor included in it, a costly omission both therapeutically and ethically. The failure to provide simultaneous support in the home is likely markedly to lessen the impact of the intervention in the school (Yoshikawa, 1994), particularly as the parents would be justified in feeling angry about not being informed. The procedures make no provision for the long-term maintenance of improvements in the bullies' behavior or the prevention of new behavior problems. Finally, both procedures are inconsistent with the established empirical and clinical knowledge that has been built up about bullying (Olweus, 1988).

With respect to the Pikas method, Olweus (1988) contradicts the claim that bullies feel guilt about the victim, on the grounds that there is an abundance of clinical evidence (Besag, 1989) showing that bullies do not show empathy for the victim's feelings. Rather, they are prepared to fake remorse on finding out that punishment is not involved. Olweus's most stringent criticism of the Pikas method is that it is built on manipulation and latent threats disguised as cooperation between the teacher and the bullies and hence is unethical. He thinks that it would be more honest for the teacher to state that the bullying is unacceptable and severe negative sanctions will follow if it continues. In other words, he favors the direct method of handling the bullying problem.

Comment

In discussing the empirical support for the efficacy of the Norwegian Campaign Against Bullying, Olweus (1993a) has been critical about the lack of empirical evaluations for many of the specific interventions in current usage in other countries, particularly those in the United Kingdom:

> The recent English literature on bully/victim problems in school abounds with suggestions about measures against these problems. Almost none of the proposed measures have been scientifically evaluated, however, and consequently it is difficult to know what their effects, if any, are likely to be. (p. 128)

There is no question that empirical support is virtually nonexistent for some of the specific interventions in this chapter. But blanket acceptance of such a requirement should be tempered by Dubos's caveat that "Sometimes the more measurable drives out the most important" (in Siegel, 1986, p. 20). The realities of setting up an empirical test of the *direct effects* of bully courts, for example, present formidable obstacles. Or consider the case of a whole school program that includes the use of video cameras that provide unequivocally valid information about bullying. If after 2 years the incidence of bullying drops, how could a numerical value be attached to the contribution made by the use of these cameras? Other variables may well be operative.

These methodological difficulties may be outweighed by the *indirect benefits* that can accrue from the use of specific intervention programs. These, too, lack empirical evidence, but strong theoretical support for their existence comes from social learning theory (Bandura, 1969). They are difficult, if not impossible, to measure, given the current state of the art, but it is highly likely that they do exist. Their potential is considerable. The inclusion of specific interventions in a whole school campaign allows a number of students to be actively involved in combating bullying, and in the process to acquire skills such as conflict resolution, problem solving (quality circles), and an understanding of trial and other court procedures that would likely be of long-term value. Seeing antisocial behavior punished with the bullies visibly working off their sentences should have a powerful modeling effect on those with bullying tendencies (Bandura) and provide substantial reassurance and hope to the victims of bullying. Perhaps most important of all is the fact that the student body would see the difference between mandatory telling and being a tattle-tale, and in the process the bullies would be stripped of their greatest source of protection—the code of silence.

7 Teasing: An Overview

TEASING IS PRESENT in many bullying episodes, although typically its various forms, such as name calling, taunts, and derision, are of only secondary importance to the other components of bullying. That the function of these verbal barbs may be more to heighten the threat inherent in the bullying episode than to draw attention to specific characteristics of the victim is evident in this account from an 11-year-old boy:

> It don't matter who it is or what I'm doing like beating up on him or messing up his books or just picking up the rent (payment for protection) . . . I go, "You gleeb, you lesbie, you wimp. . . ." It gets him more scared, all the names and stuff. (E. M. Allen, personal communication, July 17, 1991)

Teasing that is unquestionably cruel also occurs independently of the other components of bullying and should be accorded the status of a behavior problem in its own right. This category of teasing is the focus of this chapter.

However, before we turn to the cruel and destructive qualities of teasing, aspects of teasing in general will be discussed, with emphasis on the developmental sequence that it follows from the preschool period through adolescence. Unlike bullying, teasing can be fun, playful, and unequivocally constructive. Teasing between parent and child, for example, can be used to build up strong relationships in the family. Using references that only the family understands can enhance feelings of solidarity and closeness (Eisenberg, 1986). It is important to recognize the differences between this teasing that can be beneficial and teasing that is unquestionably cruel and should be stopped. Further, teasing and being the target of teasing enable young children to acquire competence in some of the social skills that they will need in adolescence and adulthood (Kutner, 1981). In America, teasing also is a tool of socialization used by black inner-city mothers to prepare their young children for the challenges of the street (Miller, 1986), by black adolescents to teach self-restraint in the face of intolerable taunts and insults (Abrahams, 1962), and by white middle-class parents to toughen their children and hone their verbal gamesmanship skills (Blau, 1993).

THE NATURE OF TEASING

The Many Meanings of Teasing

Although early derivations of the word "tease" tended to emphasize the destructive and vicious aspects, as in the English meaning "to pull apart" and the Norwegian "to tear to bits" (Pearce, 1989), contemporary definitions and synonyms also include the more positive dimensions of humor and fun. Pearce (p. 15), for example, offers a two-component definition of teasing as (1) making fun of someone in a playful or hurtful way, and (2) making an offer and then delaying giving what had been offered or withdrawing it altogether. The Oxford English Dictionary (1993) defines teasing as a "mildly annoying, harassing, or irritating occurrence done in sport or mischief—typically of a trifling or petty nature." The same range of affect is apparent in the synonyms of teasing. Some are more hostile (badgering, harassing, tormenting), but others are more playful (bantering, kidding, chaffing).

The effect of the positive affect implicit in these definitions and synonyms has been to engender a misconception common among adults that teasing is "only joking" and, as such, is not to be taken seriously. In fact, as Pawluk (1989) has pointed out, teasing differs from joking in that it involves a perpetrator and victim and often occurs at the latter's expense by relating specifically to one of the victim's characteristics. Joking, by contrast, reflects a more equal dyadic relationship and can relate to people other than the victim and to impersonal topics. Whereas teasing may elicit reactions ranging from extreme upset to amusement, true joking usually results only in amusement. It also lacks the essential serious component of teasing, namely, the potential for developing into something that is painful and destructive.

The Ambiguity of Teasing

Teasing is characterized by ambiguities and intangibles that make it a difficult problem for parents and other adults to handle effectively. What distresses one child may not bother another at all and even the same incident may not consistently elicit distress in the child. As a result of this variability, children's complaints about being teased often are more likely to exasperate adults than to arouse sympathy. In addition, ongoing teasing interactions typically are often difficult to document because they can be virtually invisible to onlookers: For example, the casual observer sees a group of girls giggling but may miss the immediate and transient aftermath of tears and a flushed face. Furthermore, it is relatively easy for persuasive teasers to convince adults that they were "only fooling," thus placing the victim in the category of one who makes a fuss about nothing. (This defense may have an element of truth to it: Besag [1989] reports that many teasers genuinely appear to see their teasing as far milder, and of less consequence than the victim sees it, and Shapiro, Baumeister, & Kessler [1987] found that elementary school teasers were more likely to see teasing as being good sometimes than were nonteasers.)

Added to the ambiguity is the fact that it is sometimes difficult for the child who is teased to know whether to take a specific tease seriously. As Blau (1993) has noted, the very essence of a tease is that its meaning is always open to interpretation, a feature that is not characteristic of most other components of bullying, such as physical aggression, extortion, and social exclusion. Some light has been cast on this dilemma by Pawluk (1989) in a scholarly dissertation that is by far the best treatise on teasing that has appeared in the literature to date. Pawluk has identified several characteristics of teasing episodes that should determine whether teasing is taken seriously. It is often not so much what is said or how it is said, but rather *who* says it that determines whether a specific tease will be seen as offensive. Sometimes the teaser means the teasing to be taken lightly and conveys this by certain contextualization cues (Gumperz, 1977) such as a singsong intonation, facial expressions of exaggerated sorrow or alarm, or winks and smiles at apparently inappropriate times. Certain characteristics of the content of the tease also may determine its reception. If the tease contains negative comments that the onlookers know are patently false, the recipient is more likely to take it lightly.

Consider the case of the attractive, mature 13-year-old girl in a new school whose first date is with a popular and prestigious star of the school football team. Her older brothers, who secretly are enormously impressed, feign exaggerated relief with comments such as, "She's got a date! Man! He must have been *desperate!*" "We better help her all we can, Mom, she may never have another chance." "Buy her a great dress, Mom, and he might not notice how plain she is." While the girl pretends annoyance verging on outrage, she clearly enjoys the whole exchange and wishes it would continue (E. Patterson, personal communication, May 10, 1988).

WHEN DOES TEASING BEGIN?

Anthropologists agree that in childhood, teasing is a universal form of social interaction. The same teasing patterns found in the inner-city children of Philadelphia, for example, have been observed among the Kaluli aborigine children of New Zealand (Kutner, 1981). Visitors to non-English-speaking countries report their surprise at hearing children chanting the melody and format of the familiar singsong taunt of their own early school years: "Pattie's a pooper, Pattie's a pooper." However, teasing occurs long before the child is capable of this level of speech. Like most attempts to assign clusters of behavior, such as teasing, to age categories, the boundaries are blurred and individual differences rampant. Nevertheless, the categories do provide a framework for ordering progressions in developmental sequences.

The Preschool Years

Kutner (1981) has described the most primitive form of teasing as that seen among toddlers when one child holds a toy out to another and then pulls it back out of reach as the other child's hand makes a grab for it. Two- and 3-year-olds can accurately identify the cues signaling the playful nature of a teasing interaction and can join in it (Eisenberg, 1986; Miller, 1986). In preschool settings teasers often say silly things that are not specifically related to the target. A group of 4-year-olds, for example, suddenly started amidst raucous laughter to call a boy playing nearby "fruity" names such as "You're a slippery banana, a squishy peach." They quickly lost interest when the intended target's only reaction was a puzzled glance before he resumed play. At this age level the playful nature of most teasing serves the important function of providing practice in beginning to acquire a certain tolerance for name calling that is a distinct advantage when the child enters kindergarten.

Opinions differ on the age at which teasing with a deliberate intent to hurt begins. Besag (1989) believes that toddlers are well aware of the feelings of others and the irritation they can arouse with teasing. Kutner (1981) agrees that teasing begins at the toddler stage, but he contends that, although young children may recognize that their gibes can anger their targets, they are still unaware that someone might feel hurt by what they say. Maccoby (1980) argues that teasing designed to be deliberately hurtful cannot occur until children have reached a level of cognitive development that provides them with an understanding of the self and the feelings of others. Reaching this level can be facilitated by teaching children at an early age that their comments can hurt others, and this intentional training can be strengthened through the incidental learning that occurs as a result of witnessing familial and televised verbal aggression. That preschool children are able to identify and implement ways of deliberately upsetting other children is evident in the following conversation that the author overheard at the Stanford Nursery School:

MITCH: Let's go and say mean things to Petie (another four-year-old). He's a gunk.

KENNY: Yeah, Mitch, and *do* some real mean things. Make him cry and bleed his nose.

MITCH: [Reluctantly] No, just say mean things and make him cry a *lot*.

They are also capable of making value judgments. Sigelman and Begley (1987) have reported that preschool children tend to devalue peers who are physically or behaviorally different; for example, they have negative stereotypes of the obese (Jarvie, Lahey, Graziano, & Framer, 1983).

Middle Childhood

Many 6- and 7-year-olds are capable of more varied forms of teasing: They are able to present the tease as playful or as a deliberate attempt to hurt (Eder, 1991). At this stage children are particularly vulnerable to others' opinions because they are struggling to feel confident in the public school situation. Consequently, they are easily upset by unkind comments. Being one of the group is very important. Conformity is the rule, and those who are noticeably different (for example, shy, small for age, particularly for a boy, dressed differently) frequently are the targets of unkind comments. If these elicit visible upset, the comments may change to teasing that is both individualized and deliberate. Such teasing is especially likely if the differences are ones that the group regards as babyish (Klein, 1975).

At this level most children know some of the taunting rhymes:

Ha, ha, ha, he, he, he,
You've got a face like
A chimpanzee.

Roses are red, violets are blue.
If I had your hair I'd be in the zoo.

These rhymes become part of the teasers' arsenal as much to show mastery and membership in the group as to attack, but a target is still needed regardless of the motive.

As children move through the middle childhood years three qualitative changes occur in their teasing. In the first of these, the teasing becomes sharper, more incisive, and cutting, partly because of their increasing verbal skill but also because acceptance by the peer group now has become a top priority. Teasing at this level can be a way of showing other children that *they* are not one of the group. Conversely, it can be a sign of social acceptance:

> An 11-year-old girl, a newcomer in the school, was the first to wear knee socks with horizontal stripes. Despite an element of nastiness in some of her peers' comments, she clearly perceived remarks about going out for the boys' soccer team and wearing jail garb as indicative of a degree of social acceptance. She told her mother, "It was the best day so far, the other kids, especially the guys, made more cracks about my socks than they've made the whole time I've been here." (J. S. Ross, personal communication, 1964)

At the same time, there is a trend toward a more positive judgment of teasing, a recognition of some teasing as being funny or as an effective way of sending useful messages to the recipient. In one of the few studies of the child's view of teasing, Shapiro et al. (1987) asked third- and fifth-grade children if they thought that teasing *was* or *could be* good or bad. Twenty percent of the third graders thought that teasing could be good sometimes, as compared to 33% of the fifth graders. Children who viewed teasing as potentially good were more often self-acknowledged teasers.

The second change is a gender difference that was not apparent in the early school years. Boys "go for the jugular" (Blau, 1993, p. 67): They challenge each other's masculinity ("You like girl things," "You're a gay-gay."). They try to identify another boy's Achilles' heel, and when they do, they focus on it while doing their best to embarrass him. By comparison, girls are more subtle: They spread rumors about other girls and use social exclusion rather than confrontation. Some of their teasing may appear to be playful, but the playfulness masks thinly disguised hostility (Eder, 1991; Pipher, 1994).

The third change is characterized by an underlying sexual quality to the teasing. The child who is often seen talking to one of the opposite sex is at risk for being teased about "liking" the other child. The effect of this heterosexual teasing is to construct and monitor boundaries between the sexes, keeping them as separate groups having only limited informal contact in public. In a study of 5- to 11-year-old children, Thorne and Luria (1986) commented that the probability of being teased for such contacts is so great that cross-gender friendships that originated in other settings sometimes "go underground" during the school day.

Adolescence

In early adolescence unfriendly teasing of a general nature starts to disappear partly because young adolescents often are more empathic and so more reluctant to attack certain attributes of others, and partly because they begin to look at negative attributes in others in terms of controllability (Royal & Roberts, 1987). They usually react more punitively to peers with apparently controllable negative attributes, such as obesity, than to those with uncontrollable conditions such as cerebral palsy.

By the end of the eighth grade most adolescents have experienced, witnessed, and in some cases subjected others to a variety of teasing in the form of name calling, needling, abrasive mimicry, and derision. Their reactions to these experiences are the basis for being recognized as one "who can take it" or being labeled as "a wimp." As one 13-year-old girl commented, "If you can't keep your cool about a few names and cracks by the time you're our age, you'll never make it in high school." Those who have mastered these teasing experiences are indeed well equipped to handle the bantering, ribbing, and exchange of pseudo-insults (insults that are really a sign of goodwill or friendship) that characterize much of the social intercourse in adolescence.

However, when teasing does occur, it is more likely to be cruel in a deadly way. With increasing cognitive maturation there is a concomitant increase in verbal skills, particularly in the ability to convey more subtle and punishing barbs. The adolescent is often very adept at pinpointing the most private areas of vulnerability in the victim. An example of this level of teasing appears in the autobiography of Graham Greene (1971) in which he describes the vicious teasing he had experienced from a schoolmate. The teasing related to the conflict of loyalty position that Greene was in because he and his older brother attended a school in which their father was the headmaster:

> . . . there was a boy at my school called Carter who perfected a system of mental torture based on my difficult situation. Carter had an adult imagination—he could conceive the conflict of loyalties, loyalties to my

age group, loyalty to my father and brother. The sneering nicknames were inserted like splinters under the nails. (p. 82)

In adolescence the heterosexual teasing that begins in the middle childhood years intensifies and branches out into three clusters. One of these is teasing that serves to initiate heterosexual interactions. Much of this teasing is characterized by playfulness and ambiguity, a combination that allows the teenager to express liking for a person of the opposite sex without being held accountable for these feelings (Oswald, Krappman, Chowdhuri, & von Salisch, 1988).

In another cluster, the teasing becomes somewhat insulting, with the content often focusing on sexual patterns such as homosexuality and lesbianism. This focus often functions as a way for the teaser to deal with his own sexual fears by attributing them to others, particularly to the least prestigious targets such as the isolates in the group (Evans & Eder, 1993). It is interesting that many adolescent girls are aware of the cruelty inherent in these sexual taunts and go so far as to reprimand the teasers (Evans & Eder).

When jealousy is a factor (Hazler et al., 1993) in combination with the sexual aspects, the mix is particularly potent. The following quote is from a letter to a dance magazine column:

. . . you wrote about boys being teased in ballet. Well, I was one of those bullies. When my cousin dared to be different and took ballet, I gave him a hard time because I was jealous of his guts. Then I had a growth spurt, and my gym teacher suggested that I take ballet because I was so uncoordinated. I took flak from all my friends. (Hamilton, 1992, p. 54)

Teasing in the third cluster is sometimes extremely crude, as McCoy (1992) has reported:

. . . a social service professional asked her 13-year-old daughter, a good-looking star soccer player, why she seemed so unhappy. The girl started sobbing, then admitted that for the past six months whenever one boy saw her in the hall, he would lean toward her and say things like, "You big fat whale, you zit faced slug, you ugly witch." He did this up to ten times a day and used a lot of four-letter words. (p. 199)

THE PROBLEM OF CRUEL TEASING

The discussion so far has centered around aspects of teasing in general, with the emphasis on the developmental steps from preschool through adolescence. The remainder of the chapter focuses on teasing that consists of destructive verbal attacks (P. K. Smith, 1991) that are usually, but not always, repeated over time, the goal being to create increasing misery in the victim. There is no ambiguity here in what is said or how it is said: The intent is to hurt, annoy, upset, or goad the victim to tears. A deliberate attempt is made to find fault with the victim and to bring this fault to the attention of any onlookers in an embarrassing and humiliating way. The potential for upset is even greater if the topic of the tease is true, negative, and beyond the victim's control. Such teasing is a test that most victims are likely to fail unless they have been trained in coping effectively with teasing or have been exposed to models who were able to field destructive verbal attacks without too much difficulty. The ability to generate an effective response is one of the more difficult verbal interaction skills because the response can manipulate the meaning of the tease. As Willis (1977) has pointed out, it takes some skill to initiate a teasing attack, but it takes far more to respond quickly and decisively.

From the teaser's viewpoint teasing is most successful when the victim's reaction is one of visible upset. Colloquially, this behavior is recognized as having "got a rise out of him," "scored a direct hit," been "right on target," or achieved a "put-down." One of the most detrimental reactions the victim can make is to reject the teasing in a weak defensive way coupled with visible upset. Although walking away, theoretically, should mean that the teasing has failed, in practice it is extremely difficult for the victim to carry it off without appearing to be making an escape. Walking away is usually accompanied by further taunts such as, "What's the matter, Mark, are you too chicken to stay?"

From the reports of children who have experienced a substantial amount of teasing and from interviews with self-acknowledged teasers (D. M. Ross, Case studies, University of California, San Francisco, 1978), hurtful teasing generally follows an orderly sequence. The tempo of the teasing begins slowly and then accelerates. The teaser first probes rather tentatively with some exploratory insults and negative comments. If the potential victim responds appropriately with visible upset or anger and appears to be avoiding the teaser, the teaser goes ahead with the tried-and-true teases. However, he or she still spends some time trying to identify new "sore spots," which are then added to the repertoire. Thus teasing is, in most cases, almost a leisurely process in which the teaser gradually accumulates a set of effective teases for a specific victim. From the point at which the first probes clearly work, the teaser feels in complete control of the teasing interactions.

The Incidence of Teasing

Although there is a paucity of incidence data, there is no question that teasing in school-age children is widespread in parts of Western Europe, particularly Norway and Sweden, the United Kingdom, the

United States and Canada, as well as Japan, Australia, and New Zealand. The few studies that have been published support the view that the incidence of teasing is a problem in the schools, but there is less firm empirical support than might be expected because teasing usually is included as a component of bullying in the questionnaires. The child is asked some form of the question, "How many times have you been *bullied* in the past week, month, etc.?" whereas to determine the incidence of teasing as a separate problem, the question should distinguish between *teasing only* and teasing as *secondary to other components of bullying*. Some investigators have used questions that permitted this distinction. For example, Yates and Smith (1989) asked 234 pupils in secondary schools, "In what way have you been bullied in school?" Seventy-one percent of the respondents stated that they had "been teased only." Similarly, when Boulton and Underwood (1992) asked 296 elementary school children to check specific categories of bullying, they found that 58% of the group said that the bullying they had experienced consisted of teasing only; and in an important review article, P. K. Smith (1991, p. 245) stated that most respondents who reported being bullied said that it took the form of teasing.

Who Is a Target for Serious Teasing?

No theory adequately explains why one child and not another becomes the target of teasers. For a long time it was assumed that being different in some way was the criterion. Then in 1984 Olweus introduced the victim theory discussed in Chapter 4, that is, that children are bullied, or in this case teased, because their whole demeanor labels them as easy targets who are unlikely to retaliate. Olweus (1993a) has never suggested that this theory explains all teasing, however, popular acceptance of it has tended to obscure its limitations. The fact is that both the difference and victim theories make a contribution.

Differences Likely to Create Problems

Differences play an important etiological role in the teasing problems of four groups of children who, when teasing is first initiated, are not characterized by the victim syndrome. The first group are children who are beginning public school, usually kindergarten, and have two characteristics. One is a *significant lack of social experience* with other children because of living in an isolated area or some other reason not related to any inadequacy in them that repels their peers. As a result, these children are inexperienced in even mildly negative social interactions with children other than those in their own families. The other characteristic is *some visible difference* in dress, speech, or gait, that sets them apart from the other children. When the differences elicit negative comments of a general nature, these children usually are unable to handle them. More often than not, they become angry, visibly upset, or they withdraw. Any one of these reactions is sufficiently rewarding to other children so that they continue along the teasing track. Although a victim personality may develop as a result of the teasing, it is not the cause of it.

The second group is made up of those who are extremely shy with strangers and overly cautious in new situations to the point where they may withdraw altogether. Although almost all children are shy sometimes, the children in this group consistently exhibit shyness to an almost debilitating degree. A mother with an extremely shy son attributed his shyness to newness: "If something is new and different his inclination is to be quiet and watch. . . . It's unfamiliarity that is the cause of his behavior. Not just new people, but *newness*" (Galvin, 1992, p. 41).

Jerome Kagan, who has been studying shy children since 1978, at first thought that their extreme shyness was an acquired trait, the result of rejection by family or peers, poor school performance, or some other identifiable reason (Galvin, 1992). He now believes that, although one cluster of these painfully shy children has acquired shyness as Zimbardo (1982) has demonstrated, the remainder were born with this temperament, a quality that Kagan calls *inhibition*. Kagan has documented impressive empirical support for genetic and physiological bases being partly responsible for inhibition.

Because shyness in our society can be a major handicap, it is fortunate that both acquired shyness and inhibition-related shyness are modifiable. Zimbardo (1982), through his Shyness Clinic at Stanford University, has made a major contribution to those whose shyness appears to be acquired, particularly those in the adolescent through young adult age groups. His texts on overcoming shyness (Zimbardo, 1982, 1990) offer invaluable help for the parents, teachers, and other professionals who seek to modify shyness in those in the grade school through young adult age groups. Kagan (Galvin, 1992) has data on changes with age in inhibition-related shyness. Some changes may occur spontaneously, but more likely they are the result of determined parental intervention. On the basis of his findings with the group of extremely shy children studied from infancy, Kagan estimates that for every 10 children who are extremely shy at age 2, only five will still be shy by kindergarten or first grade, and only three by adolescence (Galvin, 1992). The behaviors characteristic of extreme shyness could be viewed by peers as a negative difference such as standoffishness, thus creating a logical link to peer rejection and teasing.

A third group of children who are teased are those with differences that are extremely unsightly, the salient characteristic being a marked degree in deviation of their negative attributes from the physical appearance norm. The aftermath of serious burns, facial disfigurement from an accident, and unsightly skin conditions that border on the grotesque are the kinds of differences that draw immediate attention. In this group the cases that we have seen were all children who previously had been "normal" in all respects, including popularity with peers.

We first became aware of this group when we asked children with leukemia to tell us what was the worst pain they had experienced (Ross & Ross, 1988). The answers we expected were some treatment-related pain such as spinal taps or bone marrow aspirations. Instead, for many of these children and for those with the aftermath of serious burns, the worst pain was going back to school and being teased about their appearance. Treatment with prednisone and chemotherapy typically result in leukemic children being bald, obese, and having a curiously spongy look to their skin along with extreme pallor. Often the children look like aliens from another planet, as do some children with the aftermath of severe burns.

The slowly accelerating tempo of the teasing described earlier is not a characteristic with this group. These children are not selected by the teaser but, instead, more or less burst into his or her sphere on their first day back to school. The teaser typically initiates an all-out attack from the first point of contact and this high-power verbal assault continues unabated. The teasing always focuses on the markedly deviant attribute, such as baldness, regardless of the target's other teaseworthy negative characteristics. The teasing also tends to be highly repetitive, with little or no variation.

It is our opinion that these tempo and content differences are indications that the teaser feels a loss of control, and the all-out teasing attack is a fear reaction to seeing the dramatic change for the worse in a previously normal-appearing child. It was clear in talking to the teasers that the changes in the leukemic children came as a terrible shock. The teasers clearly did not know how to cope and some said that they were frightened. One 8-year-old boy said, "I just started yelling at him (the leukemic child), I said all kinds of terrible things, I couldn't stop." The same sequence of shock at changed appearance leading to fear and attack has been documented in animals (Bergman, 1973). We recently observed it in two dogs who had been close friends for more than a year. When one returned from the veterinary hospital wearing a temporary 12-inch-wide white plastic collar designed to prevent scratching, the other dog first became extremely agitated and then attacked his former friend. They never regained their previous level of friendship.

The fourth group whose teasing problem is etiologically related to a difference are children in the first or second year of school who are different in some conspicuous but minor way and whose teachers set them up as targets for teasing by their classmates. To understand how such a thing can happen, it is important to remember that the teacher has a great deal to do with how children see themselves and how others in the class see them. The power of teachers is tremendous: They can take a boy who is different in some way from his classmates, set him apart from them in a negative way, and in the process possibly do him lasting psychological damage; or they can make him a valued member of the group.

An impressive empirical demonstration of this phenomenon has been provided by Whalen and Henker (1976). They have unequivocal evidence that the world of the classroom can function as a *provocation ecology* that accentuates the differences between average children and those who are different in a way that their classmates can be led to see as negative, or as a *rarefaction ecology* that diminishes such differences. It is the teacher who determines and controls the ecology of the classroom, as the following examples clearly show. Robert, an unusually bright 6-year-old, suffered frequent mortification and shame in kindergarten because he was unable to tie his shoelaces. His teacher clearly had rigid norms about what boys in kindergarten should be able to do:

> She frequently would ask in a world-weary tone that conveyed complete scorn for Robert's lack of agility, "Will someone please come up and tie Robert's shoes for him so we can go outside for recess? He can't seem to do it for himself yet." And there Robert would stiffly sit—no recourse but to face front—toward tables lined with jeering faces, hearing the barely suppressed giggles, the stage whispers behind loosely cupped hands. There he would sit while some better-coordinated classmate, sometimes a boy, sometimes a girl, would bend over him condescendingly and tie his laces into a bow. (Klein, 1975, pp. 127–128)

Given this scenario, the potential teasers in the class would feel with justification that their teacher was tacitly endorsing the teasing of Robert. As Zimbardo (1982) has commented: "The power of a teacher to erode a child's self-confidence is overwhelming. And the power of a teacher to turn otherwise nice children into tormentors is frightening" (p. 12).

Zimbardo (1982, pp. 125–126) describes Suzy, a pretty child even with her thick glasses. She was friendly and outgoing until she was in first grade, at which time she changed to an unhappy, solitary child who often went to her room after school and cried. When her mother asked her what was wrong, all that Suzy would say was, "The kids don't like me."

Soon after this change occurred Suzy's teacher requested a parent conference. One issue was that the child was failing in school, the other explained the recent change in her behavior. The teacher told the mother that she had to do something about Suzy's thumb sucking and said righteously that *she* was doing all she could. Several weeks earlier, when she had first seen Suzy sucking her thumb, she began to have her sit at the front of the class facing the rest of the children, who were told to watch her and remind her not to suck her thumb. Reminding Suzy was effected with such taunts as, "Suzy is a baby, born in the navy," and "Suzy is a four-eyed thumbsucker." Note that the same children who had originally accepted Suzy's thick glasses changed, under the teacher's tutelage, to teasing her about them. Suzy's mother was horrified. She took her out of the class, complained to the principal, and, with great success, set about the arduous task of reversing the damage.

What Are the Effects on the Victim of Being Teased?

Adults would not be so ready to brush teasing aside as a passing problem that all children go through if they realized that teasing has important immediate *and* long-term effects on the victims. The immediate effects, which are felt throughout the elementary and high school years, are for the most part like those of bullying. The victims come to dread school, are reluctant to attend formal and social groups that the teaser attends, begin to see themselves as worthless and inferior beings, avoid other children, including former friends, and suffer from anxiety, acute loneliness, and depression. Fabian and Thompson (1989), for example, have reported a significant relationship between the current level of depression in 13- to 15-year-old girls and their history of being teased. If the teasing continues over a long period and if the girl receives no social support from parents and others, her depression about her inability to cope with what she sees as a hopeless problem can have drastic results. Her thinking may become confused to the point where only one action occurs to her: If I destroy myself, then the problem is destroyed. The case of Nathan Faris is a textbook example of this sequence (Greenbaum, 1989).

Nathan was a bright, slightly overweight boy in seventh grade who had been teased relentlessly by his classmates since the third grade. He hated going to school: The others continually harassed him and called him names such as "fatso," "chubby," and "walking dictionary." Nathan felt tormented and vowed to take revenge. One day in 1987 he brought a gun to school, killed one boy who tried to take the gun away from him, wounded two others, and then killed himself.

From the newspaper accounts and from post-suicide interviews with classmates, the teasing that Nathan was subjected to seems rather mild. As one girl said, "Nobody really had anything against him, he was just someone to pick on." But it was bad enough from Nathan's viewpoint for him to kill himself. This points to the *subjectivity* of the pain of being teased: Others' opinion of the teasing is completely irrelevant because their judgments have no relation to how the victim feels. Children's appraisals *must* be accepted at face value: If they say it is terrible, then it *is* terrible. This is an extremely important point that cannot be overemphasized.

The long-term effects, that is, in post high school and adulthood, continue to exert a punishing influence on the victims. People teased about their appearance by peers in childhood more often evaluated their appearance in adulthood negatively than those who had not been teased. As a woman whose nickname in childhood was "elephant legs" said: "I still can't bear to look at myself in a full-length mirror. . . . My legs still look huge to me even though my husband tells me they look fine" (Cash & Janda, 1986, p. 33).

Thompson and Psaltis (1988) report that those teased about their appearance in childhood also more often have high levels of eating disturbances in adulthood. Minor deviations singled out for teasing in childhood may, without intervention, escalate in adulthood. Wiehe (1991) reports the case of a woman in her early 30s who was teased and ridiculed so often as a child about a minor speech problem that she is reluctant even now to speak up for herself. What started as an inability to say certain words correctly developed into the belief that people would laugh at the *content* of her conversation:

> My brother would tease me about not saying certain words correctly. Some words I could not pronounce correctly, so he would get me to say them and then would laugh at me. (Now) I feel like people will laugh at what I have to say or they will think it's dumb. (p. 29)

Even when the victim of childhood teasing achieves impressive success in adulthood, the residual effects of the teasing may linger, thus lessening the satisfaction that should accrue from success. A classic example of this destructive sequence is that of Yasmeen

Ghauri, a beautiful 21-year-old model who is the daughter of an Indian father and a German mother. Despite her popularity and the enormous financial success that she has achieved in only 4 years of modeling, she has mixed feelings about her career that appear to result in part from her painful memories of growing up in Canada and being called names such as "chocolate-cake face" (Scott, 1993).

What Do Parents Do When Children Complain of Being Teased?

When children complain to their parents, they are likely to handle the problem in any of the following ineffective ways:

Suggest Paying No Attention

The suggestion to ignore the teaser often is accompanied by the old adage, "Sticks and stones may break my bones but names will never hurt me." This is a myth perpetuated by adults who have forgotten how stressful being teased can be for a child. This advice has little or no effect on the victims other than to convince them that their parents do not understand how much the teasing hurts and, in fact, will be of no help.

Minimize the Problem

The parent attempts to downgrade the seriousness of the teasing by making a joke of it and encouraging the child to laugh it off as nothing of any importance. One father told his daughter it was "just a blip on the computer screen of life"; a mother told her 8-year-old son, "When you're nine you'll look back at this and wonder what all the fuss was about." In the previously described case of Robert, the kindergarten child who could not tie his shoelaces, his mother did not offer social support in the form of comfort and sympathy, nor did she make suggestions about how to handle the problem when he went home that first day and told her about it. Instead, she laughed, kissed him, and asked gaily, "Who cares about such a silly thing? I promise you by the time you go to college you'll know how to tie your shoes" (Klein, 1975, p. 15).

What parents do not understand is the effect that their failure to take some constructive action or offer sympathy or helpful advice has on the victim. It is the interaction between the cruelty inherent in teasing and the tendency of parents and other adults to treat the teasing as trivial that is demoralizing to the child. One 8-year-old boy reported that the worst thing about being teased was that none of the people who he thought would help him did. He said sadly, "It's the most alone I've ever been."

Complain to the Teaser's Parents or to the School

Rarely is this a successful tactic because two essential conditions are seldom met. The interaction must be handled with unusual skill and tact, and the adults involved must be genuinely sympathetic about the problem and concerned about possible negative effects on the victim. Otherwise, this tactic could be disastrous: The child could be labeled as a tattle-tale by the peer group and viewed as a trouble-maker, wimp, or worse, by school personnel, leaving the victim in an even more unenviable position than prior to the "help."

Present It as "Character building"

Teasing is presented as something that almost everyone experiences at some time, a statement that does have an element of truth to it. What is missing, however, is the fact that not everyone is subjected to the extended periods of teasing that drive them to complain to their parents. The parents tell the children that it is their problem and they have to tough it out. Handling it themselves is important because they have to learn to stand up for themselves. The effect of this advice on the children is to convince them that they are wimps and that their parents either will not or cannot help them.

Do Nothing

Parents may take this approach because they view teasing as a common and transitory event in childhood that will work itself out. Sometimes this choice is made because the parents do not know what to do, or they think that anything that they could do might exacerbate the problem.

On a superficial level it is easy to feel critical of these ineffective actions. But parents today lack a traditional framework as a support for many child-rearing decisions. Very little that their own parents did is viewed as applicable to today's children. So each generation is, in effect, starting from scratch. Also, consider the barrage of mixed messages about handling almost any problem that parents get from professionals. In the case of teasing, in the advice columns, magazine articles, and talk shows the volume of contradictory advice offered as fact is extraordinary. If parents were given as much conflicting and inappropriate advice about physical health problems as they get about behavioral problems, many children would never reach adolescence.

What Parents Should Do When a Child Is Cruelly Teased

Start by listening with empathy. This involves putting aside all the parents' ideas about teasing and making an effort to see the problem from the child's view. The parents (or parent) should sit down, look interested, and ask the child to describe the teasing, starting from the beginning. A child who is upset often has difficulty talking about it. By listening patiently, almost never interrupting, and nodding in agreement at appropriate times, the parents can help the child to provide a reasonably coherent account of the teasing. The child's account of the teasing and appraisal of it must be accepted as *fact*. Arguing or criticizing the child's handling of the problem will almost certainly inhibit further communication. The child's self-confidence is in too precarious a state to cope with blame or criticism. At best, any further conversations would be censored, and at worst, further communication about the teasing problem and other similar emotionally laden topics would be cut off.

The parents should offer unqualified social support in the form of clearly understanding the child's misery and sympathizing with it. They should assure the child that they know how painful it is to be teased because one or both of them (and any other family members of importance to the child) were teased and did not know how to handle it effectively. In casting teasing as a problem common to many, including members of the immediate family, it is essential that this not diminish the seriousness of it. Teasing is not to be endured: The child should neither accept it nor wait for it to be over. The parents must give assurances that they know of ways to stop the teasing *now* and will teach the child how to do it (see Chapter 8).

When the child has finished, the following information should be obtained if not already included in the child's report. Throughout this discussion the focus should be on the teasing rather than on the personality of the child. Without sounding indifferent, the parents should try to keep the discussion as impersonal as possible.

1. Who is the teaser and what is his or her status? Is it someone the child knows well? A friend? If so, is it likely that the purpose of the teasing is to exclude the child from a group or sever membership in it?

2. If the identity of the teaser seems unimportant, then ask about the *content* of the teasing. Is it directed to some characteristic of the child that is reversible? Or is it something such as a speech deficit that is largely irreversible?

3. Does the child appear to feel to blame for the teasing and therefore to deserve to be teased?

4. Are there problems with the teacher(s)? Does the teacher set the child up for teasing?

In the light of the information provided by the child, the parents or professionals now have a base on which to attack the problem.

Concomitantly, the parents should consider the child's pluses and minuses as objectively as possible and obtain opinions from other reliable and discrete sources. Is there anything about the child that should be worked on? Any shortcomings or faults? Great care must be taken here to avoid conveying that there is something wrong with the child.

It is pointless for the parents to advise the child simply to ignore the teasing. Such advice merely confirms the child's suspicions that they do not understand. It is almost impossible to ignore being teased without appearing to be a coward. Further, being ignored causes the teaser to intensify the verbal attack, the child's reactions become increasingly ineffective, and any remaining self-confidence dribbles away. As Kutner (1991) has noted, when the victim reacts ineffectively, the battle is lost and the child becomes an easier target next time.

Mention should be made of two courses of action frequently advocated to parents as solutions to the teasing problem. One of these, complaining to the school (Scialli, 1991), is not recommended unless it is one of the very rare schools in which there is genuine concern about teasing, combined with skill in handling it without branding the child as a tattle-tale or worse. Unfortunately, most teachers are not sympathetic about the problems of teasing (Olweus, 1993a). The other involves rewarding the teaser in some way (Spock, 1986), such as having the victim's mother invite the teaser over for a snack and friendly chat, and offering some privileges. This approach should be avoided at all costs. What it teaches the victim is first, that if someone bothers you, try to buy them off (a course of action difficult to distinguish from paying for protection) and second, that parents cannot be trusted to deal with their children's problems because they are likely to defect to the enemy.

What Parents Can Do If Their Child Is Teasing Other Children

The parents of the alleged teaser should listen to the complaint from the school or the victim's parents and make a note of specific instances and behaviors. Ideally, such complaints should be received in a low-key, objective way with the emphasis on obtaining specific details of the teasing incidents. Rebuttals at this point should be avoided, the only commitment being that the parent will talk to the teaser and get back to the complainant. Next, the parents should sit down with the child and discuss the complaints with him. If he denies the teasing, define it for him using the reported instances as examples, and discuss why the complainants would make the charges if they are untrue. Drawing on their own assessment of the child and of the complainants, the parents should come to some conclusion about the validity of the complaints. If the child appears to be telling the truth in denying the accusations, then a meeting with all involved persons might shed some light on the problem. If both factions are adamant about their interpretation of events, then the parents of the accused child should in private spell out what they mean by teasing, emphasize that the child must not engage in teasing of others, and that there would be negative consequences should he do so.

If, on the other hand, he admits to the teasing, then the parents must make it very clear that the teasing must stop immediately. They should define behaviorally what is meant by teasing, and the consequences to the child if the teasing continues. Some time should be spent with the teaser discussing the immediate and long-term effects of teasing on the victim. Have the teaser read some fictional accounts of teasing; discuss the importance of having a sympathetic imagination (seeing what a stressful event is like for another child); emphasize the potentially serious effects on the victim of being teased; and discuss some age-appropriate examples of victims who committed suicide.

Independently of the child, the parents should consider the state of the child's life. Is he under stress? Frustrated by specific ongoing events or by his failure to achieve in some respect such as making the team or being chosen for some office? Is there anything about his life that can and should be changed?

What the School Can Do for a Child Who Is Teased

As we have already noted, most schools show a discouraging lack of interest in bullying, and teasing ranks even lower on the agenda of interest and action. However, if a teacher is genuinely concerned about stopping teasing and helping a specific victim, some steps can be taken:

1. If the victim has some behaviors or other modifiable attributes that annoy others, or is lacking in skills that enhance his presence in the peer group, the teacher could work with the parents and victim to effect changes in the victim.

2. Class discussions about teasing (with no reference to the victim) could evolve from stories, role play, and problem questions about common teasing situations such as, "What should you do if you see a big boy teasing a small boy?"

3. Situations could be set up in the classroom that allow the victim to perform well. Contests or other activities involving chance could be rigged occasionally so that the victim wins.

What Is the Optimum Solution to the Problem of Vicious Teasing?

In the case of Nathan Faris described earlier, many letters to the newspaper charged his parents with negligence in failing to protect him from his tormentors. What these writers failed to grasp was that in most instances real protection is not having a stressor such as teasing eliminated by some kind of parental intervention. Instead, real protection is to teach children how to cope effectively *themselves* with most of the stressors of childhood. The fact that there are no physical or instrumental aggressive components in verbal teasing sets the stage for the victims to handle it themselves. What they need is a strategy, a plan of action to use in confronting the teaser. With a strategy they will feel less helpless, and this will reduce their anxiety and distress. With a successful strategy, children who are teased will feel an enormous sense of accomplishment. Other children will see them as ones who can manage: They may not like them any better, but they will treat them with some respect.

Admittedly, teasers enjoy some clear advantages: They can take as long as they want to think of a taunt and then wait for the ideal time to deliver it; they have the protection of strong sanctions against tattling, coupled with the known embarrassment of admitting to parents that one cannot cope with being teased. There is also the element of surprise: Victims are often caught off balance and are usually disconcerted, yet they must respond quickly and decisively if they are to stop the verbal attack and save face in front of onlookers.

Even so, it *is* possible for children to devise successful strategies, particularly if they have reason to anticipate that they will be teased. Consider the following instances:

A teenager whose school locker was adjacent to those of two boys was continually harassed with suggestive comments that were clearly intended to upset her. For some time she followed the advice of her parents and other adults and just ignored them, but it had no effect. Finally, she said, she got fed up and counterattacked:

"When they started in on me, I turned around, put on a big smile, and said in the most sultry voice I could manage, 'Well, *hello!*' They got this real shocked look on their faces and mumbled about how they had to be somewhere and they left me alone for the rest of the year." (Minton, 1994, p. 30)

A 10-year-old boy whose grandmother had knitted him a pink and blue cap wore it to school of his own volition to show appreciation of the gift. An older boy accosted him and asked what was the pink and blue for, was it his old baby bonnet or was he having twins? The 10-year-old, who had anticipated teasing, successfully silenced the teaser by snapping, "Get real, man! Don't you know what football team has these colors?"

The interviewer, who was an avid football fan, was puzzled and asked, "What team does?" The boy laughed and replied, "Heck, I don't know if any team has them. With guys like Nathan it's best to come right back and sound convincing about what you say." (J. C. Mitchell, personal communication, December 17, 1986)

Even children with markedly deviant negative attributes have been successful in devising coping strategies in the school setting. In the following instances children who were well aware that they might be subjected to verbal harassment on returning to school were able to initiate strategies to prevent teasing from occurring. Their strategies were both bold and brave:

An 11-year-old girl with leukemia who looked (in her own words) "gross, grim, and ghastly" after chemotherapy decided to bring her appearance to the attention of other children in a positive way on her return to school. On her first morning back in school she immediately took off the cap her mother had knitted for her, discussed her baldness, allowed other children to feel her head for ten cents, and set up a contest, with entrance fees, for guessing the date at which the hair at a specific point on her head would be an inch long. Her mother helped by knitting endless caps that were the envy of other girls. The caps became status symbols—she gave them out to other girls. The principal helped by giving permission for the girls to wear them in class. The girl was never teased. (D. M. Ross, Case study, Children's Hospital at Stanford, 1980)

Another example in this mode of taking the initiative before the onset of any teasing was a strategy that involved describing in detail how awful the negative attribute was: This made teasing pointless because everything that could be said had been freely acknowledged by the potential victim. The boy who thought up this tactic had an unsightly and serious skin condition that imposed severe limitations on his activities. On his first day in his new school he gave an unemotional account of the problem to the class: He described the painful treatment, showed photographs of his skin at its worst, explained the limitations, and discussed his depression about the grim outlook as well as the financial problem for his family. He was never teased and, in fact, was welcomed by the group.

Some children with deviant negative attributes were teased but were able to put an end to it very neatly. The first time he was teased, a 10-year-old boy in a wheelchair challenged his teaser to compete with him on a speed and accuracy basis in a wheelchair race. To the delight of the spectators, the teaser was hopeless in the wheelchair. This led to a schoolwide competition, with elimination trials and runoffs along with a hilarious betting system. He had social support: The principal allowed the competition including the betting, and several of the teachers helped set up the track and monitor the races.

These examples are not at all representative of the children who are established or potential victims of teasing. Very few children in this group would have the necessary attributes of bravery, confidence, and risk taking, as well as creativity in planning a novel strategy. They are included here as emphasis for our view that strategies *can* be developed for coping with teasing and that the victims *can* carry them out successfully with no negative fallout. In order to achieve these goals programs specifically designed to teach the child the skills for managing teasing are needed.

It is clear that in some respects teasing presents more problems for the target child than does bullying. Whereas bullying is invariably seen as antisocial and negative, teasing is not. It takes many forms, as evidenced by its many meanings, and the act of teasing often is characterized by an ambiguity that the target child must interpret correctly because the "right" response is of great importance in the peer group. As children wend their way through the developmental stages from early preschool to late adolescence, there is a concomitant series of changes in the teasing interactions that confront them. At each stage there is a fine line between constructive and destructive teasing and the target child or adolescent must know which side of the line the teasing is on. Cruel teasing can be an unremitting source of misery, with both short- and long-term effects of a negative nature. Some children are able to take such decisive direct action that the teaser searches for another victim. Sometimes social support is forthcoming. But for many children the outlook is dismal. Often they are unable to generate solutions to the teasing and they come to view themselves as incompetent and to blame. However, even for these children there is reason for optimism. There are teasing programs that can be easily mastered with an adult or older adolescent's help. In Chapter 8 four of the available approaches for handling teasing will be described, concluding with a detailed description of the highly successful program developed by the author (Ross, 1973; Ross & Ross, 1984).

8 Teasing Programs

UNLIKE THE PROCEDURES for stopping ongoing bullying that were described in Chapters 5 and 6, those for stopping teasing are designed to equip victims to handle teasing situations themselves. Thus, in addition to ending the misery of being teased, the victims have the immense satisfaction of having pulled off this coup with no adult present.

Since the development of the first teasing program (Ross, 1973; Ross & Ross, 1984), three other programs (Kellerman, 1981; Phillips, 1989; M. J. Smith, 1986) have appeared in the literature. All four use some or all of the following elements, in varying combinations: *Nonreward* involves not reacting overtly to the teaser in any way that would encourage further teasing. *Verbal punishment*, by contrast, has the victims striking back verbally in a way that actively discourages continued teasing. *Assertive training* focuses on changing the demeanor of the victims so that they cease to be passive recipients who appear to have no rights. *Understanding the teaser's motives* helps victims select the most effective retaliatory verbal responses and also shows them that they are not totally responsible for their status as victims. This chapter describes these programs and discusses their various strengths and weaknesses, beginning with Kellerman's nonreward approach.

KELLERMAN'S PROGRAM

Kellerman's (1981) Program is based on the fact that behavior that is consistently nonrewarded will eventually drop out, that is, extinction occurs. In his text, *Helping the Fearful Child*, Kellerman states:

> There is only one way that I know of to get rid of teasing behavior. And that is to ignore it. Most children tease, and most are teased. Teasing is

a special kind of power play. The payoff that comes from ridiculing someone else is the loss of control that the victim exhibits in terms of an angry or frustrated response. The object in teasing is to "get to the other guy" or make him "lose his cool" (translation: lose emotional control). By removing the payoff for teasing, we *extinguish* such obnoxious behavior. (pp. 97–98)

As Kellerman points out, a problem with extinction is that it does not occur immediately. Nor does the unwanted behavior follow a steady downward gradient. Instead, when behavior such as teasing has been consistently rewarded, the immediate effect of withholding reward is to intensify the teasing. Only if the victim can maintain a nonrewarding stance will the teasing eventually stop altogether. The crucial question with this program then becomes, *Can the victim hold out until the teasing stops?*, which, Kellerman cautions, may take weeks.

Should victims attempt to use nonreward, but fail, the consequences are punishing: Their misery increases and their already shaky self-esteem is further damaged. Consider our hypothetical case of two 10-year-old girls, Karen and Mary. Karen teases Mary at school every day about her clothes ("where'd you get the dress, Mary, the Salvation Army, or are you just learning to sew?") or her protruding teeth ("Here's some celery for lunch, Mary, I told my Mom we had a new little bunny at school"). Mary gets upset and shows it. Sometimes she cries. She tries unsuccessfully to avoid Karen, and her attempts at counterattacking are pathetically weak. Finally, she tells her mother, who assures her that if she just ignores Karen completely the teasing will stop. Because her mother is almost always right, Mary goes happily to school and tries to ignore Karen, only to find that Karen redoubles her efforts and the teasing becomes more severe. Mary is unable to maintain a nonreward demeanor. She lapses into her old pattern of upset and weak rejoinders, and Karen continues to enjoy teasing her.

Kellerman would attribute this result to a "maybe-the-next-time" attitude on Karen's part. Her first thought when Mary fails to respond with upset to the teasing is, "I'll keep trying. Maybe the next time I'll get her to cry." However, it also points to a failure on the part of Mary's mother to prepare her adequately: She needed to be warned about the strong possibility that the teasing would increase and she should have been given practice in ignoring the teaser. Note that Kellerman (1981) has emphasized the importance of warning the child that the teasing is likely to increase if the teaser is ignored. He also has recommended that the period between the child's first attempts to extinguish the teasing and the point at which it finally stops will be easier to endure if the power struggle can be presented as a game, a Science Experiment. In this game the victim is a scientist who is observing the teaser (an animal) and keeping a record (data collection) of the frequency of teasing. With sufficient preparation (and a child who is able to meet the demands of the nonreward method), Kellerman's approach should be successful. Consider our hypothetical case of Stevie, aged 10:

MOTHER: Hi, Stevie. How was school today?

STEVIE: That Gary! In P.E. he called me a *pansy*, and he got the guys to smell me like I was a flower. And at lunch he said I was a drip and to turn off the tap. Very funny! *They* all laughed.

MOTHER: I bet you didn't like that at all. I would have hated it.

STEVIE: He makes me feel terrible and kinda stupid. And the guys *always* laugh.

MOTHER: You know, this reminds me of how I was teased in fifth grade. I was *really* fat and they'd say, 'What's shaking? Oh, it's just Porky Peggy. Hi, Fatso.' I used to cry. I hated them and I hated going to school.

STEVIE: *You* were teased, Mom?

MOTHER: Sure. So were Daddy and Roger (older brother). It doesn't mean there's anything wrong with you. Most kids get teased. I know how you can stop it. I know a way that worked for Roger. You want to try it?

STEVIE: Sure, Mom. Hey, imagine *Roger* getting teased!

MOTHER: Well, when Gary teases you, don't look mad, don't look upset, act as if Gary isn't there at all. Look very, very interested in something else that's going on.

STEVIE: That sounds hard to do. Like Gary is *right there* calling me a cupcake or something.

MOTHER: It *is* hard at first. But you can do it. Gary only teases you because he can see that it makes you mad. Being able to make kids like you mad makes Gary feel good. He feels powerful like Superman. What would help you a lot is if you could get *interested* in the teasing like you would in a game.

STEVIE: [Outraged] Mom, this *isn't* a game.

MOTHER: It could be a sort of game. How many times does Gary tease you in a week? Five times, ten, twenty?

STEVIE: Hundreds of times.

MOTHER: [Laughing] This game is called Lucky Number. [She gets out playing cards excluding face cards, and two envelopes which she labels "Mother" and "Stevie."] Now pick two cards and don't look at them and put them in a sealed envelope with fifty cents. Here's a card with 16 squares. Starting Monday you put an X in a square every time Gary teases you. Keep the card where other kids can't see it and on Friday we'll count up the Xs and look at our cards and whoever has a card closest to the number of Xs wins all the money. If there are a lot of Xs you can add up your two cards if that would get you closer. If your card(s) is exactly the same as the number of Xs you win *double* the money.

STEVIE: Wow! It's like what we do in science, data collection.

MOTHER: That's right. Now when Gary teases you and you ignore him, what do you think will happen?

STEVIE: He stops teasing me. Right?

MOTHER: Wrong. He tries harder to make you mad, he gets meaner. He knows you've always been a good one to tease—you get mad. Gary thinks, 'Why isn't Stevie upset the way he used to be? I'll have to try harder.' And he does. So what do you do?

STEVIE: Keep ignoring him?

MOTHER: Right. You have to say to yourself, 'I can outlast you, Gary, keep trying, it won't get you anywhere.' And you must not slip up and get upset, not even once. Now, I wonder who will win the game. Let's practice. I'll be Gary and I'll tease you and you show me how you ignore him. [They practice, then reverse the roles. Stevie performs competently.]

MOTHER: Good work, Stevie. You didn't look upset at the things I said and you didn't even look as if you heard me. Remember this will work as long as you can outlast Gary. He is sure to get meaner the minute he sees that you are trying to put a stop to the teasing. After a few more tries he'll probably go off and find someone else to tease because you know what?

STEVIE: What?

MOTHER: You're stronger than he is. You know what's going on so you aren't going to slip up and get mad when he teases. I wonder who has the lucky card.

Although Kellerman does not make any specific suggestions about the mother's behavior during role play, we recommend that the following procedure be used. When the child is first acting as the teaser it is essential that the mother (victim) make errors, for example, she should look upset and look as if she is trying to ignore the teaser but cannot quite manage it. In other words, she must act as a *coping model* (Thelen, Fry, Fehrenbach, & Frautschi, 1979), one who performs poorly at first but gradually improves. The rationale for this procedure is as follows: Being teased has been a very painful experience for the victim. It is not easy for him to acquire these new responses even in the safety of role play with his mother. By having his mother experience some difficulty, the child is unlikely to feel discouraged by his own less-than-perfect performance. However, if the mother acts as a *mastery model* (Thelen et al., 1979) by immediately exhibiting effortless competence and great self-confidence, the child may be easily discouraged and decide that the task is too difficult for him.

Note that the game serves a dual purpose. It adds a note of interest to the teasing experience with a consequent lessening of the victim's negative response to the teasing. If the victim tends to exaggerate the negative aspects of the teasing situation, that is, to catastrophize (he is teased "hundreds of times"), the game provides an accurate record of the frequency of teasing.

Comment

Kellerman's program has a narrow focus, with its emphasis on nonreward. As a concept, nonreward has both theoretical and applied support and is unquestionably an effective tactic. The problem lies in the difficulty most teasing victims have in meeting its no-response requirement. It is often difficult for victims to remain completely silent in a teasing interaction. If they walk briskly and purposefully away from the teaser, remaining silent should not pose any problem, although it could result in the teaser taunting them about being too "chicken" to stay. But if they are rooted to the spot by the teasing, it may be very difficult for them not to reply. Because there is no provision in this program for teaching the victims effective retaliatory verbal responses, they may respond with weak rejoinders or ineffective denials that lessen the impact of showing no upset and cancel out the strategy of ignoring the teaser. It would be easier for the victims to remain silent if in addition to presenting a calm front they were also taught some nonverbal behaviors that they should exhibit. The teaser's sense of being ignored would be heightened if the victims yawned sometimes and looked around the area. If others are present, the victims could occasionally laugh at some ongoing event at a distance from the teaser. These behaviors would convey an important positive message to the teaser and at the same time give the victims something concrete to do. One final point: It takes longer to bring an end to the teasing because the teaser does not grasp that the victims are slipping away until some time after their nonreward strategy has been introduced. During this interval the victims are subjected to an intensified attack and are equipped with only the one strategy to handle it.

PHILLIPS'S PROGRAM

Phillips (1989), like Kellerman (1981) uses nonreward for helping a victim put an end to painful teasing. In the following case study she preceded the teasing training with a series of therapy sessions because the child was singularly lacking in assertive skills. Phillips defines assertiveness in operational terms, for example, being able to express one's feelings easily and calmly rather than aggressively or with hostility; being straightforward and forthright in difficult situations rather than embarrassed or defensive; and being an active person rather than a passive one. Note that being assertive does not involve being overbearing, pushy, or aggressive. Rather, it is the ability to act in a confident way, be competent in social situations, and cope effectively in everyday social interactions as well as in conflict situations. Phillips's approach to teaching a child assertive skills and how to combat teasing is described in sufficient detail in her book (*How to Give Your Child a Great Self-Image*, 1989) that any competent and caring parent could use it to help a school-age child or adolescent to become more assertive in teasing interactions and consequently more competent in handling such attacks.

It is our opinion that most children who are teased could benefit from learning how to be more assertive, which does not mean that they need therapy sessions. Instead, most children who are experiencing ongoing teasing can benefit from some practice in looking and sounding confident and untroubled when teased, maintaining a relaxed stance and eye contact with the teaser, and not backing off when confronted by the teaser.

The case of Rachel, age 10, reported by Phillips (1989), provides a good example of her approach. Rachel's problems started when she entered a new school. Although she was unquestionably intelligent and quite creative, all her fellow students saw was a short, underdeveloped, unimpressive-looking girl who seemed to be a good target for teasing. She was teased wherever she went in her school. Although there were other students who normally would have been friends with her, they were intimidated by those who were harassing her, and the teasing had escalated to being vicious. A boy on her school bus, for example, told her, "You're ugly. You're the ugliest girl on the bus." Another boy in her homeroom said, "I bet you don't even wear a bra yet," and a girl whose name she did not know approached her and said, "No boy will ever ask *you* out." When the class had to fill out medical forms, someone said, "I wonder what Rachel is going to put down for 'sex' " and everybody laughed.

Rachel's parents knew that she was miserable, but only gradually was Rachel able to tell them that she was being teased and did not like anything about the new school. They did what most caring parents do—they assured her that the teasers were insecure and that many people that they had known as children had grown up to be successful and popular despite earlier teasing. Rachel's parents then went further by admitting that they had been teased and had tried unsuccessfully to stop the teasing by such tactics as crying, lying, running away, fighting back, one-upping, tattling, and changing their behavior to "suit" their tormentors. They then sought professional help from Phillips.

Phillips focused first on training Rachel to become more assertive, the goal being to help her to feel stronger, which, in turn, could be expected to manifest itself in an assured, confident demeanor that would discourage teasing. Through a combination of positive reinforcement and empathic listening Phillips was able gradually to get Rachel to express her feelings freely. She was not allowed to be merely a passive recipient of treatment but, instead, was assigned homework that required her to think about her feelings and translate her thoughts into action by expressing her feelings to others in her family. None of this was easy for Rachel, but with Phillips' help she persevered with great success. Only when Rachel showed that she could express her feelings to a variety of people within and outside the family did Phillips turn to the teasing problem.

Knowing how uncomfortable Rachel was about the teasing, Phillips proceeded cautiously. She elicited information about a great moment in Rachel's life when, at her previous school, she had been given a standing ovation for her performance in the school play. Phillips then instructed Rachel in how to use this experience as an escape hatch whenever talking or thinking about the teasing made her anxious or upset. Rachel's task was to substitute thoughts about her success in the play whenever any aspect of the teasing or any other aspects of her life bothered her.

Phillips had also learned who was teasing Rachel, what they said, and how she reacted. Using role play, including reversal of roles, she taught Rachel to respond to teasing in an assertive and nondefensive manner by standing up straight, making extended eye contact (looking the teaser straight in the eye and not looking away), not showing any upset, and never arguing. In fact, not responding verbally at all unless what the teaser said was true, in which case Rachel was to agree in an unemotional but nondefensive way

("You're right. I do have hundreds of freckles."). Agreeing is disconcerting to the teaser, it deflates him or her and reduces the impact of the teasing.

To combat the problem of remaining silent, a demand most children find difficult, Phillips taught Rachel to use an *emotional shrug*, that is, to assume a demeanor that conveys "So what," or "Who cares, I don't." It is a look of confidence and indifference that indicates that the teasing really does not matter at all. Although this method was hard to master, Rachel persevered and soon noticed that she was being teased less and less. She also found that when she was teased she felt "stronger and more in control" (Phillips, 1989, p. 133). Her weekly therapy sessions dwindled to monthly sessions and then stopped altogether. At last report Rachel was no longer being teased. A measure of the value of Phillips's approach was that Rachel attributed the change to her self-confidence and assertiveness rather than to a change of heart on the part of the teasers.

Comment

Phillips's program offers a number of important features for the adult who wants to help a child combat teasing. It is easy to teach. Procedures such as role play along with reversal of roles, homework assignments that put some responsibility on the victim, thought substitution, the emotional shrug, and positive reinforcement are clearly described and skillfully incorporated into the teaching sessions. For children such as Rachel, beginning with assertive training means a significant delay in attacking the teasing problem with its attendant misery. Phillips's program, like Kellerman's, requires the victim to remain silent in the teasing interaction (except in Phillips's case when the victim agrees that a tease is indeed true); it is often difficult for a child to do this. We suggest having some nonverbal behaviors that the victim should exhibit in order to fill the verbal gap.

SMITH'S PROGRAM

The third teasing program was developed by M. J. Smith (1986) and included in a guide for parents to use in teaching children and adolescents to be assertive. Titled *Yes, I Can Say No*, it describes his Social Thinking and Reasoning Program, referred to as STAR. The emphasis throughout the program is on teaching the child what to say in social conflict situations such as coping with peer pressure, rather than on what to do. To this end Smith teaches a set of general verbal strategies and skills for use in coping with a wide variety of conflict situations. Included in this set are:

- *Free Information.* Information you provide spontaneously without having to be prompted. It is the basis of good social conversation.
- *Self-Disclosure.* Making personal statements about yourself, expressing opinions about what you think, and describing how you feel. This strategy makes it easier for the other person to talk to you because he or she can become involved by following up on your personal statements: It can turn a stilted verbal exchange into a two-way conversation.
- *Fogging.* Agreeing with another person's critical comments about you when there is no objective way of proving whether they are correct. It involves responding to the other person's *observations* about your behavior, ideas, and so on, but not to his or her *judgment* about them ("Perhaps I am." "Maybe.").
- *Mirroring.* Repeating back what has just been said.
- *Broken Record.* Saying what you want to say over and over again until the other person realizes he or she is getting nowhere with you. Prefacing a Broken Record comment with a Mirroring statement helps to convince the other person that he or she is getting nowhere.
- *Positive Assertion.* Stating that you are right. Asserting your positive qualities.
- *Negative Assertion.* Agreeing with a critic that what he or she says about you is true, or admitting that you have made a mistake. Note that where Fogging is somewhat ambiguous, Negative Assertion is clear-cut.
- *Negative Inquiry.* Exploring the other person's opinion in a nonchallenging and nonthreatening way rather than apparently accepting it (as in Mirroring).
- *Workable Compromise.* Assuming that something can be worked out so that both participants gain something from the interaction.

Smith (1986) states that the teaching format for his program is based on one principle: Give an idea, then practice on an example. The child must learn the strategies by rote, understand what each one can accomplish, and then practice them in as many different social interactions and conflict situations as possible. Considerable practice is required because children do not easily transfer skills, such as those learned in one situation in this program, to similar situations outside, if there is anxiety associated with the second situation. To provide the practice needed for such transfer of training to occur, Smith includes sample dialogues demonstrating their use in a wide variety of social interactions that are likely to be encountered by children and adolescents. When the specific topic is teasing, Smith (1986) asserts unequivocally that chronic teasing can be extinguished simply and effectively with his method. Children learn how to respond to teasing in an assertive but nondefensive and unemotional way. With the help of selected assertive verbal skills, the child's behavior when teased changes from an automatic and ineffective response ("can so," "it is not," "are not") to a voluntary thinking response.

In support of the efficacy of his program, Smith (1986) describes its use with 8-year-old Mary, a shy self-conscious girl who was teased unmercifully by her brother and her second-grade classmates. When Mary's rate of absenteeism increased with a concomitant fall in her grades, her teacher and a psychologist experienced in the use of the STAR program devised a plan to help her. First, they gave a few students in Mary's class demonstrations on how to cope assertively with teasers. The children were told that using the STAR techniques would lessen a child's upset when teased and at the same time would exhaust the teaser by repeatedly seeking explanatory information about the topic of teasing without any sign of upset. After several demonstrations, Mary volunteered to participate in a trial. The rest of the class were told to tease and criticize her. For 20 minutes the psychologist coached Mary on how to respond assertively to her classmates' taunts. Smith (1986) states that by the end of the demonstration Mary could handle their teasing. Further, during the following weeks she used her newly acquired skill repeatedly with no help from others to cope with being teased.

In evaluating the coaching by the STAR psychologist, it would be helpful to know whether he or she provided Mary with *specific responses* (for example, "I don't understand. What is it that I do that makes you call me stupid?") or made *general suggestions* about how to reply ("Keep asking her questions about why she doesn't like your dress."). In any case, what this classroom demonstration shows is that during what was probably a 40- to 45-minute session that included discussion by a psychologist about a single assertive response, Negative Inquiry, demonstration of its use by peer models, and 20 minutes of intensive coaching of the target child, Mary learned to use this procedure and transferred the learning to the playground. It is a far cry from this level of competence with one assertive response to the level of expertise with multiple assertive responses to teasing that is demonstrated in Dialogues 70 (pp. 202–204) and 72 (pp. 207–209).

In our following hypothetical dialogue illustrating the application of Smith's procedures, a 12-year-old girl struggles ineffectively in a defensive and nonassertive way to deal with teasing by her 15-year-old sister. The younger girl is working on a poster when her sister enters the room:

OLDER SISTER: What's the great Picasso doing now?

YOUNGER SISTER: [Reluctant to show work but does so after persuasion.] It's my Safety Contest poster. I think it might win a prize.

OLDER SISTER: Get real! A dumb poster like *that*? Well, if no one else goes in the contest . . . or if only preschoolers do.

YOUNGER SISTER: *That's mean!* Why do you always make fun of me?

OLDER SISTER: I'm saving you from making a fool of yourself and looking even stupider than you are. You're too stupid to know you should just forget the contest.

YOUNGER SISTER: All you know is how to be mean. I thought it was looking good and now you've ruined it.

OLDER SISTER: What's ruined? There's nothing to ruin.

YOUNGER SISTER: There is so. I've been working on this for more than two hours.

OLDER SISTER: Well, you must be *really* stupid to spend that long on a pathetic poster like this.

YOUNGER SISTER: [crying] It is *not* pathetic.

OLDER SISTER: Sure it is. It's making you cry, isn't it?

YOUNGER SISTER: Mother!

A second dialogue shows the younger girl responding according to Smith's program, that is, in a nondefensive but assertive way in the face of her sister's gibes:

OLDER SISTER: What's the great Picasso doing now?

YOUNGER SISTER: [Reluctant to show work but does so after persuasion.] It's my Safety Contest poster. I think it might win a prize [Self-Disclosure].

OLDER SISTER: Get real! A dumb poster like *that*? Well, if no one else goes in the contest . . . or if only preschoolers do.

YOUNGER SISTER: You think it's dumb [Mirroring]. What's dumb about this poster [Negative Inquiry]?

OLDER SISTER: I just told you. It's dumb like all your pitiful attempts at art. Like when something's *dumb*, it's dumb.

YOUNGER SISTER: Maybe [Fogging]. But I still don't know what's dumb about it [Negative Inquiry and Broken Record]. I'd like it if you'd tell me some specific things in it that make it seem dumb to you [Self-Disclosure].

OLDER SISTER: You go on and on like a stuck record. It's like you don't know many words. Like you're as dumb as your poster.

YOUNGER SISTER: How about if I give you time to think what *exactly* is dumb about it [Workable Compromise]?

OLDER SISTER: I'm getting out of here. [Leaves in disgust.]

In sensitive situations such as being overweight, just learning not to be unduly upset is rewarding for the child being teased. In the following dialogue based on Smith's method, an obese girl keeps her composure by responding in a nondefensive, assertive, and unemotional way to a teaser:

TEASER: Here is Hippo the Blimp getting fatter every day.

VICTIM: You're right. I am getting fatter [Fogging].

TEASER: You're the fattest kid in the whole school. Soon you'll need two desks.

VICTIM: I probably will. I've never seen anyone fatter than me at school [Fogging].

TEASER: I hate looking at you.

VICTIM: Why do you look at me if you hate it [Negative Inquiry]?

TEASER: I just told you, you bucket of lard. Because you're so fat, you're *gross!*

VICTIM: What else makes you hate looking at me [Negative Inquiry]?

TEASER: Would you stop asking so many questions?

VICTIM: I don't understand why it bothers you [Self-Disclosure].

TEASER: I've got better things to do than talk to you [Leaves].

VICTIM: I'm sure you do [Fogging].

Comment

On the basis of his experience in using the STAR program to teach children assertive skills, Smith (1986, p. 202) contends that "chronic teasing can be extinguished simply and effectively" with the foregoing procedures. This statement implies that his assertive training can be readily mastered by the average child. It is an erroneous conclusion. A child would have considerable work to do before approaching the level of competence evident in the Chronic

Teasing Dialogues No. 70 (pp. 202–204) and No. 72 (pp. 207–209) in *Yes, I Can Say No* (Smith). Learning the general strategies by rote first and then understanding what each one can accomplish is a major task in itself. Furthermore, a substantial amount of practice would be needed in a wide variety of social situations for a child to become competent in selecting at a moment's notice the appropriate strategy for a specific ongoing conflict situation. To use the strategy effectively constitutes a further challenge. However, once a child has mastered the assertive techniques in Smith's program there is no question that there would be immediate and long-term benefits.

A surprising omission in the STAR program concerns the *nonverbal* components of assertiveness. No mention is made of teaching children to stand up straight, look the teaser in the eye, and try for a neutral look devoid of upset. Nor is any attention paid to eliminating defensive behaviors such as backing away from the teaser, folding arms across one's chest, or fidgeting from one foot to the other. It is a mistake to assume that the nonverbal components of assertiveness will appear spontaneously as the child experiences some success in coping with teasing by using the verbal procedures in this program.

THE ROSS TEASING PROGRAM

Ross (1973; Ross & Ross, 1984) designed the Ross Teasing Program to teach victims of ongoing teasing strategies to stop the teasing.* The underlying rationale of this approach is as follows: Teasers expect their victims to show upset, exhibit avoidance or withdrawal, and be ineffective in retaliation attempts. They are unlikely to continue teasing children who appear to be untroubled by the teasing, who stand their ground in an assertive but not aggressive way, and, above all, who counterattack promptly and effectively. Effecting these changes in children who are teased is the goal of this program.

The program is for individual school-age children and adolescents of normal or above-normal intelligence for whom ongoing teasing clearly is a problem. It can also be used as a preventive intervention with children who are unequivocally at risk for teasing, such as the facially disfigured child. The program should *not* be used with children for whom teasing is a problem secondary to other kinds of bullying, particularly physical aggression. It should never be used in schools in which guns and knives are commonplace.

---

*© 1973, Ross. Reprinted by permission.

Most children complete the program in 3 to 5 hours, spread over several days or a week. No teaching session should exceed 1 hour, and for some younger children, a full hour may be too long. The program falls logically into four parts. It is essential to stay with one part until the tasks in it have all been mastered. Children must be allowed to work through the program at their own pace. Should a child clearly be unable to handle the demands of the program, some other intervention should be considered. Under no circumstances should the child be forced to continue. There should be no direct or implied suggestion either of incompetence or of terminating the program midway.

Any competent adult or older adolescent can teach the program. An assistant, who may be an adult, adolescent, or child, is needed to help with role-play demonstrations. Having the child's parent(s) teaching or assisting is an advantage because the more knowledgeable they are about the program, the more supportive they can be. Any siblings who participate must be congenial with the child, sympathetic about the teasing, and completely trustworthy about *never* discussing the ongoing program with outsiders. There have been instances of siblings telling others about the program, with the result that the victim was confronted with merciless taunts about going to "teasing school."

Between training sessions, practice in the form of homework usually reduces the time needed to complete the program. For some of the homework tasks, it helps to have someone in the home environment work with the child. Children will become proficient in handling staged teasing incidents during the lessons. But if the program is to benefit them, they must also be able to use their new skills in outside situations, that is, they must be able to generalize. Because generalization usually does not occur spontaneously, it is intentionally worked into this program through homework assignments and other procedures.

In the following description of the program the person teaching it will be referred to as the Teacher, the assistant as the Helper, and the child as the Victim. Note that whenever examples of teasing sequences are used, the teaser should be the same age and gender and in the same grade as the Victim. A brief outline of the program's content appears in Table 8.1.

Part One

Begin by giving high priority to reassurance and face saving. Victims, especially boys, often feel defensive and embarrassed about being teased, particularly if the teaser is the same age. Assure the

Table 8.1 Ross Teaching Program

Part One

Provide reassurance about the normalcy of being teased and consequent upset.
Explain that Victim's own behavior partly determines whether teasing will occur
  and whether it will continue.
Assure Victim that there are ways to stop ongoing teasing.
Discuss the concept of *payoff*.
Explain procedure for role play demonstrations.
Teach four nonverbal behaviors that the Victim must not exhibit when teased.

Part Two

Review payoff and nonverbal behaviors that must not be exhibited during teasing.
  Teach nonverbal behaviors that must be used.
Have Victim act as a critic as well as a participant in role play.
When Victim is competent, he must use the appropriate nonverbal behaviors in the
  actual teasing situation.
Explain that Victim is to collect data in the teasing situation.

Part Three

Victim learns verbal retort strategies, beginning with the mildest (nonreward) and
  continuing with the more severe (punishing) strategies.
Victim chooses strategies to use in the next actual teasing situation.

Part Four

Criteria for initiating a test run in the actual teasing situation.
Importance of reporting back after first trial.
Criteria for considering the Program a success.

Victim that it is normal to be upset about being teased. It does not
mean that he is a wimp or a sissy. Tell him that he will soon learn
how to stop the teasing. Misery loves company (Cottrell & Epley,
1977), so the Victim will feel more at ease with a Teacher who has
experienced the stress of childhood teasing and talks freely about it.
If possible, obtain anecdotes from the Victim's parents, too, about
being teased and not knowing how to handle it.

In your account of how you (the Teacher) were teased as a child,
work in the following ideas. You did not know how to handle being
teased or what to say to the teaser, and you were so upset that
sometimes you cried. You tried to avoid the teaser, but he always
found you. You were too embarrassed to tell your parents or teacher.
The teaser teased you for a long time and got other children to tease
you, too. Use your account of being teased to introduce two important ideas that the Victim must accept: How a child behaves often
determines whether he will be teased at all and, second, how he
reacts when being teased usually determines whether the teasing
will continue.

To help the Victim understand why children are teased, discuss the concept of *payoff*, that is, the effect of reward on behavior. Start with some age- and gender-appropriate examples of payoff (reward): A girl babysits because she earns money (payoff) doing it; a boy works hard at swimming so that he can make the school team and go to swimming meets (payoff). Ask would they continue to do these things if there were no *payoff*? Emphasize that payoff may take many forms, for example, satisfaction, pleasure, or feelings of accomplishment, in addition to monetary benefits.

Now discuss the payoff for the teaser in the Teacher's story. Explain that it made the teaser feel good, powerful, and in control to upset someone else, to see them cry, and have them be afraid. Stress that as long as a child makes teasing pay off by acting upset, crying, hiding from the teaser, and not telling someone who could stop the teasing, the teaser will keep on teasing. Help the Victim to see that by providing payoff, he is largely responsible for keeping the teasing going.

Next, have the Victim watch while you show him how a mean kid named Jeffrey teased a boy you know and ask the Victim to tell you what the payoff is for Jeffrey. The Teacher and Helper now role play a sequence in which the Helper, acting as Jeffrey, calls the Teacher names. The Teacher looks upset, stands in a hunched-up position not looking at Jeffrey, moves away cautiously, starts to cry, and mumbles, "I am not." The teasing continues. Discuss what the Teacher did that was payoff for Jeffrey.

The Victim may find this demonstration upsetting because he is seeing *for the first time* how he looks when being teased, an unquestionably powerful learning experience and motivator. Some Victims start to cry. One 10-year-old boy said, "I'm a *real* wimp. I oughta just hang a sign around my neck that says, 'Kick me. I won't do nothing if you do.'" But not every Victim is upset by this demonstration. Some watch the role play with interest and are able to state clearly what the payoff is and how the victim (the Teacher) should have acted.

Ask, "What would happen if the teasing did not have any payoff? What if the boy had not become upset when Jeffrey teased him? That's not much fun for Jeffrey, is it?" Role play this sequence, then tell the Victim that a teaser *may not stop* after just getting no payoff once. He will *probably* try harder to get the victim upset. Why? Because he does not want to lose someone who has given him a lot of payoff. But assure the Victim that if he keeps on not getting upset, the teasing will stop. Role play a sequence in which Jeffrey tries harder and the Teacher doesn't give him the payoff he wants so, after several attempts, Jeffrey just walks away.

Next, the Victim must learn not to exhibit the following nonverbal behaviors when teased:

1. *Any kind of upset* such as crying or looking embarrassed
2. *Physical withdrawal* such as moving away or deliberately trying to avoid the teaser
3. *Making any kind of physical contact* with the teaser because even minor physical contact can escalate into behavior, such as pushing or hitting, that is likely to result in punishment from school personnel
4. *Standing so close to the teaser* that it implies threat

Using role play by the Teacher and Helper, demonstrate behaviors from each of the above categories. Make a simple, easy-to-read list of these nonverbal behaviors, and assign for homework the task of thinking which of the incorrect ones he shows when teased. If possible, someone in the Victim's family should work with him so that he can practice not looking upset and so on.

The Victim must master the content of Part One before starting on Part Two.

Part Two

Review payoff and the nonverbal behaviors that the Victim must *not* show, then move on to the nonverbal behaviors that the Victim *should* show when teased. He must:

1. Look interested, laugh sometimes, appear to be untroubled, yawn sometimes, suddenly stare at something going on elsewhere, and then, if appropriate, turn to the teaser and ask him what he had just said.
2. Assume an *assertive* rather than a *passive* stance. He must stand his ground, feet slightly apart, arms at side or hands in pockets (this suggests confidence that nothing of a physical attack nature is going to happen).
3. Maintain eye contact with the teaser, a very important move.
4. Move closer to the teaser rather than moving away.

In trying to look interested or bored, some victims may present exaggerated versions of these expressions (De Paulo, 1992). As you use role play to demonstrate each of the above nonverbal behaviors, try to overdo some of them. Laugh too much, for example, or lean forward and stare instead of just maintaining eye contact as you would in normal conversation. When you do this, have the Helper tell you to stop, demonstrate the exaggerated behavior, and then give you a hand mirror so that you can see how you look.

It is not easy to control facial expressions under conditions of stress. The Victim will soon see that the intent to present a particular facial expression cannot always be accomplished successfully (De Paulo, 1992). Nor will it be easy for the Victim to exhibit nonverbal behaviors, such as an assertive stance, to convey an external impression that is at odds with his internal state. For homework the Victim must learn these behaviors and then practice in front of a mirror, first being the teaser making a mean remark and then being himself exhibiting the appropriate behaviors. Demonstrate these sequences for the Victim and have him practice them.

Start having the Victim act as a *critic*. Have the Teacher and Helper use role play to show a teasing interaction in which the Helper exhibits some nonverbal behaviors that he *should not* use and some that he *should*. Have the Victim sit on the sideline and when the role play ends, ask him to tell the Helper how he should have reacted. This critique procedure allows the Victim to be the "expert" as well as to have some control over the situation, both being experiences that he sorely needs.

Next, repeat the role play with the Helper following the Victim's instruction in a not too competent way that leaves room for improvement. The Helper, for example, might withdraw a bit or start by looking untroubled but then look upset. With this degree of semi-competence the helper becomes a *coping model* who initially does not perform perfectly but clearly tries hard. The rationale for some Helper incompetence is based on the following points. It is not easy for the Victim to make these quite drastic behavioral changes. If the Helper, too, is somewhat incompetent at first and gradually improves, the Victim will feel more at ease when he participates in the role play than he would if the Helper performed with the ease and confidence of a *mastery model*. Coping models are more effective than mastery models in reducing anxiety and uncertainty in the observer (Meichenbaum, 1971). Also, the idea that both the Teacher and Helper make "mistakes" serves to focus the Victim's attention.

The Victim and Teacher now role play a teasing interaction while the Helper sits on the sidelines and provides feedback in the form of specific descriptions of what was done correctly and praise for it, as well as comments on what needs to be done differently. (In these interactions, concentrate on the nonverbal behaviors that the Victim *should* show but also work in some that he *should not* show.) The Victim and Teacher reenact the sequence and then they reverse roles. Role play in which the Victim first plays himself and then takes the teaser's role serves as a vehicle for integrating and mastering the teasing experience. It allows the Victim to see teasing from the viewpoint of the teaser, thus giving him a different perspective about being teased.

When the Victim demonstrates competence in the nonverbal behaviors that he *should* show, he must use them outside when he is teased. Encourage him to reward his efforts with positive self-statements, for example, "I'm really eyeballing him, I bet he's wondering what's going on." He must also report back to the Teacher, who should show great interest and approval of any reported success. Sometimes have the Victim show how he acted, so that you can both enjoy his success. Some Victims stated that when they used the nonverbal behaviors the teasers sometimes were "real nasty, meaner, and talked louder," but did not stop teasing. Use any such reports to review the payoff idea, that the teaser might have sensed a change in the Victim and so had redoubled his attacks to ensure that the Victim remained a victim. Emphasize that the teaser's behavior shows that the Victim's tactics are having a real effect and so far, the Victim has not even said one word!

When the Victim has clearly assimilated the nonverbal behavior tasks, tell him that soon he will learn what to say when he is teased. Explain that for this step you need his help because what he says has to *fit* the teasing. Explain *fit* using examples such as clothes fitting, or having the right tool for a job. Ask the Victim to start the next time he is teased to remember exactly what the teaser says and to write it down *as soon as possible*. Give him a small notebook and treat him as an expert, an essential member of the team. Gear the job title to the Victim's age, for example, data collector, ace reporter, advance scout, or scientist.

The whole data collection experience should be as enhancing as possible for the Victim. When he reports actual taunts, show great enthusiasm, for example, "That's a winner!" "We'll get him if he tries that one again." "We'll nail him for that one, we can think of something better for you to say back." If the Teacher and Helper show clearly that the Victim's input is valuable, he will begin to see being teased as a source of ammunition to use against the teaser, rather than solely as persecution against himself.

One 7-year-old boy who was working very industriously at collecting the teaser's taunts absent-mindedly replied, "Hey, that's a great one—we can use that," after a particularly nasty crack. The teaser was clearly disconcerted at the Victim's comment and asked what he meant. The Victim, who was becoming increasingly confident, just laughed and for the first time *the teaser walked away* (D. M. Ross, Case study, University of California, San Francisco, 1976). Parents sometimes express concern that rehashing the teasing episodes will upset the Victim further. In fact, it often defuses the teasing because the Victim places a less painful interpretation on it. An 11-year-old girl said:

> It's real interesting how I feel now about Missy teasing me. Like I really have to listen carefully because I'm in the front line and the people back in the planning room are counting on *me* to bring in the reports. And I have to remember them 'till I can write them down. I just don't have time to get upset at what she says and anyway it sorta doesn't seem so bad anymore. (D. M. Ross, Case Studies, University of California, San Francisco, 1976)

Part Three

Even if the Victim handles his nonverbal behavior correctly when he is teased, his remaining silent has an element of payoff because the teaser can interpret the silence as upset or fear. What the Victim needs now is the quick, *specific* retort that fits the teaser's scornful comments. Generalities such as "Are not," "Who says?" and "You're crazy" are very weak retorts lacking any element of fit. By now the Teacher will have accumulated a list of specific taunts and topics of attack by the teaser for use in building up a retort repertoire. Retort strategies range in a hierarchy from mildest (nonreward) to strongest (punishing). We will cover the nonreward category first because even the mildest retort can become a major hurdle for the Victim who has never previously made a strong rebuttal. Although it is usually best to begin with the least threatening (to the Victim) and proceed up the hierarchy from there, occasionally a Victim will react negatively to the nonreward strategies and ask for something "more mean like what he says to me." When this occurs, bypass the nonreward strategies and teach the punishing ones.

It is important for the victim to know what not to say. If the teaser's comment about the victim is true, the victim must neither deny it nor argue. Instead, the comment should be either ignored or agreed with. When onlookers see that the victim does not deny what is clearly true, the tease is defused and the victim's other retorts gain stature.

There are three nonreward strategies: Exhausting the topic, making an asset of the topic, and giving the teaser permission to tease. The teaching procedure for all of the retort strategies is as follows. First, the Teacher and Helper enact one of the teasing interactions (with teaser payoff) that the Victim has actually experienced. Then they repeat it using a retort strategy combined with the nonverbal behaviors that should be exhibited. Next, all three discuss the strategy, think of other replies the Victim might have made, and then the Teacher and Victim reenact them. The Helper watches, offers suggestions, and gives a critique of their performance.

Nonreward Retort Strategies

1. Exhausting the Topic: This is a good strategy to use when the teaser's taunts are true. The Victim must first acknowledge in a matter-of-fact, unemotional tone that what the teaser says is true. He then shows interest in hearing more about the topic. In the following scenario the teaser taunts the victim about being fat:

TEASER: Fatty, fatty, two by four. Can't get through the kitchen door.

VICTIM: You're right . . . I am fat. [Moves closer, makes eye contact, shows no upset.] Could you say some more about fatties like me?

TEASER: You're beyond fat, you're like a hippo.

VICTIM: Yes, I am very, very, large. When did you first get interested in kids like hippos?

TEASER: Who says I'm interested? All I'm saying is you're a big blob of fat.

VICTIM: You're quite right. I am a big blob. Tell me more.

TEASER: Oh, shut up.

Some teasers lose interest at this point. Others redouble their efforts to get a rise out of the Victim. No matter what the teaser says, the Victim continues to agree, act interested, show no upset, and seek more information.

2. Making an Asset of the Topic: This strategy is most useful when the teaser's taunt is indisputably true and the Victim is *clearly* not to blame for the target characteristic. It has proven particularly successful with leukemic children whose baldness and pallor are the aftermath of chemotherapy (Ross & Ross, 1984). The Victim's task is to look undisturbed, reply quickly, acknowledge the truth of the taunt, and point out the positive aspects of the characteristic. The Teacher knows in advance what this Victim will be teased about and should help him think of replies:

TEASER: Hey, guys, look at Steve! Is that a head or a skating rink?

VICTIM: Hi, Mitch. You're right. Not one hair. You know what's great about it? [Pauses while teaser looks puzzled.] You don't *know*? It's the *only time* in my whole life that I could wash my hair in 10 seconds.

TEASER: You look like a freak from Mars. I bet it never grows in.

VICTIM: I sure do look like outer space, but I hope it doesn't grow in for a while. If it just stays this way till Halloween I'm going trick and treating as E.T. [Telly Savalas or some other bald TV or athletic star].

3. *Giving the Teaser Permission to Tease:* This strategy was suggested by Dr. Edna Durbach, who has also made a video (Durbach, 1993) demonstrating the Ross Teasing Program. At the first taunt the Victim takes control by saying kindly to the teaser that he can say that if it makes him feel good. Being given permission to tease is very irritating, but often the teaser is genuinely puzzled about why it is irritating:

TEASER: Wow, Karen, where did you get that freaky dress? Straight from Dudsville! Did your little sister make it?

VICTIM: [Smiling sweetly] You can say that if you want to, Cheryl. Don't stop.

TEASER: Gee, you're *stupid*, Karen.

VICTIM: You can say that as much as you want, Cheryl.

TEASER: [Annoyed] Stop telling me what I can do! Who do you think you are?

VICTIM: I'm Karen [this is a very effective retort to "Who do you think you are?"] I just want you to know you can keep talking about my dress.

TEASER: Oh, shut up! [Walks away. This is a typical response: The teaser cannot grapple with the situation and the Victim is clearly in control.]

Now that the Victim has had experience with the three non-reward retort strategies, give brief demonstrations of each. Ask him to pick two of these to use in an actual teasing situation, then give him intensive practice with the selected strategies. The Victim is given a choice because being allowed to choose makes him feel in control. He must feel comfortable with the strategies that he uses to counterattack otherwise he will not sound convincing. In addition, being actively involved in retort selection will make him more likely to use the retorts and he will also try harder and longer to make them work (Bandura, 1969).

Punishment Retort Strategies

The next eight strategies use verbal punishment. Here the Victim must attack, rebut, and downgrade the teaser's taunts, the goal being to annoy, discomfit, and embarrass the teaser particularly when other children are present. Onlookers are like sheep—they soon side with whomever is winning.

Remind the Victim that the three strategies that he has just learned will annoy the teaser because he is not getting the expected payoff (reward). Explain that now you are going to teach him how to *punish* the teaser. A teaser will soon stop teasing a Victim who not only is not upset by the teasing, but who also starts getting tough, picking on the teaser, and making him look dumb. Use the same teaching procedure that was used for the nonreward retort strategies.

Note that some of these strategies may sound somewhat inflammatory and likely to elicit aggression. However, the teaser has *not* been physically aggressive, *this program is designed for children who are being subjected to teasing only*, and in the first 100 times that the Program was used there were only three reports of resultant aggression. Two of these involved mild pushing and shoving, the third one resulted in a nose bleed for the teaser. Since then, the program has been widely distributed with no negative reports of any kind concerning its use.

1. Unable to Remember Teaser's Name. No matter what the teaser says, the Victim starts to reply using the wrong name. The message here is that the teaser is of so little importance to the Victim that she cannot remember the teaser's name:

TEASER: Here comes Carrot-Top. Here comes Red Light. You look like a traffic stop-light.

VICTIM: Uh, Betty. No. Your name isn't Betty. Don't tell me, I want to think of it myself. [Pause. Victim looks apologetic then says] I have the *hardest* time remembering your name. I never have any trouble with anyone else. [Victim looks around and quickly names 5 or 6 girls.] See, I know *their* names.

TEASER: It's Jessica.

VICTIM: Oh, sure, *Jennifer*. [The Victim must use a name with the same first letter.] I guess there's just nothing about you that helps me remember your name. [Pauses and looks thoughtfully at the teaser.] Or maybe it's just that I never think about you.

During this kind of exchange the Victim *must* respond quickly and smoothly and look puzzled at the appropriate times. The teaser will usually be thrown off balance by the Victim's counterattack: This gives the Victim an immediate if temporary edge and her confidence soars. There should be no trouble about alternate names: The Victim knows who is likely to tease her, so "wrong" names can be decided upon in advance and included in the practice runs. Initially, it was anticipated that the teaser would feel insulted or angry. But, in fact, most teasers were reported to be genuinely upset that the Victim could not remember their name.

2. *Turning the Tables on the Teaser.* This strategy can be used only *if* the topic is general enough that it could apply to the teaser. It consists simply of listening to the teaser's opening statement and then responding with, "It takes one to know one, doesn't it, (teaser's name)?" Often the teaser becomes really angry. Sometimes he is speechless and when this happens, the Victim should leave with a pseudo-kindly comment, "Well, I'll leave you to think about it."

3. *Reversal of Teasing.* Any kind of teasing can be reversed. The Victim must use the attribute that he is being teased about:

- *Clothes.* Pick out one item that the teaser is wearing and say, "Where *did* you get it? Did your *Mom* pick it out? Do *you* like it?" Stare. Point it out to others.
- *Hair.* "Was *your* hair *always* a bit thin? Do you know that some people go bald *before* they're 20?" Stare at hair and shake head. [Used very successfully by children with leukemia.] (Ross & Ross, 1984)
- *Hat.* "I guess you noticed *my hat* because you look so *funny* in *that* hat." [Pause.] "You don't think so? Really?"
- *Teacher's pet.* "You think *I'm* the teacher's pet. Well, it takes one to know one. I guess you're feeling a bit jealous. It's hard when someone else takes over your place."
- *General.* No matter what attribute the teaser uses, throw it back at him: "I can see why you noticed that I'm (fat, skinny, etc.) because you're getting that way, too." If the teaser denies it, ask a series of questions about it, for example, "How much do you weigh? Did you always weigh that much (or little)?"

Now follow the same procedure given at the completion of the Nonreward Retort Strategies: The Teacher and Helper demonstrate the three Punishment Retort Strategies, the Victim chooses the one that he would like to use when teased, and he is given intensive practice in it. (If he wanted to start out with "meaner" strategies, he should choose two strategies and practice both.)

For the remaining strategies follow the same procedures described earlier: discussion, demonstration, incorporation of some of the nonverbal behaviors that should or should not be exhibited, less-than-perfect role play by the Helper, reversal of roles, critiques, and ample rehearsal by the Victim.

4. *The Victim Shows He Is the Boss.* One way for the Victim to show that he is in charge is to take the teaser's taunt (for example, "You're just a cripple, you got lousy legs") and ask with a puzzled look, "What did you say?" Repeat this with, "Could you say that again?" Often the Victim can get the teaser to say this three times before the teaser catches on. When this gambit is successful, the Victim should praise the teaser in as condescending a manner as possible: "Good work, Jones, you said that three times. Come back at lunchtime and I'll have you say it some more."

Note that as part of the "boss" behavior the Victim uses the teaser's surname (boy) or proper name (girl: Margaret, not Peggy) in any verbal exchange. Whenever possible he gives orders and points with a jabbing motion but does not touch the teaser: "Be here tomorrow, Patterson. Same time. I'll talk to you some more about my ankles." He should take every opportunity to play to the spectators. In the above situation he should say in an aside to spectators, "I'm having Patterson come tomorrow."

5. *Making the Teaser Look Foolish When He Says the Obvious.* "She knows I'm in a wheelchair. Wow! What else do you know? (Points to familiar objects.) What's that, Elizabeth? A tree. Say tree." If Elizabeth is so foolish as to say "tree," tell the spectators that you are having her name things. If she does not say "tree," look sympathetic and tell her that "tree" is a pretty hard word for someone like her and suggest an easier word.

6. *Making the Teaser Look Ignorant about Medical Conditions.* The Victim with any kind of visible medical problem is almost certain to be teased. The teaser says, "You're in a wheelchair, you're never going to walk." The Victim looks surprised and says, "William, are you *able* to read newspapers? or watch TV? I *really* wonder if you can because if you could, you'd know that in medicine there's no such word as *never.*" Explain, using joint replacement or heart transplants as examples.

Or the teaser says, "You've got leukemia, you're going to die." The Victim should point a finger at the teaser and say, "Joseph, I have news for you. You're going to die, too. Everyone dies, don't you know that?" At this point the teaser is likely to say that he means the leukemic child is going to die *soon.* The Victim replies, "You're not using the right words. You don't talk about *going to die,* you say *terminal.* Now let's hear you say it again *properly.*" If the teaser hesitates, say, "Well, that is a pretty big word for someone like you. Now, I'll help you. Ter-min-al. Now you say it." If Joseph says it, praise him in a heavy-handed way, "Good boy." If he does not say it, say, "Well, even if you can't say it, Joseph, you try to remember it and *maybe* when you're older you'll be able to say it."

Or the teaser picks on an obese or underweight child, in which case the Victim says enthusiastically, "You're *right*! I'm fat. I weigh . . ." pause, look closely at the teaser and say, "I bet you don't know how much I weigh." If the teaser hesitates, say, "What's the matter? You scared to try? I'll give you a dime if you get it right." No matter what the other child guesses, laugh uproariously. Repeat his guess, " X pounds! Wait till I tell my doctor. He'll die laughing." Pause, shake head slowly, then urge the teaser to try again. Offer him three more chances. Tell him to try again the next day. If the spectators press the Victim to tell his weight, he should laugh and say, "I want to give [teaser] some more chances." Try to sound pitying and say, "X pounds! He thinks I weigh X pounds!"

7. Derogating the Teaser for Repetition of Taunts. Here the Victim nods occasionally as she listens to the teaser. The first time that the teaser repeats herself (they often do, their repertoire is generally very limited), say, "You know who you remind me of, Ruth Anne, it's a TV commercial, they say the same thing every day. So I want you to sing it this time" (To spectators: "I'm having her sing it—she says the same thing about my ankles every day.") "Oh, come on, Ruth Anne, sing it." (Pause). "Ruth Anne, is it that you don't *want* to sing or you just *can't* sing?"

This question is a useful tactic because it puts the teaser in a no-win situation. If she does sing, the Victim should praise her in a condescending manner; if she refuses, the Victim should suggest that she's lacking in ability.

8. Anticipation of Taunts the Teaser Will Use. This strategy was suggested by an 11-year-old girl who, like most of the children who worked through the program, became very interested in the retort strategies. She thought, correctly, that her strategy would throw the teaser off balance.

The procedure here is for the Victim to accost (go near but not *too* close to) the teaser *before* she says anything to the Victim and ask, "What's it to be today, Carol?" and immediately reel off several of the taunts that the teaser often uses. Then take advantage of the teaser's momentary silence to deliver the final blow: Offer to meet with the teaser to help her think up some new taunts.

When these last strategies have been covered, have the Victim choose two and follow the previously described routines for ensuring that the Victim is able to use them effectively in the real-life situation.

Part Four

Assuming that the Victim is (1) skilled in the Retort Strategies that he has chosen; (2) believes that he can use them effectively in counterattacking the teaser; and (3) wants to try them when teased, the next step is a test. In the test situation some of the retort strategies chosen by the Victim would be appropriate, but the content of the interaction is new to him. The Teacher confronts the Victim with a taunt and he must respond. Have a critique of his performance with demonstrations by the Teacher and Helper. Then repeat the same test and see how the Victim performs.

Follow the same procedure with a new test. If the Victim does well, explain that the teaser might not stop and might even become nastier (because he senses that his source of payoff might be slipping away). But this will be a temporary reaction, so the Victim should continue to handle the teasing using the strategies and behaviors that he has learned. Demonstrate this possibility with the Teacher and Helper taking the teaser and Victim roles.

When the tests have been completed satisfactorily, the Victim should now be ready to confront the teaser in the actual teasing situation. Urge him to note as many details of the interaction with the teaser as he can, so that he can report back. It is *essential* to make the Victim feel important when he does report back and to be untroubled by any slipups on the Victim's part. Enlist his help in incorporating any changes needed for the next trial. If the Victim wants to temporarily postpone the next trial, let him, but continue working on his verbal and nonverbal behaviors using the test procedure. An unexpected finding occurred at the first trial point in the training sequence: If the Victim handled the verbal responses well, the teaser's repertoire seemed to narrow and become more stereotyped, possibly because of frustration over the Victim's unusual behavior. The effect was to reduce the number and variety of taunts that the Victim had to handle, thus making his task much easier.

Of the first 100 children who were taught this program, 96 had no further difficulty with the teasers, according to the children themselves, their parents, their teachers, and their pediatricians (where the latter were involved in the case). Three of the remaining four children, two girls and one boy, were apparently too timid to put the program into action, even though they had demonstrated impressive competence in the training situation. The fourth child, a boy, had also been successful in the training situation but was unable to apply the skills that he had learned. Under no circumstances should such failures be punished in any way, including a show of even the mildest disappointment on the part of the Program Teacher. Instead, consider some other form of intervention more suited to the child's temperament.

Comment

In a number of ways the program is an apparently simple one: No professional help or training is necessary because the straightforward instructions can be followed by reasonably competent adults or adolescents who are motivated to help teasing victims. No special equipment is required and room space large enough for three people is all that is needed. So it is interesting to consider why the program has been effective in helping a large number of children to eliminate their teasing problem.

The context is strongly supportive with the Teacher and Helper acknowledging that the problem is a serious one warranting their undivided attention and help. The Victim achieves repeated successes until he no longer feels upset in the teasing situation. The training procedures defuse the Victim's attitude to being teased by having him observe and participate in role play incidents, some of which are similar to his real-life experiences. As Bandura (1969) has pointed out, fears can be mastered in this way. In addition, the Victim takes an active rather than passive part by providing essential information crucial to the training. In doing this he begins to look at the teasing situation in a more detached and, therefore, unemotional way. The extensive training generates a feeling of being in control of the teasing interaction and this inner change effects a change in his demeanor. He no longer is an obvious target for teasing.

In addition to the benefits directly accruing from participation in the Program, parents have frequently reported other positive changes in their children, changes that they found hard to describe. One man, for example, said that his 8-year-old son "was tougher about things now," and a mother described her 10-year-old daughter as "much more mature." We believe that these changes may occur as a result of coping effectively with the teasing. The victim's confidence and self-esteem are bolstered: The result is what Rutter (1987) calls a psychological stiffening or steeling (*not* to be confused with rigidity) that helps the former victim to confront new experiences of a stressful nature with greater composure than had previously been the case. It is this *increase in composure* in the face of stress that underlies the positive change that the parents report.

CONCLUSION

Cruel and destructive teasing may start as a daily hassle, but all too often it quickly assumes the status of a major life event (Lazarus, 1966), a stressor that the victim is ill-prepared to cope with. What is needed is direct action in the form of a quick sharp rebuttal, but the victim seldom manages anything more than a feeble comeback. This is not surprising because the dynamics of the teasing interaction usually put the victim at a great disadvantage. The teaser can choose the topic, which is often indisputably true and consequently difficult to refute, the ideal time for the verbal attack, and the place to deliver the barb. In the early stages of teasing, the victim often is taken by surprise and may be unable to conceal the hurt and discomfiture engendered by the teasing. At this point social support from bystanders would give the victim a tremendous boost, but such support is rarely forthcoming. More often the bystanders side with the teaser when the victim is clearly unable to handle the situation. It is not surprising that victims in this situation often end up blaming themselves for their inadequacies. At this point it is of critical importance to provide social support.

No child should have to endure destructive teasing. It is inexcusable to have a child's life marred for weeks or months by the misery of cruel teasing and, in addition, have the possibility of negative effects well into adulthood. Any interested, reasonably competent adult with a capacity for empathy could teach the Ross Teasing Program and, in the process, equip the child to cope effectively not only with the immediate painful problem of being teased but also with the inevitable verbal sparring of early adulthood.

9 Primary Prevention of Bullying

SINCE THE MID-1980s, concern about the safety of American schools has escalated among parents, school personnel and administrators, public health officials, and law enforcement agencies, with justification. Attendance at school occupies a substantial block of time during which schools are expected to ensure adequate physical safety and psychological security for all those enrolled. In fact, however, an increasing number of schools do not begin to meet this requirement. Often there is no certainty of even minimum physical safety. Instead, the rate of weapon-related violence and other antisocial behaviors is rising rapidly, so that a climate of fear and terror exists in many schools, to the detriment of academic and social progress (Prothrow-Stith, 1991).

The term *terror* is used advisedly. Three million incidents of attempted or completed assault, rape, robbery, theft, and destruction of others' possessions occur inside American schools or on school property every year, a rate of one every 6 seconds. Five percent of teachers in public schools are assaulted annually, and 12% are reluctant to confront some students who misbehave because they fear some form of reprisal (Zinsmeister, 1990). A senior U.S. Public Health official, Dr. Mark Rosenberg, has gone so far as to say that violence in our schools has reached epidemic proportions and that combating it will require public health resources in addition to educational intervention and action by the criminal justice system (Rosenberg, 1993).

In the face of this social anarchy, it is not surprising that over 100,000 students in junior and senior high schools reported taking a gun to school on a daily basis, with an additional 800,000 carrying knives as weapons. Although these figures are alarming, the weapon-carrying behavior also can be seen as a rational response to a potentially dangerous situation. If schools cannot ensure physical safety, it is reasonable for students to take steps to protect themselves—or not go to school at all, which was the case in New York City in 1989 when nearly half the high school population stayed home on Halloween because they were afraid that there would again be trouble on what had often, in recent years, been a violent occasion.

Particularly disturbing is the fact that the level of violence in the schools is so widespread that it is beginning to be treated in the media and by the population at large as just another part of American life like the hazards of smoking, teen-age substance abuse and pregnancies, and pollution. A Seattle realtor told a prospective buyer that "You're always going to have violence in city public schools" (M. Bell, personal communication, September 8, 1995). The tacit acceptance of violence as a fact of school life is evident even in young children. When a kindergarten teacher in a fairly affluent suburb in California told her class that one of their classmates, a 5-year-old boy, had died, another boy asked with casual interest, "Who shot him?" However, under the facade of apparent insouciance lies a genuine fearfulness. In a recent interview study of children's worries (Silverman, La Greca, & Wasserstein, 1995), anxiety about physical harm from others was the single most frequent response and also one of the most intense worries reported by a group of 205 second- to sixth-grade children who lived in a low-crime area.

Bullying is one component of the school violence problem. In the school setting, hundreds of thousands of bullied children are in a constant state of misery escalating to terror, with even the youngest children suffering from grossly inadequate protection. Besag (1989) has commented that only adults who are imprisoned physically for criminal acts or psychologically by hopeless marriages experience the misery that some children encounter daily in school. Some victims become truants, pay for protection, or as a last resort become suicidal. A substantial number of victims and bullies alike will suffer negative long-term effects. There is unequivocal evidence of the persistence of bullying in many children and of the heightened risk it represents for trouble in adulthood. Estimates vary, but it appears that approximately one quarter of the boys who are bullies at age 8 are headed for occupations far below their level of ability, can expect significantly more criminal convictions than their nonbullying peers, and are likely to become the abusive parents of a new generation of childhood bullies (Olweus, 1993a). The financial and psychological costs of ongoing bullying are substantial, and in many cases the latter are difficult or impossible to reverse.

When the first reports of research-based findings on the frequency of bullying in school-age children began to attract attention, the media in the United States, Canada, and the United Kingdom (particularly England) tended to sensationalize the problem as a school-based phenomenon. Headlines in Britain claimed "Bullying in Our Schools Is Worst in Europe" (*Sheffield Star*, September 28, 1989), and other publications, such as *Psychology Today* (February, 1988), ran articles about the "Schoolyard Menace: Millions of Bullies Are Making Life Miserable for Millions of Victims." Some countries, particularly those in Scandinavia (Olweus, 1993a; Roland, 1989a) and the United Kingdom (Smith & Sharp, 1994) made determined efforts, with considerable success, to combat bullying: The whole school campaigns, first in Norway and then in the United Kingdom, established beyond any doubt that ongoing bullying was amenable to intervention. Others, notably Japan, made little headway with the problem despite strenuous efforts to effect change.

At this point the media again entered the fray with wildly enthusiastic accounts about bullying being eliminated. For example, the normally level-headed *Times Educational Supplement* ran the headline, "Bully Success" for an article on the report from Maines and Robinson (1992), who had stated that their no-blame approach to bullying had had a 100% success rate in primary schools. Other features, such as the "Bullies Licked at Lunchtime" (Burstall, 1995, p. 3), presented the problem of bullying as being greatly improved by making a school a telling school and having a student watch group. Following publication of two excellent companion volumes based on research carried out by investigators on the Sheffield Bullying Project (Sharp & Smith, 1994; Smith & Sharp, 1994), the headline was "Bullying: It Needn't Happen." As a result of the media reports of the efficacy of intervention in the schools, optimism soared: To the reader it must have appeared that a cure for bullying was at hand.

Throughout the media accounts the emphasis was and has continued to be on bullying as a school-based phenomenon. Action has been demanded on the part of the schools, the implication being that the schools *cause* bullying and, therefore, are responsible for eliminating it. What the media fail to recognize is that bullying is a *symptom* whose causative antecedents are in the home, for example, in parental practices and attitudes, and that many children come to school (and preschool) with bullying tendencies or as full-fledged bullies. Although the schools do cause some bullying in that some teachers set children up to be bullied, the school's contribution to bullying consists largely of providing opportunities for it to occur through inadequate supervision and the failure to take decisive action when it does occur. Because of the passivity of most school personnel in the United States, bullies often are able to avoid sanctions for even the cruelest offenses that in many countries would result in their being tried as adults. Instead, the emphasis in the

United States has been on curbing the spread of weapon-related violence. Little thought has been given to the antecedents of this antisocial aggressive behavior. Children do not start out with guns and knives in kindergarten, at least not yet, but bullying already is a problem when children enter school. The possibility that early childhood bullying is an antecedent of other classes of antisocial aggression and that stopping bullying might partially reduce the spiral toward weapon-related violence has not been explored.

The point is that the effective school programs that have been described in this text should be viewed as an essential step in reducing *ongoing* bullying, but as *secondary preventive methods* they rarely get at the cause of the bullying and should never be viewed as *the* solution. If there is a solution, it can lie only in the development of *primary prevention programs* supplemented by other forms of intervention.

Consider the case of the polio epidemic of 1952 in terms of the primary versus secondary prevention approach. If the United States had continued to rely solely on secondary prevention measures after that epidemic had killed 3,152 adults and children and left thousands more partially or seriously incapacitated, survivors would have received the best possible medical care. Treatment in the form of life on an iron lung, physiotherapy, special education, and later vocational training would have cost the taxpayers millions of dollars if the prevalence of polio had continued unabated. Instead, the federal government set their sights on primary prevention, in the form of procedures to forestall the onset of polio with immunization. While continuing diligently to pursue secondary prevention, they also targeted the cause (lack of immunity to the virus) and funded research by Jonas Salk and Albert Sabin, who worked independently of each other on developing an effective polio vaccine (Gould, 1995). The success of this bold move was dramatic. Two effective vaccines were produced, primary prevention was made possible, and polio was virtually eliminated in the United States and most of the Western world. The strident complaints that had been voiced initially about the funding required for not only one but *two* research projects were silenced when it became obvious that the expenditures were more than justified in terms of the cost–benefit ratio: The vaccines produced tangible returns far in excess of the development costs (Cousins, 1979). The impressive success with polio was not an isolated occurrence. The efficacy of primary preventive interventions is well documented in the annals of pediatric medicine (Nicoll & Rudd, 1989).

Since the 1970s, professionals in the mental health disciplines have been increasingly endorsing the use of primary preventive interventions at developmentally significant points of childhood, the rationale being that the optimal approach to the behavioral problems of childhood is to prevent their onset. Although significant progress has been made in the development of viable preventive interventions that can be used effectively in real-life settings, there are as yet no primary prevention programs that might forestall the onset of bullying. However, some effective interventions for other antisocial behaviors have the potential to serve as models for the primary prevention of bullying.

Of relevance here is a review of research on violence prevention (Yoshikawa, 1994) that should be mandatory reading for investigators who are interested in the primary prevention of bullying, because the risk factors for violence and delinquency overlap with some of those for bullying. Yoshikawa's review described how intervention programs that combine comprehensive family support with early childhood education helped to prevent the onset of juvenile violence and crime. Because these two-generation preventive programs resulted in greater economic independence among participating families, more harmonious households (measured, for example, in terms of reductions in child abuse), and fewer special education placements, they also proved to be cost-effective. To explain this phenomenon, Yoshikawa cites evidence from longitudinal studies that risk factors for developmental disorders can operate cumulatively and interactively (Rutter, 1979), and that interventions that target multiple risk factors can have a far more powerful impact than those that affect only one or two risk factors. On the basis of these findings, Yoshikawa has proposed a cumulative protection model that states that it is the *interactive effects* that result from the simultaneous provision of support in the two major contexts in the child's life (home and school) that are of crucial importance in helping to prevent the onset of violence. For example, positive parenting practices (the family support component) and age-appropriate verbal ability (the early education component) interact to protect against the development of antisocial behavior such as violence in children in low-income households. The probability that an intervention that targets only one or two risk factors would have the same impact is extremely low.

COMMON ELEMENTS OF SUCCESSFUL PREVENTION PROGRAMS

In his review, Yoshikawa (1994) identified the common elements of several programs that have proven successful by achieving long-term reductions in antisocial behavior, that is, delinquency and behaviors whose purpose is to inflict harm on others or damage to their property. Among these programs are the Perry Preschool Program (Berrueta-Clement, Schweinhart, Barnett, Epstein, & Weikart, 1984) and the Yale Child Welfare Project (Seitz, Rosenbaum, & Apfel, 1985). Elements common to these projects are discussed, followed by a brief description of the Perry Program:

1. These programs were basically ecological in design and effect in that they provided comprehensive family support as well as early childhood education and in the process achieved long-term results benefiting both the families as a whole and the children.
2. They were started in the early preschool years. Although some investigators advocate intervention beginning at or before birth (see, for example, Crockenberg, 1987), others (McCall, 1981) dispute this suggestion on the grounds that the environmental influence on mental development (which is of prime importance in this type of intervention) is greater in early childhood than in infancy.
3. The period of intervention was 2 years or more.
4. Day care with an educational focus in the broadest sense, or preschool with an explicitly educational focus was provided.
5. A trained home visitor provided social support of an emotional kind in the form of discussing family and other problems with one or both parents and support of an informational nature, including a focus on facts related to child development, the advantages and disadvantages of specific parenting practices, and the educational and vocational goals of the parents. Visits were weekly or monthly, depending on the specific program.

The Perry Preschool Program

The Perry Preschool Program (Barnett, 1993; Berrueta-Clement et al., 1991) began in 1962 in Ypsilanti, Michigan, under the auspices of the local public school district. The participants were 123 African American children age 3 or 4 who had been born in poverty and were believed to be at high risk for failing in school. They were randomly assigned to either (1) a program group who were given a high-quality, active learning preschool program; or (2) a control group who had no program and thus were typical of minority children born in poverty. The teachers in the program group all had public school certification; one teacher was assigned to every six children. The sessions ran for 30 weeks, from October to May, for 2-1/2 hours on weekday mornings. In addition, the teachers met with the mother and child in the home for 90 minutes once a week. The program began as a traditional nursery school, but over the 2-year period, it gradually adopted an explicitly Piagetian approach. It encountered the problems that almost all school and home interventions do; for example, average attendance in the first year was only 69% and home visit appointments were not always kept.

Data were collected on the program and control groups annually from ages 3 through 11, and thereafter at ages 14–15, 19, and 27. The evaluations were meticulously done, in marked contrast to the methodological limitations that characterize the evaluation procedures of many early intervention studies.

The findings were impressive. There was strong support for the hypothesis that a good preschool program with parental involvement could help children in poverty make a better start in their transition from home to community and thereby set them on the road to becoming economically self-sufficient and socially responsible adults. By the age of 14, those in the Perry Preschool Program had significantly higher achievement scores and at age 19, had significantly higher literacy scores than those in the control group. By age 27 the program group had half as many criminal arrests; significantly higher earnings and property wealth, such as owning their own homes and cars; and had a significantly greater commitment to marriage (Schweinhart, Barnes, & Weikart, 1993). It was clear that the program produced economic benefits to both the participants and the general public far in excess of the costs of the program. In fact the cost–benefit analysis was 1:7.16, that is, for every dollar invested in the program, the public received $7.16 in savings from lower prison costs, lower welfare expenditures, and so on. This statistic represents just part of the benefits because the cost–benefit analysis makes no allowance for the less tangible benefits accruing from the program, such as personal satisfaction and heightened self-esteem.

THE OPTIMUM APPROACH TO THE CHILDHOOD BULLYING PROBLEM

It is our opinion that a preschool and school program consisting of three components would have a realistic chance of success in effecting a marked change in the bullying problem. The components are:

1. A 2-year primary prevention program for 3- and 4-year-old children designed to forestall the onset of bullying and victimization. It includes a school-based cognitive and social skills training compo-

nent and a home-based parent-training component that would help ensure continuity between school and home expectations.

2. A secondary prevention program targeting children who are already bullies and victims. It would be similar to the whole school campaigns against bullying programs that have proven successful. Active, but not overly demanding, involvement by the parents would be strongly encouraged.

3. A voluntary program with the goal of achieving community-wide involvement in combating bullying and other antisocial behaviors such as vandalism. Such a program would take the form of heightened awareness concerning the neighborhood children's welfare and willingness to intercede on their behalf when their physical safety or psychological well-being was jeopardized by bullying or other antisocial behaviors.

For a fair test of this approach, the proposed program should go into effect in an entire school district, with the participating preschools under the jurisdiction of the school district (as they were with the Perry Preschool Program), rather than operating independently of any supervision, as most American preschools do. With this arrangement children with bullying tendencies or propensities to victimization would start school in an unselected heterogeneous group of children rather than in a same-problem group open only to referrals of children with bullying tendencies. If these tendencies are well established, special attention must be given to modifying them without drawing undue attention to the target behaviors.

Under no circumstances should these children be labeled as bullies or victims. Labeling young preschool children as potential bullies and restricting their early school experiences to a homogeneous group of other children with bullying tendencies is short-sighted at best. It also is a gross misuse of special class placement: Being assigned to a group with the same negative tendencies is tantamount to an immersion experience in bullying behavior. What these children need is practice in learning how to coexist peacefully with the kind of heterogeneous group of peers who will be their classmates for the next 10 or 12 years.

The Primary Prevention Program

The preschool program itself would be modeled on the general procedures of the Perry Preschool Program: one teacher to every 7 or 8 children; regular home visits to involve parents in their children's education by providing information and emotional support tailored to the child's needs. The primary goal of this 2-year program would be to equip the children with the cognitive, social, and emotional skills that are prerequisites for school entry, that is, to send them off to kindergarten both sociable and socialized. Of relevance here is an outstanding program that is admirably suited to the goals of the approach to bullying advocated here. The *Early Violence Prevention Program* is intended for preschool and early school children in the age range of 2 to 7 years. It was recently developed by Ronald Slaby and his associates (Slaby, Roedell, Arezzo, & Hendrix, 1995). It provides teachers and other adults who work with children in this age group with the requisite knowledge and practical strategies for helping to reduce aggressive behavior, preventing violence, and building skills in constructive conflict resolution. Furthermore, it teaches children to be more assertive, empathic, and willing to share and cooperate with others. It combats tendencies to bullying, becoming a victim, and being a racist. Most children who are exposed to this program will be equipped with the social and emotional skills that facilitate entry into the peer group and becoming a good friend. They will be better able to resist peer pressure to engage in antisocial and other harmful activities, and their ability to protect themselves from abuse will be increased.

In addition to the excellent content of the program, it is easy to use. The materials needed are readily available to most teachers. Everything that an adult needs to know or do is spelled out clearly; for example, the rationale underlying the use of positive and negative reinforcement is presented in such a way that it is completely clear why a particular step is introduced. The 13 chapters in the program set out the objectives so that the material can be used effectively despite the wide age range of 2 to 7. One advantage of this age range is that it bridges the transition from preschool to the primary grades. We strongly recommend that preschools and public schools use this excellent program.

The Secondary Prevention Program

It is essential that all schools in the neighborhood, including those in which the preschool programs are located, should have whole school campaigns against bullying similar to those of Olweus (1993a) and Smith and Sharp (1994). Ongoing bullying and victimization must be stopped in the school setting for the good of the perpetrators, their victims, and the school as a whole. Parental and community efforts would be sharply undermined should the schools falter in this respect. For those children entering the school for the first time, either from outside preschools or as transfers to the upper grades, a standard presentation should be made explaining the purpose of the whole school campaign and the expectations concerning their own behavior. They must see that bullying is unacceptable and that negative sanctions are enforced should it occur. The younger children would benefit greatly from having an ongoing Big Brother or Big Sister program in effect to facilitate the transition into the new school.

The importance of parental involvement emphasized in Yoshikawa's (1994) review suggests that any attempt at changing children's behavior at school would be enhanced by such involvement. This means that the whole school campaigns for combating bullying should include the systematic involvement of all parents in the school rather than just the parents of known bullies. Not all investigators in the bully research arena agree on this point. Olweus (1993a), for example, stated that "to enlist parent cooperation is clearly desirable but not a core component of the program" (p. 124). In his program parental involvement activities were available and included discussion groups for the parents of bullies and victims and parent circles for parent–teacher discussions about bullying, but attendance was not mandatory. Similarly, in the Smith and Sharp (1994) program there was only minimal interest in parental involvement.

There is no question that these two programs and others (see, for example, Tattum & Herbert, 1993) using secondary prevention procedures have been successful in reducing the incidence of bullying and, at present, have the most potential for this task. However, there is no evidence as yet that the initial reductions in bullying will be maintained, and none of the principal investigators (Olweus, 1993a; Smith & Sharp, 1994) is making any claims concerning long-term benefits. Even in areas of behavioral problems that overlap with bullying, such as antisocial behavior and delinquency, very few interventions involving secondary prevention have reported evidence of either cross-setting generalization or maintenance of posttreatment gains of more than 1 or 2 years' duration (Kazdin, 1987; Lytton, 1990; Rutter & Giller, 1983).

Even if the initial gains reported by Olweus (1993a) and Smith and Sharp (1994) are maintained, Yoshikawa's evidence (1994) for the relative ineffectiveness of single component interventions suggests that multicontext secondary prevention interventions with an ecological emphasis might be significantly more beneficial over the long term. Support at least for the efficacy and feasibility of such an approach comes from three recent multicontext studies with an ecological base (Hawkins, Catalano, Morrison, O'Donnell, Abbott, & Day, 1992; Kazdin, Siegel, & Bass, 1992; Tremblay et al., 1992). All three combined parent training with child social skill training or collaborative classroom teaching practices, and each demonstrated significant reductions of antisocial behavior in primary-grade children.

Of relevance to the issue of parent involvement in secondary prevention is an ongoing study of the efficacy of the FAST (Families and Schools Together) Track Program run by the Conduct Problems Prevention Research Group (1992). This secondary prevention program targets conduct disorders in elementary school children through five integrated components designed to promote competence in the family, child, and school. The involvement of parents in this program was based on the assumption that parenting skill deficits, particularly in the area of discipline practices, are key factors in the onset and maintenance of conduct disorder. The investigators developed a 22-session curriculum for teaching appropriate parenting skills during weekly parent group meetings. This training was supplemented with biweekly home visits or, in some cases, telephone contacts, but underlying it all was a radically different approach to parent involvement.

All the parents of children entering first grade were approached at the beginning of the school year and were told that the FAST Track Program was a new program to help all the children get off to a good start. The parents were treated as collaborators and potential staff members. In line with their role as "expert members of the program team," they were paid for their participation in the enrichment program. Other benefits included

> teaching parents new skills, providing a support group atmosphere for parents in high-risk situations, assisting parents in learning the role of tutor and homework helper with their children, and providing a positive and supportive atmosphere in which the parents, project staff, and teachers can develop trusting relationships. This latter circumstance is quite contrary to the usual interactions between high-risk parents and school personnel where contacts are few and usually due to child behavior or learning problems. (Conduct Problems, 1992, p. 522)

Community Involvement

In most school districts there is a potentially valuable and largely untapped source of help in combating antisocial behavior. People who are at home all day often witness misbehavior but do nothing about it for a variety of reasons, including reluctance to be involved and fear of possible reprisal. An alert community is a genuine asset: Once residents begin noticing and reporting bullying, they also become more responsive to other problems such as burglary and vandalism. A neighborhood watch program could make residents feel more secure and also help the police. One effect of such programs is to change the zeitgeist about minding one's own business (the "nosy neighbor" image).

A neighborhood watch program could be a particularly potent weapon against bullying because such behavior is not confined to the school setting. Bullies are well aware of the protection provided by limiting their attacks to areas beyond the school's jurisdiction:

Miss, if I kick him will you suspend me?
Yes!
But what about if I leave him alone, but get him when he's walking down the street on Sunday afternoon? (Frost, 1991, p. 35)

Such reasoning is commonplace among bullies. Smith and Sharp (1994) reported that when their whole school anti-bullying campaign was well established, reports of bullying outside the school grounds increased. An alert community corps could also benefit children in general. The old adage from India, "It takes a village to raise a child," has particular applicability in today's world of working mothers and latchkey children.

Communitywide interventions have proven to be highly successful with a variety of problems such as promoting cardiac health (Farquhar, Fortmann, & Flora, 1990) and combating early teenage parenthood (Howard & McCabe, 1990). The benefits are not limited to the target. In the study by Farquhar et al. there was an astonishing increase in sociability as a result of group participation in a common problem. Participants told the investigators that their lives had changed for the better, that they made many new friends, and that new groups such as bowling leagues had formed. It appeared that one side effect of the cardiac campaign was a reduction in the alienation that is characteristic of large segments of our society. In describing this phenomenon one of the senior investigators said that there was "a new sense of community" in some of the participating towns (N. Maccoby, personal communication, June, 1975).

Research support for the feasibility of community involvement focused specifically on bullying comes from Randall and Donohue (1993), who set up an ambitious project in Hull, England, to mobilize the residents of an inner-city community to take action against bullying. Participants were recruited through poster campaigns, leaflet distribution, local press coverage, and workshops. The project leaders empowered parents and other adults in the community to stop ongoing bullying or to report it. All reports were guaranteed to be confidential. Counseling services were provided for families or adults whose lives had been blighted by the effects of ongoing or past bullying. Volunteer counselors were trained by project personnel.

The project had close associations with the schools but accomplished this through the community in order to avoid having the project become school-centered with only marginal community involvement. In instances where bullying problems did not stop, help and information relevant to legal rights and procedures was provided. The project is proving to be highly successful (Randall, 1995).

Comment

Although childhood bullying will never be completely eradicated, there is reason to believe that with the comprehensive intervention program proposed here it could be virtually eliminated in all but the relatively small hard-core group of bullies who are candidates for intensive psychiatric treatment. Studies with children at risk for violence (Yoshikawa, 1994) have demonstrated the efficacy of early intervention that combines school-based social skills training with home-based parent training. The latter component is included because violence begins at home and so should prevention. It is our contention that if a school district were to wholeheartedly implement the preschool program that we have described, along with the secondary prevention and community watch programs, significant improvement in the bullying problem could reasonably be expected to be apparent in 2 years; and in 4 years the incidence of bullying would be reduced to the status of the minor problem that many school personnel erroneously contend it to be now.

Unquestionably, the barriers to such a plan are formidable and they include conceptual, political, and fiscal differences. The conceptual differences alone present a significant problem. In some respects the U.S. government is prevention-oriented; for example, the safety of the country, that is, defense, is accorded the highest priority on the national agenda. Billions of dollars are allocated annually to training military personnel, stockpiling missiles, and producing B-52 bombers. The safety of the community is another matter. Here, the United States is unequivocally treatment-oriented, particularly in respect to juvenile offenders.

A case in point was an occurrence at the Washington State Conference on Violence, held in 1994 . The meeting began on a prevention note but rapidly deteriorated to a focus exclusively on new detention facilities for adolescent criminals; those who had urged the funding of early prevention procedures were decried as fiscally irresponsible and labeled as "hug-a-thug" advocates. No mention was made of the rapidly escalating rate of violence in the United States and the soaring costs associated with it. One American child is shot to death every 2 hours. The juvenile arrest rate for murder (FBI, 1991) rose 87% in the 1980s, and unless intensive intervention is implemented nationwide, it is expected to double in the next 15 years to 260,000 arrests ("Dangerous, " 1995). Nor was any mention made of the fiscal facts related to this violence. As of now, it costs $29,000 per year to keep one child in a juvenile facility and an average of more than $14,000 in medical costs to treat each child struck down by gunfire. The latter statistic led Lawrence McAndrew, president of the National Association of Children's Hospitals and Related Institutions, to comment bitterly in 1993 that when polio killed 3,152 adults and children in 1952, it sparked a massive government-sponsored effort to combat that epidemic. In contrast, people shrug off the fact that in the United States over 5,000 children alone are lost every year to gun violence ("Cost," 1993).

In keeping with the treatment-oriented approach, no mention was made at the Washington State Conference of the antecedents of violence. The kind of violence that puts a juvenile in the criminal detention system does not erupt full-blown at age 14 but, instead, has its antecedents far earlier in the young criminal's history. Bullying is one such antecedent and one that should be looked on as an early warning system requiring early intervention. Instead, it is viewed as a transient problem of middle childhood and adolescence that is caused by the schools and, consequently, is their problem.

CONCLUSION

As the beginning of the 21st century draws near, it is clear that in the space of less than two decades a substantial body of scientific and clinical information about the problem of bullying has been made available. Although new investigations spawning new directions for research must continue, there is no question that the current status of our knowledge of bullying is sufficient to justify the implementation on a nationwide scale of the primary and secondary preventive efforts described in this chapter. The critical question now is whether the federal and state governments are willing to make the expenditures needed to subject the proposed preventive intervention to a fair test.

What is needed now is a massive public outcry against bullying and all other forms of school violence, with extensive media coverage. The general public would have to mount a campaign at the grassroots level against violence, beginning with early intervention against bullying and the lesser types of antisocial behavior. Action against violence should become a political issue, with pressure for change exerted on our elected officials. Until this happens, the approach that we are advocating is likely to be taken up only by a relatively few enlightened school districts.

References

AAUW Educational Foundation. (1993). *Hostile hallways: The AAUW survey on sexual harassment in America's schools*. Annapolis Junction, MD: Author.

Abrahams, R. D. (1962). Playing the dozens. *Journal of American Folklore, 75*, 209–220.

Adams, A. (1992). Holding out against workplace harassment and bullying. *Personnel Management, 24*, 48–50.

Adlam, E. (1991, April 12). The tormented pupils. *Times Educational Supplement*, pp. 19–20.

Ahmad, Y., & Smith, P. K. (1990). Behavioural measures: Bullying in schools. *Newsletter of Association for Child Psychology and Psychiatry, 12*, 26–27.

Ahmad, Y., & Smith, P. K. (1994). Bullying in schools and the issue of sex differences. In J. Archer (Ed.), *Male violence*. London: Routledge.

Akhtar, S., & Stronach, I. (1986, September 19). They call me Blacky. *Times Educational Supplement*, p. 23.

Anthony, E. J. (1974). A risk-vulnerability intervention model. In E. J. Anthony & C. Koupernik (Eds.), *The child in his family* (Vol. 3, pp. 99–121). New York: Wiley.

Ariès, P. (1962). *Centuries of childhood: A social history of family life*. New York: Knopf.

Arora, C. M. J., & Thompson, D. A. (1987). Defining bullying for a secondary school. *Education and Child Psychology, 4*, 110–120.

Arora, T. (1991). The use of victim support groups. In P. K. Smith & D. Thompson (Eds.), *Practical approaches to bullying* (pp. 36–47). London: David Fulton.

Askew, S. (1989). Aggressive behaviour in boys: To what extent is it institutionalised? In D. P. Tattum & D. A. Lane (Eds.), *Bullying in schools* (pp. 59–71). Hanley, Stoke-on-Trent: Trentham Books.

Atwood, M. (1989). *Cat's eye*. New York: Doubleday.

Band, E. B., & Weisz, J. R. (1988). How to feel better when it feels bad: Children's perspectives on coping with everyday stress. *Developmental Psychology, 24*, 247–253.

Bandura, A. (1969). *Principles of behavior modification*. New York: Holt, Rinehart.

Bandura, A. (1977a). Self-efficacy: Toward a unifying theory of behavior change. *Psychological Review, 84*, 191–215.

Bandura, A. (1977b). *Social learning theory*. Englewood Cliffs, NJ: Prentice-Hall.

Bandura, A. (1986). *Social foundations of thought and action: A social cognitive theory*. Englewood Cliffs, NJ: Prentice-Hall.

Bandura, A., & Walters, R. H. (1959). *Adolescent aggression*. New York: Ronald Press.

Barnett, W. S. (1993). Benefit-cost analysis of preschool education: Findings from a 25-year follow-up. *American Journal of Orthopsychiatry, 63*, 500–508.

Bartocci, B. (1991, November 5). When kids gang up on your child. *Women's Day, 15*, 34, 36, 38–39.

Batsch, G. M., & Knoff, H. M. (1994). Bullies and their victims: Understanding a pervasive problem in the schools. *School Psychology Review, 23*, 165–174.

Beale, M. (1993, March). The Antipodean experience. *Report*, p. 7.

Beck, A. T. (1986). Hopelessness as a predictor of eventual suicide. *Annals of the New York Academy of Sciences, 487*, 90–96.

Bergman, G. (1973). *Why does your dog do that?* New York: Howell Books.

Berle, P. A. A. (1989). Stop the barrister bullies. *Audubon, 91*, 8.

Berrueta-Clement, J. R., Schweinhart, L. J., Barnett, W. S., Epstein, A. S., & Weikart, D. P. (1984). *Changed lives: The effects of the Perry Preschool Program on youths through age 19*. Ypsilanti, MI: High/Scope Press.

Besag, V. (1989). *Bullies and victims in schools*. Milton Keynes: Open University Press.

Besag, V. (1993). The playground. In M. Elliott (Ed.), *Bullying: A practical guide to coping for schools* (pp. 37–43). Harlow, Essex: Longman.

Billman, J., & McDevitt, S. C. (1980). Convergence of parent and observer ratings of temperament with observations of peer interaction in nursery schools. *Child Development, 51*, 395–400.

Bing, S. (1992). *Crazy bosses*. New York: Morrow.

Björkqvist, K., Ekman, K., & Lagerspetz, K. (1982). Bullies and victims: Their ego picture, ideal ego picture and normative ego picture. *Scandinavian Journal of Psychology, 23*, 307–313.

Björkqvist, K. L., Lagerspetz, K. M. J., & Kaukiainen, A. (1992). Do girls manipulate and boys fight? Developmental trends in regard to direct and indirect aggression. *Aggressive Behavior, 18*, 117–127.

Blanchard, D. C., & Blanchard, R. J. (1988). Ethoexperimental approaches to the biology of emotion. *Annual Review of Psychology, 39*, 131–134.

Blau, M. Just teasing (1993). *American Health, 12*, 66–68.

Block, J. H. (1983). Differential premises arising from differential socialization of the sexes: Some conjectures. *Child Development, 54*, 1335–1354.

Bly, C. (1988, May/June). Of bullies and mascots: Playing family roles. *Utne Reader, 27*, 72–73.

Boulton, M. J. (1994). Preventing and responding to bullying in the junior/middle school playground. In S. Sharp & P. K. Smith (Eds.), *Tackling bullying in your school: A practical handbook for teachers*. London: Routledge.

Boulton, M. J. (1995). Playground behaviour and peer interaction patterns of primary school boys classified as bullies, victims, and not involved. *British Journal of Educational Psychology, 65*, 165–177.

Boulton, M. J., & Smith, P. K. (1994). Bully-victim problems in middle school children: Stability, self-perceived competence, peer perceptions, and peer acceptance. *British Journal of Developmental Psychology, 12*, 315–329.

Boulton, M. J., & Underwood, K. (1992). Bully/victim problems among middle school children. *British Journal of Educational Psychology, 62*, 73–87.

Bowers, L., Smith, P. K., & Binney, V. (1992). Cohesion and power in the families of children involved in bully/victim problems at school. *Journal of Family Therapy, 14*, 371–387.

Bowlby, J. (1969). *Attachment and loss: Vol. 1. Attachment*. New York: Basic Books.

Bowlby, J. (1973). *Attachment and loss: Vol. 2. Separation*. New York: Basic Books.

Brier, J., & Ahmad, Y. (1991). Developing a school court as a means of addressing bullying in schools. In P. K. Smith & D. Thompson (Eds.), *Practical approaches to bullying* (pp. 25–36). London: David Fulton.

Brown, I. (1994, October 28). Nothing nice about tackling bullies. *Times Educational Supplement*, Features, p. 2.

Buchanan, C. (1992, September 12). Does your child have to face this? *Bella*, p. 8.

Burstall, E. (1995, September 8). Bullies licked at lunchtime. *Times Educational Supplement*, Primary Update, p. 3.

Carr, R. A. (1988). The city-wide peer counseling program. *Children and Youth Services Review, 10*, 217–232.

Cash, T. F., & Janda, L. H. (1986, April). Body image survey report: The great American shape-up. *Psychology Today*, pp. 30–37.

Chazan, M. (1990). Bullying in the infant school. In D. P. Tattum & D. A. Lane (Eds.), *Bullying in schools* (pp. 33–43). Hanley, Stoke-on-Trent: Trentham Books.

Cheevers, J. (1995, July 9). Schools get low marks on sexual harassment. *The Seattle Times*, p. A8.

Cillessen, A. H. N., van Ijzendoorn, H. W., & van Lieshout, C. F. M. (1992). Heterogeneity among peer-rejected boys: Subtypes and stabilities. *Child Development, 63*, 893–905.

Cohen, S., & Wills, T. A. (1985). Stress, social support, and the buffering hypothesis. *Psychological Bulletin, 98*, 310–357.

Cohn, T. (1988). Sambo—a study in name calling. In E. Kelly & T. Cohn (Eds.), *Racism in schools—new research evidence*. Stoke-on-Trent: Trentham Books.

Coie, J. D., & Cillessen, A. H. N. (1993). Peer rejection: Origins and effects on children's development. *Current Directions in Psychological Science, 2,* 89–92.

Colino, S. (1993, June/July). Fooling around or sexual harassment? *Parenting,* p. 30.

Collier, J. L. (1988, August). What your child fears most. *Readers Digest, 137,* 7–8, 10–12.

Conduct Problems Prevention Research Group (1992). A developmental and clinical model for the prevention of conduct disorder: The FAST Track Program. *Development and Psychopathology, 4,* 509–527.

Cost to treat young gunshot victim could buy year of college. (1993, November 26). *Seattle Post-Intelligencer,* p. A3.

Cottrell, N., & Epley, S. W. (1977). Affiliation, social comparison, and socially mediated stress reduction. In J. M. Suls & R. L. Miller (Eds.), *Social comparison processes: Theoretical and empirical perspectives* (pp. 43–68). Washington, DC: Hemisphere.

Cousins, N. (1979). The fallacy of cost-benefit ratio (Editorial). *Saturday Review, 6,* 8.

Cowie, H., & Sharp, S. (1992). Students themselves tackle the problem of bullying. *Pastoral Care in Education, 10,* 31–37.

Crick, N. R., & Grotpeter, J. K. (1995). Relational aggression, gender, and social-psychological adjustment. *Child Development, 66,* 710–722.

Croall, J. (1993, November 12). How to see off the bullies. *Daily Telegraph,* You and your family, p. 13.

Crockenberg, S. (1987). Support for adolescent mothers during the postnatal period: Theory and research. In C. F. Z. Boukydis (Ed.), *Research on support for parents and infants in the postnatal period* (pp. 3–24). Norwood, NJ: Ablex.

Dale, R. R. (1971). *Mixed or single-sex school* (3 vols.). London: Routledge.

Dale, R. R. (1991). Mixed versus single-sex schools: The social aspect of bullying. In M. Elliott (Ed.), *Bullying: A practical guide to coping for schools* (pp. 146–153). Harlow, Essex: Longman.

Dalenberg, C. J., Bierman, K. L., & Furman, W. (1984). A reexamination of developmental changes in causal attributions. *Developmental Psychology, 20,* 575–583.

Dangerous time to be a kid, study finds. (1995, September 8). *Seattle Post-Intelligencer,* p. A3.

Davey, A. G. (1983). *Learning to be prejudiced: Growing up in a multiethnic Britain.* London: Edward Arnold.

Davies, G. T. (1986). *A first year tutorial handbook.* Oxford: Blackwell.

Dean, C. (1995, March 17). 4,000 staff say they are bullied. *Times Educational Supplement,* News, p. 6.

De Paulo, B. (1992). Nonverbal behavior and self- presentation. *Psychological Bulletin, 111,* 203–243.

de Rosenroll, D. A. (1986). A peer counseling centre for school-based peer counseling: An experiment in progress. *Journal of Child Care, 2,* 1–8.

Deutsch, M. (1993). Educating for a peaceful world. *American Psychologist, 48,* 510–517.

Dickens, C. J. H. (1838, March). Oliver Twist: Or the Parish Boy's Progress. *Bentley's Miscellany.*

Donahue, P. (1994, October 28). *12-year-old sues school for allowing sexual harassment.* Transcript #4109, the Phil Donahue Show, New York.

Dore, A. (1992, December 4). Different strokes beat the bullies. *Times Educational Supplement,* p. 14.

Dore, A. (1993, May 7). Dipping bullies in their well of guilt. *Times Educational Supplement,* p. 9.

Douglas, M. A. (1987). The battered woman syndrome. In D. J. Sonkin (Ed.), *Domestic violence on trial: Psychological and legal dimensions of family violence* (pp. 39–54). New York: Springer.

Dullea, G. (1987, February 9). Peer pressure is used to mediate disputes at schools. *New York Times,* pp. 1, 20.

Durbach, E. (Producer). (1993). *Teasing and how to stop it* [Videotape and Manual]. (Available from B.C. Children's Hospital, 4480 Oak Street, Vancouver, B.C. V6H 3V4 Canada).

Eder, D. (1991). The role of teasing in adolescent peer group culture. In S. Cahill (Ed.), *Sociological studies of child development* (Vol. 4, pp. 181–197). Greenwich, CT: JAI Press.

Eisenberg, A. R. (1986). Teasing: Verbal play in two Mexicano homes. In B. B. Schieffelin & E. Ochs (Eds.), *Language socialization across cultures* (pp. 182–198). Cambridge: Cambridge University Press.

Ekman, K. (1977). In D. Olweus (1979), Stability of aggressive reaction patterns in males. A review. *Psychological Bulletin, 86,* 852–875.

Elkin, S. (1987). A poetics for bullies. In R. Carver & T. Jenks (Eds.), *American short story masterpieces* (pp. 173–190). New York: Dell.

Elliott, M. (1991). *Bullying: A practical guide to coping for schools.* Harlow, Essex: Longman.

Elliott, M. (1993a). Bullies, victims, signs, solutions. In M. Elliott (Ed.), *Bullying: A practical guide to coping for schools* (pp. 8–14). Harlow, Essex: Longman.

Elliott, M. (1993b). Bully "courts." In M. Elliott (Ed.), *Bullying: A practical guide to coping for schools* (pp. 44–49). Harlow, Essex: Longman.

Eron, L. D., & Huesmann, R. L. (1987). Aggression and its correlates over 22 years. In D. Crowell, I. M. Evans, & C. R. O'Donnell (Eds.), *Childhood aggression and violence.* New York: Plenum.

Eron, L. D., & Huesmann, R. L. (1990). The stability of aggressive behavior—Even unto the third generation. In M. Lewis & S. M. Miller (Eds.), *Handbook of developmental psychopathology* (pp. 147–156). New York: Plenum.

Evans, C., & Eder, D. (1993). "No exit": Processes of isolation in the Middle School. *Journal of Contemporary Ethnography, 22,* 139–170.

Fabian, L. J., & Thompson, J. K. (1989). Body image and disturbance in young females. *International Journal of Eating Disorders, 8,* 63–74.

Farquhar, J. W., Fortmann, S. P., & Flora, J. A. (1990). Effects of community wide education on cardiovascular disease risk factors. *Journal of the American Medical Association, 264,* 359–365.

Farrington, D. P. (1993). Understanding and preventing bullying. In M. Tonry & N. Morris (Eds.), *Crime and justice: An annual review of research* (Vol. 17). Chicago: University of Chicago Press.

Federal Bureau of Investigation. (1991). *Uniform crime reports for the United States.* Washington, DC: Author.

Feld, B. C. (1977). *Neutralizing inmate violence: Juvenile offenders in institutions.* Cambridge, MA: Ballinger.

Fennel, T. (1993, February 15). Fear in the hallways. *Maclean's, 106,* 19.

Fiennes, R. (1988). *Living dangerously.* New York: Atheneum.

Finkelhor, D. (1995). The victimization of children: A developmental perspective. *American Journal of Orthopsychiatry, 65,* 177–193.

Finkelhor, D., & Dziuba-Leatherman, J. (1994). Victimization of children. *American Psychologist, 49,* 173–183.

Finley, M. (1992). Belling the bully: Managing overbearing employees during meetings. *HR Magazine, 37*(3), 82–85.

Finnegan, R. A., Hodges, E. V. E., & Perry, D. G. (in press). Preoccupied and avoiding coping during middle childhood. *Child Development.*

Finnegan, R. A., & Perry, D. G. (1995). *Mother-child interaction and victimization by peers.* Manuscript submitted for publication, Florida Atlantic University.

Fitzgerald, M. (1992, December 26). Congressman bullies reporter. *Chicago-Sun-Times,* p. 15.

Floyd, N. M. (1985). "Pick on somebody your own size!": Controlling victimization. *The Pointer, 29,* 9–17.

Floyd, N. M. (1987, Winter). Terrorism in the schools. *School Safety* (National School Safety Center Newsjournal), 22–25.

Foa, E. B., & Kozak, M. J. (1986). Emotional processing of fear: Exposure to corrective information. *Psychological Bulletin, 99,* 20–35

Foa, E. B., Steketee, G., & Rothbaum, B. O. (1989). Behavioral/cognitive conceptualization of post-traumatic stress disorder. *Behavior Therapy, 20,* 155–176.

Folkman, S. (1984). Personal control and stress and coping processes: A theoretical analysis. *Journal of Personality and Social Psychology, 46,* 839–852.

Foster, P., Arora, C. M. J., & Thompson, D. (1990). A whole-school approach to bullying. *Pastoral Care in Education, 8,* 13–17.

Foster, P., & Thompson, D. (1991). Bullying: Towards a non-violent sanctions policy. In P. K. Smith & D. Thompson (Eds.), *Practical approaches to bullying* (pp. 13–24). London: David Fulton.

Foster, S. L., DeLawyer, D. D., & Guevremont, D. C. (1986). A critical incident analysis of liked and disliked peer behaviors and their situation parameters in childhood and adolescence. *Behavioral Assessment, 8,* 115–133.

Fournier, R. (1994, November 25). First mom-in-law gathers no moss. *Seattle Post-Intelligencer,* p. A20.

Fox, M., Pratt, G., & Roberts, S. (1991). Developing the educational psychologist's work in the secondary school: A process model in change. *Educational Psychology in Practice, 6,* 163–164.

Frost, L. (1991). A primary school approach—what can be done about the bully? In M. Elliott (Ed.), *Bullying: A practical guide to coping for schools* (pp. 29–36). Harlow, Essex: Longman.

Galvin, R. M. (1992). The nature of shyness. *Harvard Magazine, 94*(4), 41–45.

Gehring, T. M., & Wyler, I. L. (1986). Family System Test (FAST): A three-dimensional approach to investigate family relationships. *Child Psychiatry and Human Development, 16,* 235–248.

Gillborn, D. (1992). Citizenship, "race" and the hidden curriculum. *International Studies in Sociology of Education, 2,* 57–73.

Gilmartin, B. G. (1987). Peer group antecedents of severe love-shyness in males. *Journal of Personality, 55,* 467–489.

Ginsburg, H. J., Pollman, V. A., & Wauson, M. S. (1977). An ethological analysis of nonverbal inhibitors of aggressive behavior in male elementary school children. *Developmental Psychology, 13,* 417–418.

Goffman, E. (1963). *Stigma: Notes on the management of spoiled identity.* New York: Simon & Schuster.

Golding, W. (1955). *Lord of the flies.* New York: Capricorn.

Gould, T. (1995). *A summer plague: Polio and its survivors.* New Haven: Yale University Press.

Graham, P., Rutter, M., & George, S. (1973). Temperamental characteristics as predictors of behaviour problems in children. *American Journal of Orthopsychiatry, 43,* 328–339.

Greenbaum, S. (1989). *Set straight on bullies.* Malibu, CA: Pepperdine University Press.

Greene, G. (1971). *A sort of life.* New York: Simon & Schuster.

Greenlees, J. (1993, April 9). Harsh regime blamed for bullies. *Times Educational Supplement,* p. 10.

Growing up nasty. (1993, June). *Harper's, 286,* 13–15.

Grunsell, A. (1990). *Bullying.* London: Gloucester Press.

Gumperz, J. J. (1977) . Sociocultural knowledge in conversational inference. In M. Saville-Troike (Ed.), *Linguistics and anthropology* (pp. 191–211). Washington, DC: Georgetown University Press.

Haeselager, G. J. T., & van Lieshout, C. F. M. (1992, September). *Social and affective adjustment of self- and peer-reported victims and bullies.* Paper presented at the European Conference on Developmental Psychology, Seville, Spain.

Hagedorn, J. (1993, March). A helping hand. *Report,* 6.

Haigh, G. (1994, October 28). Blessed are the peacemakers. *Times Educational Supplement,* p. 6.

Hamilton, L. (1992, August). Advice for dancers. *Dance Magazine, 66,* 54.

Hammond, J. O. (1989). Foreword. In D. P. Tattum & D. A. Lane (Eds.), *Bullying in schools* (pp. 5–6). Stoke-on-Trent: Trentham Books.

Hawkins, J. D., Catalano, R. F., Morrison, D. M., O'Donnell, J., Abbott, R. D., & Day, L. E. (1992). The Seattle Social Development Project: Effects of the first four years on protective factors and problem behaviors. In J. McCord & R. E. Tremblay (Eds.), *Preventing antisocial behav-*

ior: Interventions from birth to adolescence (pp. 139–161). New York: Guilford Press.

Hazler, R. J., Hoover, J. H., & Oliver, R. (1993). What do kids say about bullying? *Education Digest, 58*(7), 16–20.

Heinemann, P. P. (1973). *Mobbning. Gruppvald blent barn og. vokane.* Stockholm: Natur och Kultur.

Herbert, G. (1989). A whole-curriculum approach to bullying. In D. P. Tattum & D. A. Lane (Eds.), *Bullying in schools* (pp. 73–80). Stoke-on-Trent: Trentham Books.

Hirano, K. (1992, September). *Bullying and victimization in Japanese classrooms.* Paper presented at the European Conference on Developmental Psychology, Seville, Spain.

Hodges, E. V. E., Malone, M. J., & Perry, D. G. (1995). *Behavioral risk and social risk as interacting determinants of victimization in the peer group.* Manuscript submitted for publication, Florida Atlantic University.

Hodges, E. V. E., & Perry, D. G. (in press). Victims of peer abuse: An overview. *Journal of Emotional and Behavioral Problems.*

Holmes, S. (1993). *The soldier.* London BBC Education, Post Production Script.

Hoover, J., & Hazler, R. J. (1991). Bullies and victims. *Elementary School Guidance & Counseling, 25*, 212–219.

Horne, A. M., Glaser, B., & Sayger, T. V. (1994). Bullies. *Counseling and Human Development, 27*, 1–12.

Horton, A. M. (1991). The Heartstone Odyssey: Exploring the heart of bullying. In P. K. Smith & D. Thompson (Eds.), *Practical approaches to bullying* (pp. 60–67). London: David Fulton.

Howard, M., & McCabe, J. B. (1990). Helping teenagers postpone sexual involvement. *Family Planning Perspectives, 22*, 21–26.

Hughes, T. (1857). *Tom Brown's schooldays.* New York: Harper.

Humphries, S., Mack, J., & Perks, R. (1988). *A century of childhood.* London: Sidgwick & Jackson.

Iwasaki, J. (1992, February 25). Contract law hits the playground: "Conflict managers" help keep peace. *The Seattle Post-Intelligencer*, p. B3.

James, O. (1994, May). Violent children. *Harpers & Queen, 4*, 134, 136–137, 188–189.

Jarvie, G. J., Lahey, B., Graziano, W., & Framer, E. (1983). Childhood obesity and social stigma: What we know and what we don't know. *Developmental Review, 3*, 237–273.

Jones, E. (1991). Practical considerations in dealing with bullying—in secondary school. In M. Elliott (Ed.), *Bullying: A practical guide to coping for schools.* Essex: Longman.

Juran, J. (1967). The quality circle phenomenon. *Industrial Quality Control, 23*, 329–366.

Kashani, J. H., Reid, J. C., & Rosenberg, T. K. (1989). Levels of hopelessness in children and adolescents: A developmental perspective. *Journal of Consulting and Clinical Psychology, 57*, 496–499.

Katz, A. H. (1993). *Self-help in America: A social movement perspective.* New York: Twayne Publishers.

Kazdin, A. E. (1987). Treatment of antisocial behavior in children: Current status and future directions. *Psychological Bulletin, 102,* 187–203.

Kazdin, A. E., Siegel, T. C., & Bass, D. (1992). Cognitive-problem-solving skills training in the treatment of antisocial behavior in children. *Journal of Consulting and Clinical Psychology, 60,* 733–747.

Kellerman, J. (1981). *Helping the fearful child.* New York: Norton.

Kelly, E. (1990). Use and abuse of racial language in secondary schools. In P. D. Pumphrey & G. K. Verma (Eds.), *Race relations and urban education.* Lewes: Falmer.

Kelly, E., & Cohn, T. (1988). *Racism in schools: New research evidence.* Stoke-on-Trent: Trentham Books.

Kelly, P. (1993, January 1). Up the garden path. *Times Educational Supplement,* p. 21.

Killinger, J. (1980). *The loneliness of children.* New York: Vanguard Press.

Klein, C. (1975). *The myth of the happy child.* New York: Harper & Row.

Klein, R. (1994, January 6). Where prejudice still flares into violence: Timetable of terror. *Times Educational Supplement,* Features, p. 9

Klein, R. (1995, March 31). Roughed up by justice. *Times Educational Supplement,* Features, p. 4.

Kochenderfer, B. J., & Ladd, G. W. (1995). *Victimized children's responses to peers' aggression: Behaviors associated with reduced versus continued victimization.* Manuscript submitted for publication, University of Illinois at Urbana-Champaign.

Kochenderfer, B. J., & Ladd, G. W. (in press, a). Peer victimization: Cause or consequence of school maladjustment? *Child Development.*

Kochenderfer, B. J., & Ladd, G. W. (in press, b). Peer victimization: Manifestations and relations to school adjustment in kindergarten. *Journal of School Psychology.*

Kureishi, H. (1986). *My beautiful launderette and the rainbow sign.* London: Faber.

Kutner, L. (1981). *Parent and child: Getting through to each other.* New York: Morrow.

Ladd, G. W., & Price, J. M. (1987). Predicting children's social and school adjustment following the transition from preschool to kindergarten. *Child Development, 58,* 1168–1189.

La Fontaine, J. (1991). *Bullying, the child's view: An analysis of telephone calls to Childline about bullying.* London: Calouste Gulbenkian Foundation.

Lagerspetz, K. M., Björkqvist, K., Berts, M., & King, E. (1982). Group aggression among school children in three schools. *Scandinavian Journal of Psychology, 23,* 45–52.

Lagerspetz, K. M. J., Björkqvist, K., Peltonen, T. (1988). Is indirect aggression typical of females? Gender differences in aggressiveness in 11- to 12-year-old children. *Aggressive Behavior, 14,* 403–414.

Landers, A. (1995, February 17). Advice. *The Seattle Post-Intelligencer,* p. 35.

Lane, D. A. (1989). Violent histories: Bullying and criminality. In D. P. Tattum & D. A. Lane (Eds.), *Bullying in schools* (pp. 95–104). Stoke-on-Trent: Trentham Books.

Laslett, R. (1980). Bullies: A children's court in a day school for maladjusted children. *B.C. Journal of Special Education, 4*, 391–397.

Lawson, S. (1994). *Helping children cope with bullying.* London: Sheldon.

Lazarus, R. S. (1966). *Psychological stress and the coping process.* New York: McGraw-Hill.

Lazarus, R. S., & Folkman, S. (1984). *Stress, appraisal, and coping.* New York: Springer.

Leach, P. (1986). *Your growing child: From babyhood through adolescence.* New York: Knopf.

Leach, P. (1994). *Children first. What our society must do—and is not doing—for our children today.* New York: Knopf.

Lerner, M. J. (1980). *Belief in a just world: A fundamental delusion.* New York: Plenum.

Lister, P. (1995, November). Bullies: The big new problem you must know about. *Redbook, 186*, 116, 118–119, 136, 138.

Lochman, J. (1993). Braking bullies. In R. D. Stephens, *School bullying and victimization* (p. 19). Malibu, CA: National School Safety Center, Pepperdine University.

Lorenz, K. (1966). *On aggression.* London: Methuen.

Lowenstein, L. F. (1978). The bullied and the non-bullied child. *Bulletin of the British Psychological Society, 31*, 316–318.

Lytton, H. (1990). Child and parent effects in boys' conduct disorders: A re-interpretation. *Developmental Psychology, 26*, 683–697.

Maccoby, E. E. (1980). *Social development: Psychological growth and the parent-child relationship.* New York: Harcourt Brace Jovanovich.

Maccoby, E. E., & Jacklin, C. N. (1974). *The psychology of sex differences.* Stanford, CA: Stanford University Press.

Madsen, K., & Smith, P. K. (1993). *Age and gender differences in participants' perception of the concept of the term bullying.* Poster presentation at the Sixth European Conference on Developmental Psychology, Bonn, Germany.

Maher, R. (1987, Fall). Students watch out for their own. *School Safety*, 26–27.

Maines, B., & Robinson, G. (1992). *Stamp out bullying: Never mind the awareness, what can we do?* Portishead, Bristol: Lame Duck Publishing.

Marano, H. E. (1995, September/October). Big. Bad. Bully. *Psychology Today, 28*, 50–57, 62, 64, 66, 68–70, 74, 76, 79, 82.

Marks, J. (1993, November). Our son is becoming a bully. *Parents' Magazine, 68*, 302–306.

Maslen, G. (1994, October 7) . "Subtle" bullying still leaves its scars. *Times Educational Supplement,* p. 16.

McCall, R. B. (1981). Nature-nurture and the two realms of development: A proposed integration with respect to mental development. *Child Development, 52*, 1–12.

McCoy, E. (1992, November). Bully-proof your child. *Reader's Digest, 141*, 199–200, 203–205.

McGhee, P. E. (1989). The contribution of humor to children's social development. In P. E. McGhee (Ed.), *Humor and children's development: A guide to practical applications* (pp. 119–134). New York: The Haworth Press.

Meichenbaum, D. H. (1971). Examination of model characteristics in reducing avoidance behavior. *Journal of Personality and Social Psychology, 17*, 298–307.

Mellor, A. (1991). Helping victims. In M. Elliott (Ed.), *Bullying: A practical guide to coping for schools* (pp. 90–102). Harlow, Essex: Longman.

Mellor Smith, H. (1992). *The effect of quality circles on bullying behaviour in schools*. Unpublished BA dissertation, University of Sheffield, Sheffield, England.

Miedzian, M. (1992). *Boys will be boys: Breaking the link between masculinity and violence*. New York: Doubleday.

Miller, P. (1986). Teasing as language socialization and verbal play in a white working-class community. In B. B. Schieffelin & E. Ochs (Eds.), *Language socialization across cultures* (pp. 199–212) . Cambridge: Cambridge University Press.

Minton, L. (1994, February 20). Fresh voices: Have you ever been sexually harassed? *The Seattle Post-Intelligencer*, Parade, p. 30.

Mitchel, J., & O'Moore, M. (1988). In *Report of the European Teachers' Seminar on Bullying in Schools*. Strasbourg: Council for Cultural Cooperation.

Munsch, J., & Kinchen, K. M. (1995). Adolescent sociometric status and social support. *Journal of Early Adolescence, 15*, 181–202.

Munthe, E. (1989). Bullying in Scandinavia. In E. Roland & E. Munthe (Eds.), *Bullying: An international perspective* (pp. 66–78). London: David Fulton.

My son was being bullied at school. (1989, April). *Good Housekeeping*, pp. 36, 40, 45, 48.

Nash, I. (1989, October 20). True extent of bullying hidden. *Times Educational Supplement*, p. 5.

Neary, A., & Joseph, S. (1994). Peer victimization and its relationship to self-concept and depression among schoolgirls. *Personality and Individual Differences, 16*, 183–186.

Nelsen, J. (1985). *Positive discipline*. Fair Oaks, CA: Sunrise Press.

Neustatter, A. (1994, October 7). The hurt beneath a hard exterior. *Times Educational Supplement*, p. 6.

Nicoll, A., & Rudd, P. (Eds.). (1989). *British Pediatric Association Manual on Infections and Immunization in Children*. Oxford: Oxford University Press.

O'Connor, M. (1995, April 14). Anxieties of our time addressed. *Times Educational Supplement*, p. 9.

Oliver, R., Hoover, J. H., & Hazler, R. (1994). The perceived roles of bullying in small-town Midwestern schools. *Journal of Counseling and Development, 72*, 416–421.

Oliver, R., Oaks, I. N., & Hoover, J. H. (1994). Family issues and interventions in bully and victim relationships. *The School Counselor, 41,* 199–202.

Olweus, D. (1978). *Aggression in the schools: Bullies and whipping boys.* Washington, DC: Hemisphere.

Olweus, D. (1979). Stability of aggressive reaction patterns in males: A review. *Psychological Bulletin, 86,* 852–875.

Olweus, D. (1980). Familial and temperamental determinants of aggressive behavior in adolescent boys: A causal analysis. *Developmental Psychology, 16,* 644–660.

Olweus, D. (1981). Bullying among school boys. In N. Cantwell (Ed.), *Children and violence.* Stockholm: Akademilitteratur.

Olweus, D. (1983). *Bully/Victim Questionnaire.* Unpublished manuscript, University of Bergen, Norway.

Olweus, D. (1984). Aggressors and their victims: Bullying at school. In N. Frude & H. Gault (Eds.), *Disruptive behaviors in schools* (pp. 57–76). New York: Wiley.

Olweus, D. (1985). 80,000 pupils involved in bullying. *Norsk Skoleblad, 2,* Norway.

Olweus, D. (1988). *Critical views on the Pikas method.* Unpublished manuscript, University of Bergen, Bergen, Norway.

Olweus, D. (1991). Bully/victim problems among school children: Basic facts and effects of a school based intervention program. In D. Pepler & K. Rubin (Eds.), *The development and treatment of childhood aggression.* Hillsdale, NJ: Erlbaum.

Olweus, D. (1993a). *Bullying at school: What we know and what we can do.* Cambridge, MA: Blackwells.

Olweus, D. (1993b). Victimization by peers: Antecedents and long-term outcomes. In K. H. Rubin & J. B. Asendorf (Eds.), *Social withdrawal, inhibition, and shyness* (pp. 315–341). Hillsdale, NJ: Erlbaum.

Olweus, D., & Roland, E. (1983). *Bullying: Background and management.* Oslo, Norway: Kirke-og undervisnings departementet.

Olweus, D., & Smith, P. K. (1995). *The Bully/Victim Questionnaire* (English version). Oxford: Blackwells.

O'Malley, B. (1993, June 18). Screening out the bullies. *Times Educational Supplement,* Resources, p. 15.

O'Moore, A. M. (1988). *Bullying in schools* (Council of Europe Report DECS-EGT [88] 5–E). Strasbourg: Council for Cultural Cooperation.

O'Moore, A. M., & Hillery, B. (1989). Bullying in Dublin schools. *Irish Journal of Psychology, 10,* 426–441.

O'Moore, A. M., & Hillery, B. (1991). What do teachers need to know. In M. Elliott (Ed.), *Bullying: A practical guide to coping for schools* (pp. 56–69). Harlow, Essex: Longman.

Opie, I. (1993). *The people in the playground.* New York: Oxford University Press.

Opie, I., & Opie, P. (1959). *The lore and language of school children.* London: Oxford University Press.

Osofsky, J. D. (1995). The effects of exposure to violence on young children. *American Psychologist, 50*, 782–788.

Oswald, H., Krappman, L., Chowdhuri, I., & von Salisch, M. (1988). Gaps and bridges: Interactions between girls and boys in elementary school. In P. Adler & P. Adler (Eds.), *Sociological studies of child development,* (Vol. 2, pp. 204–224). Greenwich, CT: JAI Press.

Oxford English Dictionary (1993). Oxford, England: Oxford University Press.

Parke, R. D., & Slaby, R. G. (1983). The development of aggression. In P. H. Mussen (Series Ed.) & E. M. Hetherington (Vol. Ed.), *Handbook of child psychology: Vol. 4. Socialization, personality, and social development* (pp. 547–641). New York: Wiley.

Parker, J. G., & Asher, S. R. (1987). Peer relations and later personal adjustment: Are low-accepted children at risk? *Psychological Bulletin, 102*, 357–389.

Patterson, G. R., DeBaryshe, B. D., & Ramsey, E. (1989). A developmental perspective on antisocial behavior. *American Psychologist, 44*, 329–355.

Patterson, G. R., Littman, R. A., & Bricker, W. (1967). Assertive behavior in children: A step toward a theory of aggression. *Monographs of the Society for Research in Child Development, 32* (5, Serial No. 113).

Pawluk, C. J. (1989). Social construction of teasing. *Journal for the Theory of Social Behavior, 19*, 145–167.

Pearce, J. (1989). *Fighting, teasing, and bullying.* Wellingborough, England: Thorsons.

Pearce, J. (1991). What can be done about the bully? In M. Elliott (Ed.), *Bullying: A practical guide to coping for schools* (pp. 70–89). Harlow, Essex: Longman.

Pepler, D., Craig, W., Zeigler, S., & Charach, A. (1993). A school-based anti-bullying-intervention: Preliminary evaluation. In D. Tattum (Ed.), *Understanding and managing bullying* (pp. 76–91). Oxford: Heinemann Educational.

Perry, D. G., Kusel, S. J., & Perry, L. C. (1988). Victims of peer aggression. *Developmental Psychology, 24*, 807–814.

Perry, D. G., Perry, L. C., & Weiss, R. J. (1989) . Sex differences in the consequences that children anticipate for aggression. *Developmental Psychology, 25*, 312–319.

Perry, D. G., Williard, J. C., & Perry, L. C. (1990). Peers' perceptions of the consequences that victimized children provide aggressors. *Child Development, 61*, 1310–1325.

Phillips, D. (1989). *How to give your child a great self-image.* New York: Random House.

Pikas, A. (1989). The common concern method for the treatment of mobbing. In E. Roland & E. Munthe (Eds.), *Bullying: An international perspective* (pp. 91–104). London: Fulton.

Pipher, M. (1994). *Reviving Ophelia: Saving the selves of adolescent girls.* New York: Ballantine.

Pitman, R. K. (1988). Post-traumatic stress disorder, conditioning, and network theory. *Psychiatric Annals, 18*, 182–189.

Playground person—Iona Opie. (1988, November 7). *New Yorker*, pp. 18, 39.

Pollack, A. (1994, December 18). Suicides by bullied students stir Japanese furor. *The New York Times*, p. 10(N), 20(L).

Polsky, H. (1962). *Cottage 6.* New York: Wiley.

Prestage, M. (1993, February 26). Skeleton is dragged out of the closet (Bullying incidents in schools). *Times Educational Supplement*, pp. 16–17.

Prestage, M. (1994, December 2). How to beat bullies from the inside. *Times Educational Supplement*, p. 9.

Prewitt, P. W. (1988). Dealing with ijime (bullying) among Japanese students. *School Psychology International, 9*, 189–195.

Priest, D. (1987, May 20). Why bullies do it: "To really have fun": School violence being studied. *The Washington Post*, p. 16.

Prothrow-Stith, D. (1991). *Deadly consequences.* New York: Harper Collins.

Pupils accused of spiking teacher's apple. (1992, November 20). *Seattle Post-Intelligencer*, p. F3.

Pyke, N. (1994, May 20). Bullies lurk in every staffroom. *Times Educational Supplement*, p. 12.

Randall, P. E. (1995, May). Beyond the school gates (bullying). *Special Children*, No. 84, 19–21.

Randall, P. E., & Donohue, M. I. (1993, October). Tackling bullying together. *Child Education, 70*, 79.

Reid, K. (1983). Retrospection and persistent school absenteeism. *Educational Research, 25*, 110–115.

Reid, K. (1990). Bullying and persistent school absenteeism. In D. P. Tattum & D. A. Lane (Eds.), *Bullying in schools* (pp. 89–94). Hanley, Stoke-on-Trent: Trentham Books.

Report details harassment of gays in schools. (1994, August 31). *The Seattle Post-Intelligencer*, p. B3.

Rhoden, W. C. (1993, February 6). Bobbing amid the thugs and bullies. *The New York Times*, p. 28.

Richman, N., Stevenson, J., & Graham, P. (1982). *Preschool to school: A behavioural study.* London: Academic Press.

Rigby, K., & Slee, P. T. (1991). Bullying among Australian school children: Reported behavior and attitudes toward victims. *Journal of Social Psychology, 131*, 615–627.

Rigby, K., & Slee, P. T. (1992). Dimensions of interpersonal relation among Australian children and implications for psychological well-being. *The Journal of Social Psychology, 133*, 33–42.

Riley, D. (1988). *Bullying: A study of victim and victimizers within one inner city secondary school.* In-service B. Ed. Inquiry Report, Crewe and Alsager College of Higher Education, Sheffield, England.

Rivers, I., & Smith, P. K. (1994). Types of bullying behaviour and their correlates. *Aggressive Behavior, 20*, 359–368.

Robins, L. N. (1978). Sturdy predictors of adult antisocial behaviour: Replication from longitudinal studies. *Psychological Medicine, 8*, 611–622.

Rogers, W. S. (1993). Promoting, permitting and preventing bullying. In M. Elliott (Ed.), *Bullying: A practical guide to coping for schools* (pp. 50–58). Harlow, Essex: Longman.

Roland, E. (1980). *Terror in school.* Rogalandeforskning: Stavanger.

Roland, E. (1989a). Bullying: The Scandinavian research tradition. In D. P. Tattum & D. A. Lane (Eds.), *Bullying in schools* (pp. 21–32). Hanley, Stoke-on-Trent: Trentham Books.

Roland, E. (1989b). A system oriented strategy against bullying. In E. Roland & E. Munthe (Eds.), *Bullying: An international perspective* (pp. 143–151). London: Fulton.

Rose, L. (1991). *The erosion of childhood: Child oppression in Britain, 1860–1918.* London: Routledge.

Rosenberg, M. (1993, September 6). Violence a public health problem. *Seattle Post-Intelligencer,* p. 14.

Ross, D. M. (1973). *A teasing program for children.* Unpublished manuscript, University of California Medical Center, San Francisco.

Ross, D. M., & Ross, S. A. (1982). *Hyperactivity: Current issues, research and theory* (2nd ed.). New York: Wiley.

Ross, D. M., & Ross, S. A. (1984). Teaching the child with leukemia to cope with teasing. *Issues in Comprehensive Pediatric Nursing, 7,* 59–66.

Ross, D. M., & Ross, S. A. (1988). *Childhood pain: Current issues, research, and management.* Baltimore: Urban & Schwarzenburg.

Royal, G. P., & Roberts, M. C. (1987). Students' perceptions of and attitudes toward disabilities: A comparison of twenty conditions. *Journal of Clinical Child Psychology, 16,* 122–132.

Rutter, M. (1979). Protective factors in children's responses to stress and disadvantage. In M. W. Kent & J. E. Rolf (Eds.), *Primary prevention of psychopathology: Vol. 3. Social competence in children* (pp. 49–74). Hanover, NH: University Press of New England.

Rutter, M. (1983). School effects on pupil progress: Research findings and policy implications. *Child Development, 54,* 1–19.

Rutter, M. (1987). Psychosocial resilience and protective mechanisms. *American Journal of Orthopsychiatry, 57,* 316–331.

Rutter, M., & Giller, H. (1983). *Juvenile delinquency: Trends and perspectives.* New York: Penguin.

Savedra, M. (1977). Coping with pain: Strategies of severely burned children. *Canadian Nurse, 73,* 28–29.

Schwartz, D., Dodge, K. A., & Coie, J. D. (1993). The emergence of chronic peer victimization in boys' play groups. *Child Development, 64,* 1755–1793.

Schweinhart, L. J., Barnes, H. V., & Weikart, D. P. (Eds.). (1993). *Significant benefits: The High / Scope Perry Preschool Study through age 27.* Ypsilanti, MI: High/Scope Press.

Scialli, J. (1991, November). When your child is picked on. *Parents Magazine, 66,* 47.

Scott, W. (1993, November 28). Personality Parade. *The Seattle Post-Intelligencer,* Parade, p. 2.

Segal, J., & Yahraes, H. (1978). *A child's journey.* New York: McGraw Hill.

Seitz, V., Rosenbaum, L.K., & Apfel, N. H. (1985). Effects of family support intervention: A ten-year follow-up. *Child Development, 56,* 376–391.

Shapiro, J. P., Baumeister, R. F., & Kessler, J. W. (1987). Children's awareness of themselves as teasers and their value judgments of teasing. *Perceptual and Motor Skills, 64,* 1102.

Sharp, S., Sellars, A., & Cowie, H. (1994). Time to listen: Setting up a peer counseling service to help tackle the problem of bullying in schools. *Pastoral Care in Education,* 12–17.

Sharp, S., & Smith, P. K. (Eds.). (1994). *Tackling bullying in your school: A practical handbook for teachers.* London: Routledge.

Shaver, K. J. (1975). *An introduction to attribution processes.* Cambridge, MA: Winthrop.

Siann, G., Callaghan, M., Glissov, P., Lockhart, R. , & Rawson, L. (1994). Who gets bullied? The effect of school, gender and ethnic group. *Educational Research, 36,* 123–134.

Siegel, B. S. (1986). *Love, medicine & miracles.* New York: Harper & Row.

Sigelman, C. K., & Begley, N. L. (1987) . The early development of reactions to peers with controllable and uncontrollable problems. *Journal of Pediatric Psychology, 12,* 99–114.

Silver, R. L., & Wortman, C. B. (1980). Coping with undesirable life events. In J. Garber & M. E. P. Seligman (Eds.), *Human helplessness: Theory and applications* (pp. 279–340). New York: Academic Press.

Silverman, W. K., La Greca, A. M., & Wasserstein, S. (1995). What do children worry about? Worries and their relation to anxiety. *Child Development, 66,* 671–686.

Slaby, R. G., Roedell, N. C., Arezzo, D., & Hendrix, K. (1995). *Early violence prevention: Tools for teachers of young children.* Washington, D.C.: National Association for the Education of Young Children.

Smith, M. J. (1986). *Yes, I can say no.* New York: Arbor House.

Smith, P. K. (1991). The silent nightmare: Bullying and victimization in school peer groups. *The Psychologist, 4,* 243–248.

Smith, P. K., & Boulton, M. J. (1991). *Self-esteem, sociometric status, and peer-perceived behavioral characteristics in Middle School children in the United Kingdom.* Papers presented at the meeting of the International Society for the Study of Behavioral Development, Minneapolis, MN.

Smith, P. K., Bowers, L., Binney, V., & Cowie, H. (1993). Relationships of children involved in bully/victim problems at school. In S. Duck (Ed.), *Understanding relationship processes: Vol. 2. Learning about relationships.* Newbury Park, CA: Sage.

Smith, P. K., & Levan, S. (in press). Perceptions and experiences of bullying in younger pupils. *International Foundation of Educational Psychology.*

Smith, P. K., & Sharp, S. (Eds.) (1994). *School bullying: Insights and perspectives.* London: Routledge.

Smith, P. K., & Thompson, D. (1991). Dealing with bully/victim problems in the U.K. In P. K. Smith & D. Thompson (Eds.), *Practical approaches to bullying* (pp. 1–12). London: Fulton.

Smith, S. J. (1992). How to decrease bullying in our schools. *Principal, 72,* 31–33.

Sorensen, E. S. (1993). *Children's stress and coping.* New York: Guilford.

Spock, B. (1986, August). How to tame a bully. *Redbook,* p. 36.

Stainton Rogers, R. (1991). Now you see it, now I don't. In M. Elliott (Ed.), *Bullying: A practical guide to coping for schools* (pp. 1–7). Essex: Longman.

Stein, N. (1993). No laughing matter: Sexual harassment in K–12 schools. In E. Buchwald, P. Fletcher, & M. Roth (Eds.), *Transforming a rape culture.* Minneapolis, MN: Milkweed Editions.

Stephens, R. D. (1991, September). Bullies and victims: Protecting our schoolchildren. *USA Today, 120,* 72–74.

Stephenson, P., & Smith, D. (1989). Bullying in the junior school. In D. P. Tattum & D. A. Lane (Eds.), *Bullying in schools* (pp. 45–57). Stoke-on-Trent: Trentham Books.

Stephenson, P., & Smith, D. (1993). Why some schools don't have bullies. In M. Elliott (Ed.), *Bullying: A practical guide to coping for schools* (pp. 133–145). Harlow, Essex: Longman.

St. John Brooks, C. (1985, December 6). The school bullies. *New Society,* pp. 363–365.

Strom, M. S., & Parsons, W. S. (1982). *Facing history and ourselves: Holocaust and human behavior.* Watertown, MA: International Educations.

Swann Report (1985). *Education for all.* The Report of the Committee of Inquiry into the Education of Children from Ethnic Minority Groups. London: HMSO.

Tattum D. P. (1989). Violence and aggression in schools. In D. P. Tattum & D. A. Lane (Eds.), *Bullying in schools* (pp. 7–19). Hanley, Stoke-on-Trent: Trentham Books.

Tattum, D. P., & Herbert, G. (1993). Countering bullying: Initiatives by schools and local authorities. Hanley, Stoke-on-Trent: Trentham Books.

Thelen, M. H., Fry, R. A., Fehrenbach, P. A., & Frautschi, N. M. (1979). Therapeutic videotape and film modeling: A review. *Psychological Bulletin, 86,* 701–720.

Thomas, A., & Chess, S. (1977). *Temperament and development.* New York: Brunner/Mazel.

Thompson, D. A. (1986). Developing a peer group facilitation program on the secondary school level: An investment with multiple returns. *Small Group Behavior, 17,* 105–112.

Thompson, D. A., & Arora, T. (1991). Why do children bully? An evaluation of the long-term effectiveness of a whole-school policy to minimize bullying. *Pastoral Care in Education, 9,* 8–12.

Thompson, D. A., & Smith, P. K. (1991). Effective action against bullying— the key problems. In P. K. Smith & D. A. Thompson (Eds.), *Practical approaches to bullying* (pp. 140–152). London: Fulton.

Thompson, J. K., & Psaltis, K. (1988). Multiple aspects and correlates of body figure ratings: A replication and extension of Fallon and Rozin. *International Journal of Eating Disorders, 7,* 813–818.

Thorne, B., & Luria, Z. (1986). Sexuality and gender in children's daily worlds. *Social Problems, 33*, 176–190.

Tieger, T. (1980). On the biological basis of sex differences in aggression. *Child Development, 51*, 943–963.

Townsend-Wise, K., & Harrison, H. (1991). A child's view—how Childline helps. In M. Elliott (Ed.), *Bullying: A practical guide to coping for schools* (pp. 112–118). Harlow, Essex: Longman.

Tremblay, R. E., Masse, B., Perron, D., Leblanc, M., Schwartzman, A. E., & Ledigham, J. E. (1992). Early disruptive behavior, poor school achievement, delinquent behavior, and delinquent personality: Longitudinal analyses. *Journal of Consulting and Clinical Psychology, 60*, 64–72.

Troy, M., & Sroufe, L. A. (1987). Victimization among preschoolers: Role of attachment relationship history. *Journal of the American Academy of Child and Adolescent Psychiatry, 26*, 166–172.

Troyna, B., & Hatcher, R. (1992). *Racism in children's lives: A study of mainly white primary schools.* London: Routledge.

Turkel, S. B., & Eth, S. (1990). Psychopathological response to stress: Adjustment disorder and post-traumatic stress disorder in children and adolescents. In L. E. Arnold (Ed.), *Childhood stress.* New York: Wiley.

Van Buren, A. (1995, November 7). Moms defend tormented children. *The San Francisco Chronicle*, p. E8.

Wachtel, P. L. (1973). Psychodynamics, behaviour therapy and the implacable experimenter: An inquiry into the consistency of personality. *Journal of Abnormal Psychology, 83*, 324–334.

Walvin, J. (1982). *A child's world: A social history of English childhood, 1800–1914.* Hammonsworth: Penguin.

Whalen, C. K., & Henker, B. (1976). Psychostimulants and children: A review and analysis. *Psychological Bulletin, 83*, 1113–1130.

White, M. (1987). *The Japanese educational challenge.* London: Free Press/Macmillan.

White, M. (1993). *The material child: Coming of age in Japan and America.* New York: The Free Press.

Whitney, I., Nabuzoka, D., & Smith, P. K. (1992). Bullying in schools: Mainstream and special needs children. *Support for learning, 7*, 3–7.

Whitney, I., & Smith, P. K. (1993). A survey of the nature and extent of bully/victim problems in junior/middle and secondary schools. *Educational Research, 35*, 3–25.

Whitney, I., Smith, P. K., & Thompson, D. (1994). Bullying and children with special educational needs. In P. K. Smith & S. Sharp (Eds.), *School bullying: Insights and perspectives* (pp. 213–240). London: Routledge.

Widom, C. S. (1991). Childhood victimization: Risk factor for delinquency. In M. E. Colten & S. Gore (Eds.), *Adolescent stress: Causes and consequences.* New York: Aldine de Gruyter.

Wiehe, V. R. (1991). *Perilous rivalry: When siblings become abusive.* Lexington, MA: Lexington Books.

Wiggins, J. S., & Winder, C. L. (1961). The Peer Nomination Inventory: An empirically derived sociometric measure of adjustment in preadolescent boys. *Psychological Reports, 9*, 643–677.

Williams, E. (1995, March 3). Drama out of prison. *Times Educational Supplement*, p. 4.

Willis, P. (1977). *Learning to labour*. London: Saxon House.

Wills, W. D. (1945). *The Barns experiment*. London: Allen & Unwin.

Wills, W. D. (1960). *Throw away thy rod*. London: Gallancz.

Winfrey, O. (1993, January 5). Are your children safe at school. In Harpo Productions, *Oprah: The Oprah Winfrey Show* [Transcript]. Livingston, NJ: Burrelle's Information Services.

Winfrey, O. (1994, January 6). Bully/nerd clinic. In Harpo Productions, *Oprah: The Oprah Winfrey Show* [Transcript]. Livingston, NJ: Burrelle's Information Services.

Yamamoto, K. (1979). Children's ratings of the stressfulness of experiences. *Developmental Psychology, 15*, 581–582.

Yamamoto, K., & Byrnes, D. A. (1984). Classroom social status, ethnicity, and ratings of stressful events. *Journal of Educational Research, 77*, 283–286.

Yamamoto, K., & Felsenthal, H. M. (1982). Stressful experiences of children: Professional judgments. *Psychological Reports, 50*, 1087–1093.

Yates, C., & Smith, P. K. (1989). Bullying in two English comprehensive schools. In E. Roland & E. Munthe (Eds.), *Bullying: An international perspective* (pp. 22–34). London: Fulton.

Yoshikawa, H. (1994). Prevention as cumulative protection: Effects of early family support and education on chronic delinquency and its risks. *Psychological Bulletin, 115*, 28–54.

Yoshikawa-Cogley, L. (1995, February 8). Children talk out problems. *The Seattle Post-Intelligencer*, pp. B1, B3.

Zablow, S. (1991, November 5). In B. Bartocci, When kids gang up on your child. *Women's Day*, 15, 39.

Zarzour, K. (1994). *Battling the school-yard bully*. Toronto: HarperCollins.

Ziegler, S., & Rosenstein-Manner, M. (1991). *Bullying at school: Toronto in an international context* (Report No. 196). Toronto: Toronto Board of Education, Research Services.

Zimbardo, P. G. (1982). *The shy child*. Garden City, NY: Doubleday.

Zimbardo, P. G. (1990). *Shyness: What it is. What to do about it*. New York: Addison-Wesley.

Zimmerman, J. (1995). *Tailspin: Women at war in the wake of Tailhook*. New York: Doubleday.

Zinsmeister, K. (1990, June). Growing up scared. *The Atlantic Monthly, 265*, 49–66.

Annotated Bibliography

Books for Primary-Grade Children: Fiction

Alexander, M. (1983). *Move over, twerp*. New York: Dial Press.
Shows what happens when a child who is being pushed around by bigger boys takes a firm stand.

Berenstain, S., & Berenstain, J. (1993). *The Berenstain Bears and the bully*. New York: Random House.
When she gets beaten up by the class bully, Sister Bear learns an important lesson in self-defense and forgiveness. Discussion should stress that physical aggression is not a good strategy.

Boyd, L. (1991). *Baily the big bully*. New York: Puffin Books.
Max, the new boy in school, uses assertiveness to tame Baily the bully, of whom everyone is afraid, and teaches Baily about teamwork and friendship.

Bottner, B. (1980). *Mean Maxine*. New York: Pantheon.
Ralph is teased by Mean Maxine until he works up his courage for a confrontation with her. Note that he rehearses what he will say and how mean he will be.

Chapman, C. (1981). *Herbie's troubles*. New York: Dutton Children's Books.
After trying the advice of each of his friends on how to deal with a bully, Herbie solves his problem himself.

Cole J. (1989). *Bully trouble*. New York: Random House.
Two small boys are bullied by a bigger boy until they strike back with a clever, simple plan.

Cushman, D. (1990). *Camp Big Paw*. New York: Harper & Row.
On Cyril's first day at camp he is picked on by Nigel, the camp tease. How Cyril manages Nigel with a clever strategy makes good reading.

Freschet, B. (1986). *Furlie Cat*. New York: Lothrop.
Furlie the fraidy cat mistakenly decides that being tough is the only way to overcome his fears. He becomes a bully overnight. When something happens that teaches him to be a friend to one of his victims, he gives up being a bully.

Henkes, K. (1991). *Chrysanthemum*. New York: Greenwillow Books.
A kindergarten-age mouse is teased because of her unusual name. The story shows empathy for the victim and the power of social support.

Kasza, K. (1993). *The rat and the tiger*. New York: Putnam's.
In his friendship with Rat, Tiger plays the bully because of his greater size, but one day Rat stands up for his rights: Tiger makes amends.

Kraus, R. (1977). *Noel the coward*. New York: Windmills Press.
Shows the effect that striking back has on bullies.

Passen, L. (1991). *Fat, fat Rose Marie*. New York: Holt.

Excellent on the importance of accepting others for *who* they are and for showing that if one child takes a stand against a bully, others will follow.

Petty, K., & Firmin, C. (1991). *Being bullied*. New York: Barron's Books.
A girl bully calls another girl names, teases, and scribbles on her papers. The victim seeks social support from her mother and also gets help from her teacher.

Wells, R. (1973). *Benjamin and Tulip*. New York: Dial Books.
An animal story in which the bully is a girl and the victim is a boy. When they encounter a bigger problem that affects them both, they team up and become friends.

Wilhelm, H. (1988). *Tyrone the horrible*. New York : Scholastic.
A little dinosaur tries several ways of dealing with Tyrone, the biggest bully in the swamp (avoidance, present/bribery, being cool, fighting him), and finally hits on a successful tactic.

Books for Primary-Grade Children: Nonfiction

Berry, J. W. (1982). *Let's talk about teasing*. Newark, NJ: Peter Pan Industries.
Has some good ideas but it suggests that the victim ignore the teasing and goes no further. If using this book in the teasing program, the adult should suggest some other strategies that the child who is being teased could use if ignoring does not work.

Berry, J. W. (1985). *Let's talk about being bullied*. Chicago: Children's Press.
A simple book that helps the child who is being bullied. Strategies include facing up to the bullies, being kind, and staying away from them.

Carlson, N. (1988). *I like me*. New York: Viking.
A book about taking care of and valuing yourself. This book would be especially helpful for victimized children.

Guffe, T. (1991). *Bully for you*. New York: Child's Play.
Why it is not a good idea to be a bully. A book for overly aggressive, young children tempted to bully others.

Books for Older Children: Fiction

Bosch, C. (1988). *Bully on the bus*. Seattle, WA: Parenting Press.
"A Decision is Yours Book." When Nick Jones, the meanest kid in fifth grade, is waiting for you on the bus, you make the decision about how to deal with it. Several alternatives are presented, including talking it out, and leaving anger behind.

Chambers, A. (1983). *The present takers*. New York: Harper & Row.
Lucy is tormented by a group of class bullies who demand gifts and money. When her classmates decide to take action against the bullies, a clever solution is found.

Coryell, S. (1989). *Eaglebait*. Orlando, FL: Harcourt, Brace, Jovanovich.
A shy, unpopular 14-year-old is taunted and bullied by his classmates first in a military school, then in a regular high school. Things change for the better when he starts to feel better about himself.

de Paola, T. (1979). *Oliver Button is a sissy*. New York: Harcourt, Brace, Jovanovich.
A sympathetic account of a boy who is teased because he is interested in dancing.

Duncan, L. (1988). *Wonder Kid meets the evil lunch snatcher*. Boston: Little, Brown.
Shows all the misery of being teased. Solution is very creative.

Gardner, R. A. (1972). *Dr. Gardner's stories about the real world*. Englewood Cliffs, NJ: Prentice-Hall.
  The story, "Jerry and the bullies" (pp. 78–101), shows effects of passive withdrawal and of striking back.

Gifaldi, D. (1986). *One thing for sure*. Boston, MA: Houghton Mifflin.
  Dylan is teased when his father is imprisoned. He conquers the bullies with his strength, determination, nonviolent temperament, and positive outlook.

Kinsey-Warnock, N. (1991). *The night the bells rang*. New York: Cobblehill Books.
  An excellent World War I story about a fifth-grade boy who learns a lot about bullying and in the process recognizes his own tendency to bully his younger brother.

Mauser, P. R. (1983). *A bundle of sticks*. New York: Atheneum.
  At the mercy of the class bully, a fifth-grade boy is sent to a martial arts school where he learns techniques to defend himself as well as a philosophy that allows him not to fight.

Millman, D. (1991). *Secret of the peaceful warrior*. Tiburon, CA: Kramer.
  An old man shows Danny the importance of looking brave, of not being afraid, because fear is the enemy of the victim. Good on extortion and striking back.

Needle, J. (1993). *The bully*. London: Hamish Hamilton.
  An excellent account of school personnel's blindness to the misery of victims and the cunning behavior of bullies.

Robinson, N. K. (1980). *Wendy and the bullies*. New York: Scholastic Book Services.
  Explains a lot about bullying. Good account of the strategies that victims use. Shows the effect of assertiveness. A good story.

Shreve, S. (1993). *Joshua T. Bates takes charge*. New York: Knopf.
  Eleven-year-old Joshua, who is already worried about fitting in at school, suddenly has more problems when the new boy, Sean, whom he is supposed to be helping becomes the target of the fifth-grade's biggest bully.

Sinykin, S. C. (1994). *The Shorty Society*. New York: Penguin Books.
  Three seventh graders who are short and get teased band together to combat the teasers.

Zeier, J. T. (1993). *Stick boy*. New York: Atheneum.
  A 7-inch growth spurt in the sixth grade makes skinny, self-conscious Eric a school misfit and the victim of the class bully.

Books for Older Children: Nonfiction

Grunsell, A. (1990). *Bullying*. New York: Gloucester.
  Discusses bullying, why it occurs, and how it can be handled. Excellent on importance of telling adults, not yielding to extortion or demands, why some children are bullies, and racist bullying.

Kaufman, G., & Raphael, L. (1990). *Stick up for yourself*. Minneapolis, MN: Free Spirit Publishing.
  A guide to assertiveness and positive self-esteem that contains a wealth of ideas for victimized children.

Sanders, P. (1993). *What do you know about bullying?* New York : Gloucester Press.
  An excellent general discussion about bullying including how children become bullies and how to stand up to them. A good section on racist bullying.

Webster-Doyle, T. (1991). *Why is everybody always picking on me? A guide to handling bullies.* Middlebury, VT: Atrium Society.
> Uses stories and discussion to help children to understand bullies and to solve conflict in a nonviolent way. Shows how bullies can change their ways.

Books for Parents

Lawson, S. (1994). *Helping children cope with bullying.* London: Sheldon.
> An excellent book of practical advice on how parents can help the child who is bullied.

Pearce, J. (1989). *Fighting, teasing and bullying.* Northamptonshire NNS 2RQ, England: Thorsons Publishers.
> An excellent short book of advice on how parents can forestall or manage these problems. This book is out of print but should be available in many public libraries.

Zimbardo, P. G. (1982). *The shy child.* Garden City, NY: Doubleday.
> Shyness often elicits teasing and other forms of bullying. This is an excellent book for parents of a child who seems to have a shyness problem.

Videotapes for School Personnel to Use With Students

Bully. (1973). National Instructional Television Center, Box A, Bloomington, IN 47401.
> A new boy who is very bright is resented by others, especially by a bully who harasses him continually. The video effectively shows how frightening it is to be singled out by a bully. Recommended for grades 2 to 6.

Bully Smart. (1995). Street Smart, 105 North Virginia Avenue, Suite 305, Falls Church, VA 22042.
> An excellent 20-minute video filled with practical suggestions about how to cope with bullies. Recommended for grades K to 6.

Set Straight on Bullies. (1988). National School Safety Center, 4165 Thousand Oaks Boulevard, Suite 290, Westlake Village, CA 91362.
> An 18-minute video about a young boy who is bullied by an older one. This video shows clearly that bullying affects everyone in the school environment and cannot be allowed. Recommended for children in grades 4 and up.

Author Index

Subject Index